W9-CDU-723

# PLATONIC LOVE

# PLATONIC LOVE

*by*

THOMAS GOULD
*Associate Professor of Classics*
*Amherst College*



NEW YORK
THE FREE PRESS OF GLENCOE

*First American edition 1963*
*by The Free Press of Glencoe*



*Library of Congress catalog*
*card number: 62-15340*



*For information, address:*

The Free Press of Glencoe
A Division of The Macmillan Company
The Crowell-Collier Publishing Company
*60 Fifth Avenue, New York 11*

*Printed in Great Britain*

# PREFACE

THESE NINE CHAPTERS were delivered as lectures at the University of St. Andrews during the Martinmas Term, 1961. If the reader finds himself occasionally addressed as though he were a crowd, therefore, he will know the reason why. The audience at St. Andrews did have the one opportunity which, as Plato pointed out, book readers must always sadly be without: they could talk back, question my assertions, and teach me where I was wrong. But, as a poor consolation to the silent reader, I have at least added the footnotes which my audience had to do without. Otherwise the lectures stand very much as I read them.

I found myself, in 1961–62, a visiting lecturer in Greek and in Moral Philosophy at St. Andrews, through the kindness of the Principal, Sir Malcolm Knox, and the professors of the two departments, K. J. Dover and A. D. Woozley. I owe my invitation above all to Professor Dover, who also did much to make my stay in St. Andrews extremely pleasant. I was paid, first of all, by a grant from the Leverhulme Trust, for which I am very grateful, and also from the bequest of the late Professor Francis Fobes of Amherst College. I wish to thank the President and Trustees of Amherst College, not only for this latter grant, but also for the leaves of absence, in 1958 as well as 1961–62, without which I should not have been able to finish this study. The actual preparation of the manuscript, on the other hand, was accomplished largely in the friendly and luxurious leisure of Peterhouse, Cambridge. I wish to give my special thanks to the Master and Fellows—above all to Mr. E. J. Kenney—for their invitations, in 1958 and 1961, to live and work in this college.

In addition to the many writers whose help I have acknowledged in my notes, I also owe much to a large number of friends, colleagues, and students who have helped me to clarify my interpretation of Plato's theory of love over the years. In particular, I cannot imagine how I could even have attempted this subject if it were not for the intelligent resistance of the students in my annual seminar on Plato and Aristotle at Amherst. Of my own teachers, I owe a special debt to Professors Friedrich Solmsen and Gregory Vlastos. Of my Amherst colleagues, Professors Joseph Epstein and John Moore have taught me most. Moore's help, indeed, could not be described in terms of suggestions and corrections; inspiration is more nearly the word for what he has done for me.

In 1958 I completed, but later abandoned, an earlier version of this study, which I called "The Form of the Good." The several scholars who were kind enough to read parts of that manuscript will perhaps recognize traces of the earlier attempt in these lectures. They include especially Professors Phillip DeLacy, Adam Parry, and J. B. Skemp. Professor W. K. C. Guthrie, indeed, made detailed suggestions on almost the whole of that version. To all of these men I give my thanks—and my apologies for my frequent failures to live up to their high standards.

T. G.

*St. Andrews,*
*January*, 1962.

# CONTENTS

For my hosts
E. J. Kenney and K. J. Dover

# CHAPTER 1

*The Platonic Distinguished from the Rival Theories of the Nature of Love: The Christian, the Romantic, and the Freudian Theories.*

IN ITS ORDINARY USE in conversation, the term "Platonic love" means something like "heterosexual companionship without sexual desire". In fact, the phrase usually indicates that there is no love; we may stop speculating about this man and woman. Everybody understands, of course, that this is an appalling degradation of the Platonic theory of love. Indeed, French scholars find this use of *amour platonique* so distressing that they often change the name to *amour platonicien* when they speak of love as understood by Plato. And yet, there is just a shadow of the original idea in the vulgar phrase: Plato was indeed talking about the attraction which people have for one another, and he did most certainly deny that desire for sexual gratification was the most direct or informative explanation for this phenomenon. But he was not talking about one kind of love; he was presenting a theory of all love. As for sexuality, it is, Plato maintained, a perfectly natural, but somewhat unimaginative, manifestation of love correctly understood.

There is, in Plato's view, neither thought nor activity without love. Plato's understanding of love, therefore, naturally colors every theory and every major idea in his writings. Three of his dialogues are devoted specifically to love, however: the *Lysis*, a rather dreary early work with only two or three really interesting moments; the *Symposium*, Plato's masterpiece, written at the height of his power; and the *Phaedrus*, written some years later, brilliant but complicated by new thoughts which threatened the rôle of love as the key to everything. The impatient reader who wanted a direct statement on the nature of love as Plato understood it would naturally be directed to the *Symposium*, and particularly to the great exposition by the priestess Diotima, which is the high point of that dialogue. Let such a reader beware, however. He will either come away with the impression that he has read something quite marvelous but just not quite coherent at all the crucial points; or he will be put off entirely and declare Plato to be unfeeling, if not insane; or, worst of all, he will quiver with delight and think that he has understood everything. Nor will any of these maladies be cured merely by re-reading the central passages of the *Symposium*, however carefully. The task is much more difficult. Although in these lectures we will naturally spend more time on the *Symposium* and the *Phaedrus* than any other texts, we will find it necessary to range over a great many of Plato's works, as well as the works of writers both earlier and later than Plato. And even this will not be enough, for a major effort will have to be made to look at love itself and all the sources of our complicated prejudices as to what it is. It is, as a matter of fact, with this last effort that we must begin.

If it comes as a surprise that we must examine our own ideas before we turn to Plato, consider the difficulty which any of us ever has in receiving fairly an ancient idea contrary to contemporary feelings—especially on a matter of very great importance to us. Our only hope is to root out the various historical and psychological sources for our own thoughts and then to weigh very carefully the arguments which can be given for the more typically modern position. We must not be haunted throughout our enterprise by the vague conviction that surely much progress must have been made since antiquity and that we need not take Plato's queer-sounding talk too seriously.

Since Platonic love is not a kind of love but a theory as to the nature of all love, we must begin by asking just what we ourselves consider love to be. Actually, most of us have hornets' nests instead of clear thoughts on the nature of love. It is a thing too violent, too important to us, and it goes wrong too easily for us to be able to achieve an easy understanding of it. Also, there are several extraordinary upheavals in our past caused by men who have announced with evangelical fire that they had at last understood the form which love takes when it is best of all. One of these was started by Plato; the Christians caused another; a non-philosophic tradition with many twists and turns, which we may sum up as the Romantic, is a third source; and most recently our prejudice in favor of science has culminated in that greatest of our nightmares, Sigmund Freud. As we go step by step through Plato's writings on love, we shall find ourselves hindered at every turn by these rival interpretations, for it is never quite possible to leave their revelations behind. I propose, therefore, to devote this first lecture to the drawing of the lines which separate these various interpretations of love. At the end we should at least have a kind of negative idea of what we should be looking for when we turn to the *Symposium*.

Please notice that I am not distinguishing among various kinds of love, as one might insist that love for mother, money, girl friend, country, and whisky were different. Many interesting pages have been written on such distinctions. Hubert Benoit, for instance, distinguishes benevolent, appetitive, and adoring love.[1] C. S. Lewis finds "Need-love," "Gift-love," and "Appreciative-love," or, on another level, affection, friendship, sexuality, and Christian "charity."[2] This kind of endeavor, however, is of surprisingly little help in getting started. What we want are the rival theories for explaining love itself in its truest nature. I find roughly (very roughly) these four: the Platonic, the Christian, the Romantic, and the Freudian interpretations. Each of these is a theory, not of one kind of love, but of all love or love at its best, each claims for love that it is the key to everything important in life, and yet each is just different enough from the other three to make it impossible that all could be simultaneously true.

Christian love is the easiest. Ever since Schopenhauer, and especially since Nietzsche, we have understood that Christian and Platonic love were opposed. As Wilamowitz was able to say forty years ago in his most magisterial manner: Plato and Paul would have been able to make nothing of one another on love.[3] In 1929 Anders Nygren, a Lutheran theologian, Bishop of Lund, published in three great volumes a startling new study called *Agapê and Eros*.[4] (*Agapê* is Paul's word in the famous hymn to love in the first Epistle to the Corinthians; *eros* is, of course, the word preferred by Plato.) By now the fame of Nygren's distinction has spread around the world, and there is hardly a minister in Christendom so dull and uninformed that he cannot discourse for hours on the superiority of *agapê* to *eros*. (I shall avoid the use of these famous terms, by the way, because our association with the derogatory uses of "erotic" prejudices the discussion unduly and because the refusal to use one word, "love," for both affections separates them unnaturally.)

To understand Christian love, according to Nygren, we should concentrate not, as Plato does, on a man's love for the supremely good, but on the love which the supremely good has for men. In the former case, Platonic love, the supremely good is hardly distinguishable from the man's own happiness, the well-being of the lover; in the latter case, the love of God for man, the supremely good can remain an inexplicable independent being. What the human lover loves, according to Plato, is excellence and beauty. What God loves in us is—well, whatever it is, it cannot be that. The two loves simply cannot be the same. We human beings get nowhere without desire for good; God has no need of us whatever.

Plato talks about our surge upward toward an understanding of reality which will fill us with joy; Paul speaks of the overflow of God's goodness which does not deny benevolence to the most wretched of sinners. Plato tries to show men the way out of corruption and stupidity to immortal happiness; Paul implies that our salvation is not in our own power at all, but subject to a will which may be neither understood nor encouraged. Plato tells us that the trick is to find out what is truly excellent, so that we may lavish all our care on that, and what is worthless, so that we may shun or cripple that. The Christians say that we must make no such distinction: as God loves the sinners with no qualified love, so we must love our enemies indiscriminately with our friends. "Love your enemies. . . . For if ye love them which love you, what thanks have ye? for sinners also do even the same . . . and your reward shall be great, and ye shall be the children of the Highest: for He is kind unto the unthankful and the evil."[5] According to Plato it would be grotesque not to think, act, perfect ourselves, and make works of art of our lives; according to the Christians such self-assertion is as grotesque as the sight of a helpless child responding to its parent's love and care with restless criticism instead of gratitude and trust. Such is the difference between Platonic and Christian love.

In summing up Nygren's position, I have left out much that is tendentious and unsound. But even on this central point, which we must surely accept, two cautions must be given. In the first place there is the problem of man's love for God in the New Testament: that, unlike God's love for man, cannot be without consideration for the goodness of the object. Man's love for God is not the product of the overflow of his own goodness but the product of his need and upward surge toward happiness. Man's love for God, therefore, is love of the kind on which Plato concentrates. Now, could anyone deny that Paul's works vibrate with love for his God and ambition to serve him? Nygren suggests that this upward hunger should be called "faith" (πίστις) rather than "love."[6] That begs the question, however. Surely it would be better to say something like this: while love of goodness, the kind of love which Plato extolled, exists, indeed is quite prominent, in many parts of the New Testament (especially John),[7] this love is eclipsed by the message that another form of love, indiscriminate benevolence, is infinitely more important as the source of everything good. Nygren is recklessly destructive and revels unnecessarily in his paradoxes. Plato, he says, "is fundamentally unaware of any other form of love than acquisitive love. . . . It is plain that there can be no room in Plato for any spontaneous and unmotivated love: for acquisitive love is motivated by the value of its object."[8] We must avoid prejudicial language of this sort or we shall never understand anything.

The second difficulty in accepting Nygren's account comes when we review the history of Christianity with this new distinction. The very mention of such names as Augustine and Aquinas, let alone Dante or St. Teresa, reminds us of all the ecstatic upward longing for union with the supreme being which has gone on in the name of orthodox Christianity. There are several attitudes which one may take toward this discovery. The most uncompromising is Nygren's own: between Paul and Luther, he maintains, beginning with John and continuing with the Catholic tradition even after Luther, the Christian world has been tainted almost ubiquitously with the evil of Platonic love, and the great work of the Protestant revolution has been to return to the pure Pauline love of the first generation and to disown all the history in between. It hardly needs pointing out that horror at or enthusiasm for such a view does not depend purely on scholarly research. For our purposes, however, there is something to be said for Nygren's ill-tempered position. So long as we realize that we are indicating elements in a complicated composite feeling which we have inherited about love, and do not have to commit ourselves as to what is "truly Christian" in some absolute sense, it is not unreasonable to call the upward longing for union with God "Platonic" and the indiscriminate downward overflow of benevolence "Christian." To deny the name of Christianity to the former altogether, however, is another matter.

Denis de Rougemont, in his famous book *L'Amour et l'Occident*,[9] offered a startling suggestion. Are the history of Platonic love in the Christian centuries and the history of one special virulent strain of heresy perhaps really the same, he asks. He comes astonishingly close to proving this suggestion for one moment in Christian history. His book mainly concerns the connection between the outbreak of Courtly Love in the twelfth century and the heresy fought in the Albigensian crusade. This was Platonic love, he argues, and the Church knew it, and fought it. Perhaps the Church always knew what it was doing, he suggests, and always recognized Plato as the enemy, however much it seemed to compromise on occasion. A lightning review of the writings of the Fathers and the Saints, however, is enough to convince us that de Rougemont's discovery does not really illuminate very much of Christian history. Abélard was quickly squashed by St. Bernard, but who was there to shake a finger at St. Augustine? Actually de Rougemont's discovery is important in the delineation of yet another tradition about love, which we shall turn to in a moment.

In an exciting book called *The Mind and the Heart of Love*,[10] the Jesuit priest M. C. D'Arcy tries to redress Nygren's dour slight to the Hellenized and Romanized Christianity of the Middle Ages. As a Catholic, he could not dismiss so lightly as Nygren could the vast body of Christian literature which continued the Platonic tradition. "How egocentric love is compatible with pure love of our neighbor," he says,[11] is an abiding puzzle, one which exercised the best minds of both Pagans and Christians. It is too simple to call egocentric love the sign of Pagan evil and to claim that only Christians loved their neighbor unselfishly. The puzzle of the relation between these two loves was brilliantly and sanely treated by many scholastics, he argues, and we gain nothing by turning our backs on them as lost souls just because they learned from Plato as well as from Christ.

D'Arcy noticed something curious: Platonic love is identified by some, like Nygren, as brilliant, clear Rationalism, fully conscious and ever ambitious, by others, like de Rougemont, as a violent, dark, self-destructive passion. Surely it is both, he argues. In the hands of Plato, he says, "what was Dionysiac has become Apolline, the feminine and clinging the most masculine and self-assertive."[12] But the Dionysiac did not die out in Plato's new interpretation, he argues. Far from it. There continued to be these two sides to Platonic love, rational control *and* self-obliteration. But they existed together in an uneasy and unsatisfying oscillation. When the Christians came, however, the news was out that God himself was love, and this news made it possible for the first time to achieve a kind of pure friendship, for one's fellow man and for God himself, which alone was capable of bringing peace and true harmony. At this point, to be sure, we must part company with D'Arcy, temporarily at least. For, after all, if we assume at the outset that only the love extolled by Christ is ultimately worth having, we may well find ourselves in no frame of mind to comprehend what Plato is talking about.

With all its confusing gyrations and contradictions, we can see in Christian love a single strong theme; and, in any case, we always have the Greek Bible to go back to for the original germinative idea. The same is not true for the next tradition which I should like to consider, the Romantic. There is agreement neither on its origins, its nature, nor its prophets. The very name I give to this strain in our past may be called arbitrary. But what can I do? The truth is that Platonic, Christian, and Freudian interpretations do not account among them for all the persistent ideas on love which we cherish so tenaciously. By Romantic love I wish to indicate a popular, or at least non-philosophic prejudice, more noticeable in literature than in rational arguments, and more noticeable in vulgar tastes than in literature, which has Platonic, Christian, and even "Freudian" components, but is simultaneously more and less than all of these. Since there is no authority and no text to return to from time to time to renew an orthodoxy, the Romantic changes disconcertingly from generation to generation and has taken notably different forms in different countries (in France and in America, for instance). Nevertheless, such as it is, it has a grip on us and takes its toll when we try to read the *Symposium*, so we must attempt to understand it.

Who can tell its origins? There are the Greek mysteries and the melancholy story of Persephone who married Death. There are the violent and querulous poems of the lyricists of Greece, who sang of *Eros Tyrannos*. And there are Euripides' unhappy women, Phaedra, Medea, and Andromache. Then there were the Hellenistic pastorals. Finally, in the fourth *Aeneid*, the first full-blown love story.[13] I take it that a love story is possible as a subject for high tragedy only when we believe that love is as important (and therefore as dangerous) as war, salvation, and morality. Achilles' love for Patroclus was not really the cause of his tragedy, but Dido's love for Aeneas *was* the cause of hers. The sign of such a love story is that the protagonist, usually a woman, chooses love and death at one and the same time. In the sixth *Aeneid*, Virgil creates a special place for tragic lovers, the *lugentes campi*, though he can find only women to put in it, with the dubious exception of Caeneus.

In the centuries which followed, Virgil was, of course, much read. So was Ovid, who had dug up love stories heaven knows where and published them in a profusion which says as much for his audience as it does for his taste.[14] Little can be told about love in these centuries, however. At least, there are no great revealing books. But with the return of lively literature in the twelfth century, among the Troubadours of Provence, we find love now almost the only theme. This development is a critical one for us, but one not easy to explain. If de Rougemont and others are right, this new love, Courtly Love, is not only the heir to Ovid and Virgil, it owes a great deal also to a Neoplatonic form of Platonic love and was made strong and self-conscious by intense and determined opposition from the Church. ROMA, according to the new lovers, was a perversion of AMOR.[15] This new ideal had several startling features. First, marriage was not a sacrament but a sin: does marriage not turn the act which is the essence of love cold-bloodedly to the uses of worldly society and gain? Love truly understood could be realized only in adultery. Second, love was invariably manifested in a slavelike adoration of the man for his lady. The lady, on the other hand, who is ideally the wife of her lover's lord, should be pure and disdainful, *la belle dame sans merci*. (The Church, by the way, with an unusually graceful turn, responded by introducing an extraordinary new emphasis on the Virgin Mary as *Regina Coeli*.) Third, the passion seems not to have been a passion for the lady at all, but a passion for passion, the love of being in love which Augustine had spoken of. Lastly, this love for love betrayed itself again and again as a dark love for oblivion and death. The most compelling love stories, like the fantastically popular ones of Tristram and Iseult or Guinevere and Lancelot, had to be immeasurably sad, preferably ending in a death which should be like the act of love itself. Virgil already understood this when he had Dido kill herself with Aeneas' sword, but how much more conscious Shakespeare is in describing Cleopatra's death! A comparison of Plutarch and Shakespeare on Antony's ruinous love, by the way, is very instructive: Antony was a Romantic lover in fact, but Plutarch knew no ideal which would allow him to revel in it. Shakespeare did.

On the other hand, Platonic love (as it was transmitted through writings, orthodox and heterodox, which kept alive the Neoplatonic or Stoic visions) suggested other interpretations of Romantic love which the church would not have to fight—interpretations which were less obviously sexual or suicidal while they yet continued to give expression to the basic idea: an upward climb by the awareness of beauty to an escape from this world. The sermons of St. Bernard were immensely successful attempts of this sort. The quest for the Holy Grail was another acceptable version. The lifelong inspiration which Dante found in Beatrice and (with a difference) Petrarch in Laura, was yet another. One feels that these were all still but disguises for the old longing, however. With the Renaissance, of course, came a new appreciation of antiquity, including, above all, Plato, and with the Reformation, a bold attempt to go back to the beginnings of Christianity. But, curiously enough, the great love stories do not change in their essentials. *Romeo and Juliet* (and indeed *Anna Karenina* and *Farewell to Arms*) could have been written in the Middle Ages except for their sense of form. The plot is still the same: the lover chooses love and death at the same time. In the history of the idea of love, at least, the Renaissance does not appear to have been a crucial turning point. After all, there is not really much more Plato in Spenser or Ficino than there is in Dante.

But that the "Romantic" movement of the last two centuries has brought with it some profound changes in our ideal of love would be hard to deny. These changes are notoriously difficult to define or explain, however. The Reformation, as I said, brought with it a renewed fervor for anti-Pagan ideas in early Christianity, and the revival of learning a renewed sympathy for certain anti-Christian ideas in Pagan philosophy. The "Romantic" movement fermented only very slowly from these discoveries. Often as not it is characterized by the feeling that neither the Pagan world nor the early Christian world but the Dark Ages were the true lost homeland. Why this should have been, it is not easy to say.

One very important cause of the "Romantic" revolution, surely, was the acceptance of science and its extraordinary progress. As time went on, the scientific vision of a mechanical nature became less and less inspiring, even as it got ever more difficult to deny. The "Romantic" was a man who was disillusioned with reality. The scientific explanations for human motives and for the origins of human institutions also proved to be as depressing as they were convincing. There was a vulgar new optimism that all men would be happy when they were liberated from three unnatural injustices: the division of wealth, the class structure, and repressive morality. Yet how could a man of sensibility take any pleasure in such an estimation of the important things in life? The "Romantic" was apt to feel himself as one who was searching restlessly for the lost key to high feelings and a receptivity to beauty. Sometimes he brooded on antiquity, sometimes on the Passion of Christ and on the experience of the earliest Christians, but most often, for a long time at least, it was the Gothic centuries that provided the models for his new tales. Love and death were the only things worth dwelling on, of course, but only extraordinary men were able to feel this now, and at that only if they fell into a hopeless love.

For a while we believed men like Goethe and Wordsworth when they told us that there were peasants out there who were still innocent and still felt the great things in life. But the hardiest innovation of the "Romantic" movement was not the sentimental romance; it was the realistic novel. We tend to think of the "Romantic" movement as best characterized by a rosy vision of a never-never land. But the far away and long ago were cherished by the "Romantics" not because they liked the world as it is, but because they hated it—felt it was ugly and meaningless. It was inevitable, therefore, that a serious attempt to be honest would mean to the "Romantic" a recognition of the sordid, the petty, and the stupid. And so, in many tales the tragic couple is set down in a world pictured "realistically" in a new sense—a world of brutal officials, vicious fathers, grim back alleys, broken windows, refuse, and meaningless ill-tempered conversation. After all, the sentimental romance set in an impossible fairyland and a realistic novel or film (in this new "Romantic" sense of realism) have this in common: both find that the old high seriousness and beauty do not exist in ordinary life as it is lived today, and both agree that the highest, most serious, most beautiful thing is still tragic love.

Now comes the difficult part: how to characterize Romantic love as it exists in our minds today? Has anyone expounded it clearly? There is Stendhal's splendid book,[16] but that is much too French. There is Ortega y Gasset,[17] but his work is too personal and disappointingly thin. We get closer when we turn to those of the psychologists, like Theodor Reik and Erich Fromm,[18] who have broken away from Freud precisely on his theory of love—recanted, we might say, and returned to the Romantic fold. But the best place to find Romantic love enshrined as a conscious theory is the marriage manuals and handbooks for mating counseling.[19] From there one can go back to literature, both good and vulgar, and to prejudices obviously operating in every phase of modern life.

Here are some of the catch phrases by which this love is known today. If a man has a girl who loves him and will do anything for him, he has the most important thing in life. If two people love each other, nothing else matters. To marry for any reason but love is immoral. Love prevents even adulterous sex from being really immoral. Anybody who can tell the reasons for his love is not in love. Love between a man and a woman which does not culminate eventually in sexual expression is unnatural, but the great thing is to tell true love from mere sexuality. A man who loses everything for a love, even an illicit love, is to be both pitied and envied; but a man who loses everything for sex should be locked up. True love is very rare and few are capable of it. The only really unthinkable catastrophe that could befall a man is to prove to be not man enough. (Once war, moral ties, and temptation threatening the immortal soul were the tests of manhood; now the supreme test is the ability to satisfy a woman. It is hard to say whether homosexuality or impotence is the greater nightmare.) For a woman, on the other hand, the great thing is not to be treated as a woman only. It is immoral to neglect her appearance and not do everything in her power to make men have erotic desires whenever they look at her, and if she does not have at least one man at any given time who adores her, her life is pointless; but she must remain chaste, individual, and must never quite surrender, even in the sexual act. The natural expectation of every boy and girl is that each will fall in love, once, in the bloom of youth, suddenly, intensely, and at first unhappily, desiring infinitely more than sexual fulfillment but desiring that as well; that each will fall in love with a person of the opposite sex, also young and beautiful, who is unattached and falls just as much in love in return; that they will marry and experience a bliss which cannot even be talked about; that their sexual pleasures will quietly cool, in six months to six years, but that they will then love each other for what they *really are*—a far more satisfying thing than their youthful passion. The man, of course, will have his fling now and then, but if the woman does she cheapens herself beyond repair.

There is a good deal of confusion and contradiction in this picture, but if you think that this is my fault, just consider this one item. When asked, most people take it as a truism that very few people ever really fall in love; yet in one survey of American college women 71 per cent reported that they were currently in love, and another group of 200 adult men and women reported that they had been in love a total of 1,358 times![20] Actually, a little order can be made of the current ideals by remembering the history of Romantic love as we just sketched it, and then noticing the following new departures. First, the weakening of the connection between marriage and the Church has apparently had the effect of lessening the tension between love and marriage. The Church has given up the fight against marriage for love. The sentimental dream of Jane

Austen's young heroines has therefore become the inalienable right of every schoolgirl. Second, as the commands of religion became something we had to apologize for, the call of patriotism dangerous and insincere, our duties within society a bore, and the countryside a jumble of hideous architecture torn by smoke and roaring cars, we have had to bank more and more on the faraway hope of salvation through personal human love (meanwhile titillating ourselves with erotic suggestions in every song and advertisement). Finally, we have begun to fear that maybe salvation through personal love is not really possible after all, for maybe science is right: all love is really sex at bottom and all sex somehow perverse. We cannot make up our minds whether love is fulfillment or escape. We long for it but are ashamed of it at the same time.[21]

This brings us to the last of the great rivals to Plato's theory of love: Freud. We are all familiar with that wearisome phenomenon, the Freudian, who either enlists the great figures of the past into Freud's camp or explains their genius away in those invariably defiling terms of his. Now, I am not a Freudian. But neither am I anti-Freudian. I am post-Freudian; and so are you. We are all indelibly Christian, whether we still believe or not, and we are all still products of Romantic and Neoplatonic ideals; but for most of us, surely, the thing that nags most insistently at the back of our minds, preventing us from taking any ancient writer seriously on the subject of love, is neither Paul to the Corinthians nor the sorrows of Werther, it is the knowledge that there are those wretched clinical histories piling up somewhere, all pointing to the same ghastly conclusion: whatever it is that we may have trained ourselves to long for, what we originally wanted, every time, was sexual gratification —or rather, what we long for nostalgically is that wonderful "polymorphously perverse infantile sexuality" which we have missed ever since we left our mothers' breasts. "Love," according to the master, "originates in the capacity of the ego to satisfy some of its instincts autoerotically through the obtaining of organ pleasure. It is primarily narcissistic, is then transferred to those objects which have been incorporated in the ego, now much extended, and expresses the motor striving of the ego after those objects as sources of pleasure."[22] As for beauty, "there is to my mind," Freud says, "no doubt that the concept of 'beautiful' has its roots in sexual excitation and that its original meaning was 'sexually stimulating' (*das sexuell Reizende 'die Reize'*). This is related to the fact that we never regard the genitals themselves, which produce the strongest sexual excitation, as really 'beautiful' (*Es steht im Zusammenhange damit, dass wir die Genitalien selbst, deren Anblick die stärkste sexuelle Erregung hervorruft, eigentlich niemals 'schon' finden können*)."[23] That is, the whole business is so important to us, the "great reservoir of libidinal energy" so volatile and so easily threatened by reality and authority (which, we have discovered, are, alas, not really part of ourselves), that we have suppressed the true nature of our desires and are attempting to satisfy them by elaborate fantasies, conscious and unconscious, social as well as personal, which find expression, among other ways, in basically dishonest theories as to why this object is beautiful, why that person is worth personal sacrifices to help, why these duties must be performed, and so on, on every level, awake or asleep.

Do not listen to those who tell you that Freud is already passé. The state of affairs in the Freudian camp today, twenty years after Freud's death, bears a striking resemblance to that within the Platonic school twenty years after Plato's death. We would be as wrong, I think, to listen to the current Freudian deviations rather than to Freud himself as we would be to study the latter day Platonists in preference to Plato. It is Freud's imagination which has conquered the lay world, and I have no doubt that his writings will be influential long after psychoanalysis ceases to be a lively profession. Certainly in these lectures Freud will loom very large—indeed a more considerable challenge to Plato than any which we have found in all the centuries between.

The reduction of love to a bodily function was not sprung on the world by Freud to its complete surprise, of course. D. H. Lawrence and Havelock Ellis did not have to learn this from Freud. It had probably been a lively possibility in many minds, especially since the disillusionment with reality and the triumph of scientific thinking which we have identified as part of the "Romantic" movement. But Freud deserves special consideration as a philosopher, and it is not grotesque to put up his theory of love as a rival to Plato's. That they are talking about the same thing, for all their differences, it is surely impossible to deny. Freud even borrows the word *eros* from Plato, and took great pleasure in an article published in his lifetime demonstrating the resemblance between Plato's theory and his own.[24] To all the enemies of his new ideas Freud said, "As for the 'stretching' of the concept of sexuality . . . anyone who looks down with contempt upon psychoanalysis from a superior vantage point should remember how closely the enlarged sexuality of psychoanalysis coincides with the Eros of the divine Plato (*wie nahe die erweiterte Sexualität der Psychoanalyse mit dem Eros des göttlichen Plato zusammentrifft*)."[25]

Let us see just how closely they do coincide. Both begin with a concern for human unhappiness and both diagnose this as a civil war within the *psyche*.[26] One of the antagonists, the life-giving one, is in both cases desire, an upward desire for union, happiness, and fulfillment. As to the exact nature of its opponent, neither Plato nor Freud gives the same answer through his life. Both, however, recognize the play of a longing for release from life, the death wish, or *μελέτη θανάτου*. Both assert that self-knowledge is the only hope for happiness, and that this, in turn, consists of two things: an appreciation of that part of the self which is revealed only in dreams,[27] and rationality—that is, an understanding of reality. Maturity is identical with scientific knowledge. In both cases the cure is effected by conversation. *Logos*, Freud says, is his god.[28] The aim is to establish a harmony within the *psyche*, the ideal being "the man who dreamed in a way no different from that in which he thought while awake."[29] The result would be a recapturing of a happiness lost at birth: every discovery is a rediscovery. Both men admit their profound debts to the poets, but both came finally to distrust the arts as antirational. On the other hand, art, like all great achievements and brave deeds, can be traced to love. Love in both philosophies is the great narcissistic pleasure principle to which all life-giving energy can be traced, including altruism, generosity and self-sacrifice. There is even an elaborate comparison by Freud between the power structure within the *psyches* and the situation within various happy and unhappy cities, remarkably like that which Plato worked out in the *Republic*.[30] Although Freud, as a doctor, had regularly to accept society as a "given" in his attempts to help his patients to happiness, he was, like Plato, very well aware that neurosis was a social as well as a personal matter, and that whole societies, though creations of the *psyches* within them, might be so constructed that the love inspiring these individual *psyches* might not have a Chinaman's chance of fulfillment.[31] Finally, both Freudian and Platonic theories, in contrast to Christian and some forms of the Romantic idea, happily accept the powerful and ubiquitous occurrence of the desire for sexual release as an absolutely integral and natural manifestation of the love which is the key to everything.

No sooner do we say this, however, than the feeling comes flooding in on us that there are profound differences between Plato and Freud. One: the nature of the opposition between love and the other principle was understood very differently by the two thinkers. Freud supposed that love was a pleasure principle in a fairly simple sense, and that rationality discovered a reality which must unhappily limit this at every turn. Plato believed that the world as understood by the lover *was* reality, and that that which limited this insight was by definition irrational and therefore neither comprehensible nor ultimately very important compared to the other. Two: the coincidence of a drive in man and in the other animals signified very different things for the two men. For Freud the lower the drive the more it is to be honored—not only as being ineradicable but also as a key to what we really want and therefore what we must pursue if we are not to drift inevitably farther and farther away from fulfillment. For Plato, on the other hand, to say that the lowest common denominator was the important thing was to be unforgivably blind to the necessity of civilization and intelligence and to court bestiality, the most unhappy of states for any man. Three: the search for happiness as an attempt to recover a lost vision was understood in very different senses by the two. Freud could only conclude that we are forever hoping vainly to recapture a sexual bliss lost in infancy. Plato thought we longed for a true vision of the world as it really is —incomparably more beautiful than the young, the simple, and the ignorant suppose it to be. Finally: the two men came to opposite decisions as to the relation between sexuality and the other activities which can be traced to the same source of energy. Freud supposed that sublimated love, desexualized or partially desexualized attachments to people and things, though the source of great and necessary achievements, could never arise if we did not need a substitute for frustrated sexual longings. It never occurred to Plato, on the other hand, that it would make any sense to say that the more beautiful, necessary, and admirable expression was less natural or direct. From Plato's vantage point, Freud is the product of one side of the "Romantic" movement, carried to its wildest limit.[32]

Here, then, is the promised negative definition of Platonic love. Unlike Christianity, which typically forbids us to take into consideration the deserts of the objects of our love, Plato tells us that this is the key to everything: pour your love on the excellent and you are a good man, on the unworthy and you are bad. Also unlike Christianity, but like the Romantic and Freudian interpretations, Plato recognizes human attachments with sexual longings as the primal manifestation of true love and the only one which the multitude, like animals, will ever be entirely conscious of. Like Christianity, however, and unlike the other two, Plato assumes that the finest form which love can take is so far above the personal that we in effect fall out of love even with those who were once nearest and dearest to us. Also like Christianity, and unlike the other two, Plato assumes that the world is better understood by the lover than the non-lover, that the glowing surroundings seen through the burning eyes of the true lover are more, not less, real than the ugly or indifferent nature which surrounded him before. Finally, like Freud, Plato sees in love the key to civilization, art, justice, and all great, brave achievements in this world, while the Christians and Romantics, in different ways, thought that love destroyed society or offered an escape from it.

Although all four of these interpretations of love make it the key to everything important in life, only Plato and Freud have worked out the philosophical implications of this assertion. But compared to Plato, Freud hardly got going. The exciting thing about Plato, the reason why he deserves our most alert and sympathetic attention after all these centuries, is that he alone has tried to spell out all the consequences, ethical, political, epistemological, and metaphysical, of the assumption which we evidently still believe: that without love neither thought nor activity is profitable or perhaps even possible.

# CHAPTER 2

*Non-philosophic Assumptions about the Nature of Love, Ancient and Modern Ideas Compared. The Five Preliminary Speeches of the* Symposium.

IN BEGINNING THIS EXAMINATION of Platonic love by gathering in all the conscious and half-conscious ideas which we habitually entertain about love, I was but imitating Plato himself, who devotes the first half of the *Symposium* to a series of speeches representing all of the important traditions which he wished his Greek readers to recall before he led them on to a better understanding. A comparison of the non-philosophical ideas on love in antiquity with those in our own times ought to be very helpful at this point. Before we turn to the preliminary speeches in the *Symposium*, therefore, let us review once more the complex of ideas which make up our own attitudes.

We distinguished four strains in our history: the Christian, the Romantic, and the Freudian, in addition to the Platonic. Let us consider how each of the four might characterize the other three.

Love, the Christian would want to say, is not the same as desire—not love in its purest, finest form. God did not need or desire anything when he created the world or gave his only begotten son to it. Nor does God need or desire us when he loves us. We, therefore, should neither need nor desire our neighbors. If God had love only for the truly beautiful, how would he ever have come to love us sinners? So should we also, in imitation of God's love for us, love our enemies equally with our friends. If we love only those who love us, what thanks have we? For even the publicans are capable of that. We must demand no conditions before we love—neither that the person be worthy in any way nor, certainly, that he bring us any pleasure. Sexuality, therefore, is inconceivably remote from the love which is the key to everything. Sexuality pulls us in the wrong direction altogether. If, instead of treating sexual pleasure as the simple animal mechanism for reproduction which it obviously is, you concentrate on the pleasure itself, quite divorced from any intention to have offspring, if you make a cult of this pleasure in the incredible way in which some of the Greeks did, and come to think that that is the highest experience life has to offer—even if you say that the pleasure is eventually so refined that no single person or act has anything to do with it any more —then you have sold everything for your own pursuit of self-gratification. You lose God and you must end up a selfish, unsatisfied, profoundly unhappy man. As for the Romantics and the Freudians, they are merely latter day Platonists, grown ever worse. The Romantics, despairing of the divine vision altogether, hope only for comfort and oblivion in some other person's sympathy and response. The Freudians play obscenely like wicked children with the most degrading possible interpretation of every generous inclination toward man or God.

A Romantic (in the modern fashion) might object to the Christian: ah, but you are reveling heartlessly in your paradox. Consider what you are asking of us—really that we lose our humanity. Christ could love all mankind, perhaps, but you and I cannot. What a lonely spectacle is the man without a special, exclusive, intense bond with at least one other human being! An all-consuming love between a young man and a young woman is worth losing everything for. It is the most important thing in life. And the Platonists are just as bad, in that they beg us to fall out of love with our special loved ones as we go on to love ever higher, broader abstracts. Both you and the Platonists seem to think that reality itself is somehow lovable, which is an appalling mistake. Reality is indifferent, meaningless; it is we who, by our special attachments, give it meaning. As for the Freudians, their lives must be even bleaker than that of the Christians and the Platonists. To confuse love with mere sexual need is almost the worst mistake a person can make. Sexual need is a tension which is easily satisfied and vanishes with the satisfaction; love is exclusive, unpredictable, ever demanding, and grows rather than dies when it is fulfilled. As the man who will subordinate everything else to true love is the best of men, so the man who subordinates everything to sexuality is almost the worst of men. The Freudians, like the Platonists, make the unforgivable error of trying to analyze the unanalyzable. It is not surprising that it turns to dust at their touch.

To which the Freudian would say: well, in a way you are right about reality itself being meaningless or worse, but about the nature of the desires which give form to our lives, you are just not very scientific. You cannot simply put your head in your hands and *think* about a phenomenon like that; you must investigate. You must accumulate evidence and be prepared to follow that evidence wherever it leads. The fact is that prolonged analysis of many individuals has given us overwhelming proof that the love which you take to be so foreign to sexual gratification is actually aim-inhibited desire for organ satisfaction. This desire is merely partially desexualized, partially suppressed, and badly distorted by the hostility of society. The romantic lover is living a fantasy, his own fantasy, but one suggested by society, invented in order for him to be able to act out in a socially acceptable way the true, unconscious sexual drive that is still the source of all his emotion. The desire is completely narcissistic, actually, and attachment to another person is really only the incorporation of the other person in the self, which results when one discovers how necessary the other person is to one's own pleasure.

Sexual energy is in itself bisexual; it usually develops into heterosexual attachments, however, partly because society demands it that way for reasons of survival, and partly as a natural consequence of the physical difference between the male and the female. Above all, the discovery, usually quite early in everybody's life, that male children are apparently better equipped for organ satisfaction than female children has a profound effect. As a result of this discovery the boy child fears that he, too, may be castrated; the female child, on the other hand, knows that she already has been. The male child finds the terror unbearable, for that pleasure is threatened which means more to him than anything else. To make the anxiety tolerable, therefore, he internalizes the threatening authority within himself. It is then this process of identification with authority which makes the male the preserver of justice and civilization. The loyalty which women feel toward such super-personal things, notice, is notoriously weaker. They have suffered no comparable cause to internalize the commands of culture. It all becomes sensationally clear if you only remember how paramount the importance of organ pleasure is to all of us, however successfully we may have suppressed that fact from our consciousness.

Platonists, Christians, and Romantics are all talking about sublimated love, and are thus being dishonest insofar as they claim to be talking about love in its most basic reality. The Christians are the most naïve. They merely repeat in their mindless way an absurdly exaggerated command which was invented by a repressive society in order to hold in check both of the two basic human drives, the drive to hold on to specific love objects and the drive to destroy. The Platonists at least recognize that there is a connection between the will toward civilized activity and the drive for sexual pleasure. They have the connection upside down, however. The Romantics are better in this regard, for they do seem to understand that the love of two persons is more fundamental than the derivative energy. But even the Romantics are forced to act out their sexual drives in extraordinary neurotic patterns—patterns, by the way, which were imposed upon them, among other things, by the Christian prejudices.

Plato would object against all of these ideas that they were not worked out philosophically. To the Christian assertion that love is not a desire, he would say: strictly speaking, even your noble and generous desire to love freely and to wish the well-being of all regardless of deserts is nevertheless a *desire*. You find such a life rewarding, somehow desirable. You cannot get away from it. To feel no desire is to be unmoved, to have no energy, no thought, no inclination—certainly no dedication. Now, to desire everything indiscriminately—have you considered all that is involved in that assumption? It must mean that all of reality is, as it were, desirable. I do agree with this implication, but this vision can be won, not as you suggest by killing our desires for individual excellence, but by training ourselves to desire only the truly excellent—that is to say, to understand what is truly desirable, which is the same as the truly real, as I can prove to you.

To the Romantic Plato would say: the most characteristic

thing about your ideal form of love is also its most damning feature. You seem to assert that happiness is compatible with a vision of the world as meaningless, irrelevant, or even ugly. Illusion, you seem to argue, is somehow better than a clear grasp of things as they really are. But this shows a gross naïveté about the relation between desire and knowledge. Knowledge is a correct grasp of that which we must assume to be real if we are to get our true desires. The correctness of our grasp of reality, therefore, is tied to the correctness of our desires—that is, our attainment of knowledge depends to some extent on whether or not what we are in fact pursuing will turn out really to have been the most rewarding thing we could have been pursuing. But if the object of knowledge and the object of desire are the same in this way, then reality, the object of knowledge, must be desirable. After all, this makes good sense: happiness, the object of our true desire, whatever else it may involve, must surely be a deep and lasting delight in life and the world as they are—that is to say, in reality.

You Freudians, Plato would say, share the Romantic idea that the world could appear ugly even to the happy man, but at least you do (rather inconsistently!) demand knowledge if we are not to fall into unhappiness. This is an important advance. I applaud, too, your notion that discord in the *psyche* is the true description of unhappiness, also your conclusion that desire for happiness must inevitably be narcissistic first before it can find altruistic expressions. On the other hand, your incredible assumption that sexual love gives man his greatest gratification and is inevitably the prototype of all happiness, no matter how intelligent or civilized he is, seems arbitrary and bound to have a bad effect. It is probably the product of your Romantic past. Really, you ought either to go along with your wilder colleagues, such as Wilhelm Reich, and assert that the pursuit of the largest number of the most successful sexual releases is the only rational path to happiness, or, if you accept social, artistic, and intellectual pursuits as ultimately more satisfying for the adult than the pursuit of organ pleasure only, then you might as well accept civilized pleasure as the more basic. The evidence for unconscious sexuality in all adult pursuits and the complete dominance of sexuality in the infant do *not* make it necessary to assume that the delights which the adult finds when he turns in frustration away from the tyrannous appetites of childhood are merely safer and not actually better than his best sexual memory. You may *say* that you are glad of man's capacity to sublimate, and you may admire those who are capable of sublime sublimation, but your real feelings are still betrayed by your insistence that the key to this process lies in the physical experiences of such men when they were infants. The hidden assumption here, as I say, is the one which you have inherited from the Romantics, that the world to which the adult must accommodate himself is evil and contrary to his inevitable wishes. If you admit that a direct attempt to return to infantile sexuality would be disastrous, why not begin with the assumption that, in an adult, the all-important thing is the conscious life of his intelligence—how successful he is in discovering the truly rewarding things in life and in the world around him? You are living a strange nightmare indeed when you assume the residual appetites of childhood to be a man's true self and reality to be an unavoidable horror. Like your predecessors, you have not understood the connection between the pursuit of the truly desirable and the comprehension of the truly real.

The subject of the *Symposium* is just that: the identity of the pursuit of the truly desirable and the comprehension of the truly real—the identity of desire and learning, of love and philosophy, Eros and Socrates.[1] Now this idea was just as foreign to the ordinary way of talking in antiquity as it is to our thoughts on love today. The suggestion, therefore, is not presented in this bold form in any of the speeches in the *Symposium* before the long speech by Socrates. That does not mean that Plato wastes the earlier speeches on completely misleading suggestions, of course. Plato, who was the first to state explicitly the theory of organic unity in works of art, a Greek ideal already ancient by his time, could hardly have been guilty of that.[2] But some critics, like Léon Robin, have thought that maybe Plato was merely collecting the wrong ideas on love which were current in his time in order to sweep them away.[3] And this is indeed one of the things accomplished in this part of the dialogue. The other critics, however, like Werner Jaeger, who assume that Plato must be attempting to extract the greatest possible truth out of these popular positions even while rejecting them, have a far greater probability on their side.[4]

The *Symposium* describes one long, gay evening in the house of Agathon, a famous tragedian who had just won the prize in the festival of Dionysus. The party is a very civilized one indeed, for the main part of the evening is spent in a series of competitive speeches in praise of the god Love (that is, Eros). That the party should be celebrated in this manner is first suggested early in the dialogue by the pedantic doctor, Eryximachus.[5] He calls the young Phaedrus the "father of the idea," however.[6] Phaedrus, he explains, had often remarked with astonishment that neither poet nor sophist had ever produced a decent encomium of Love—and this although men had composed praises of everything from Hercules to salt.

Here we are stopped in our tracks: can this be so? Are there not famous hymns in praise of Eros in the *Antigone* and the *Hippolytus*? And what of all the occurrences of that god even in the meagre fragments which have survived of the lyric poets? But Plato turns out to be right. Love is usually sung of in the tragedies as a hostile god[7] who takes away our wits and makes even the just act unjustly to their harm,[8] even though the wonder and the beauty of Love's power are sometimes understood as well. In the lyric poets, Love is often called a madman, liar, bringer of woe, tyrant, deceiver, or mischievous opponent,[9] and he is usually praised (in half lines and epithets) only when he characterizes the gaiety of light-hearted attachments,[10] or when his representation as a lovely youth offers a way of complimenting the poet's boy love.[11] There is great uncertainty as to Love's parents or his relation to Aphrodite,[12] and the Loves are often mentioned in the plural[13]—making them very minor deities indeed. Plutarch, who of course had much more of the early lyrics than we have, complains that the poets never did take Eros seriously, so far as he could find.[14] The truth is that Love, although, unlike Aphrodite, a native of Greece, was a major deity only in two isolated and unimportant cults that we know about, and even in literature was very quickly subordinated to the great goddess from the East.[15]

Why, then, did Plato choose Eros instead of Aphrodite as the subject for his competitive speeches? But just consider how different the whole tone of the *Symposium* would have been had he chosen Aphrodite! For one thing, we have a feeling that this company, except perhaps for Aristophanes, would not have worked up so much enthusiasm for the lady as for the boy. In Hellenistic times, when romantic affairs between men and women became the dominant theme in literature, Eros shrank to the familiar chubby infant who flits about at the command of his beautiful mother; in Plato's time, however, he was an athletic youth, the ideal of a different kind of lover. Second, there may have been a tendency to think of Aphrodite as Beauty and Eros as Desire. At least, that is how Plato turns it.[16] But probably as important as either of these considerations was the simple fact that the most common words for *sex* in Greek were derived from Aphrodite's name or epithets. This circumstance undoubtedly reduced the usefulness of this goddess for Plato's purposes. (Later, also, we shall see how one of the speakers is able to distinguish between two kinds of Eros in a parody of Hesiod's distinction between two kinds of Eris—that is, Strife[17]—and how Socrates, with Alcibiades' unwitting help, is able to draw a picture of Eros which comically resembles old Socrates himself. These fine touches would both have been impossible had love been represented by Aphrodite rather than by Eros. Who knows, perhaps the very absence of general attention to Eros made that god the more desirable for Plato's needs. Certainly Plato had more freedom in concocting a novel genealogy for Love than he would have enjoyed had he chosen Aphrodite.)

Phaedrus begins the contest because he was the father of the idea. He launches the competition with an apparently unimaginative encomium in a very traditional manner.[18] Love, he says, is to be honored because he is the eldest of the gods, being in fact, unbegotten, as Hesiod and Parmenides both tell us.[19] Love well deserves our praise also, he goes on to say, because he is the greatest of all our benefactors. How? By inspiring lovers with a sense of honor and dishonor, and thus inspiring men to great and selfless deeds. He proves this by the old stories, the self-sacrifice of Alcestis for the love of Admetus and that of Achilles for the love of Patroclus.

Despite Phaedrus' simple-minded procedure, supporting his points by genealogies and myths, he has actually started off the investigation with great force and economy. He has said, in effect: there never has been a time since the beginning of things when there was no love, for love is first of all that sweet desire which has brought us all into being, every man and god. But this pleasure is more than a longing for procreation, he says. It is at the heart of every noble deed and every act of generosity. The reminders of Hesiod and of the ancient stories have different effects. Hesiod's haunting lines[20] are moving because they instantly speak of something which has always been understood, hard as it is to speak of rationally. The stories, such as Homer's tale of Achilles' choice, remind us of how much we do indeed admire the man who can care for another. There is no reason why Phaedrus cannot be literally correct: without love, there could be neither "excellence nor happiness," neither the energy for doing anything great nor reward for the effort. But just what is the connection between the desire which keeps life going in the race and that which makes life possible and worth while for each individual? Ah, that Phaedrus does not say.

Pausanias is the next speaker.[21] Pausanias was well known to be a crank on the subject of the superiority of male love to boy-girl love.[22] His speech here is sometimes embarrassing because it is so obviously a case of special pleading. It contains, however, an invaluable survey of the attitudes of various Greek states toward homosexuality. More than that, like all of these speeches, it carries us forward toward a genuine understanding of love while simultaneously undermining our satisfaction with commonly held views.

Pausanias begins by criticizing Phaedrus for assuming that all manifestations of love are good. This is too obviously not the case, he says. In the cults, he points out, one can find a distinction between two goddesses called Aphrodite, one celestial, one vulgar.[23] So must there be two gods called Eros, one to go with each—and therefore two kinds of love. Love in itself, like eating or drinking, is neither noble nor shameful. It is the manner that counts. It all depends on which Eros is inspiring you.

The distinction between two kinds of love may well remind us of Socrates' habit of dividing all pursuits into the real and the mock activities. Perhaps the wrong love is to the right one as rhetoric is to philosophy or as cooking is to medicine.[24] But the two kinds of Eros also remind us inevitably of the two kinds of Eris, or Strife, in Hesiod. As a matter of fact we can almost equate the two distinctions: the good Eros in Pausanias' speech *is* the good Eris in Hesiod and the bad Eros, the bad Eris. The good Strife in Hesiod's poem is the spirit of competition which is the author, not only of such events as the Dionysian festival which is the occasion for the party described in our dialogue, and indeed of the competitive speeches themselves by which the party is being celebrated, but, according to Hesiod, of the whole idea of justice and civilization.[25] All this Pausanias claims for the good Eros. On the other side, the bad Eris in Hesiod is the selfish aggression which tends to break down all that its twin builds up. Exactly corresponding to this is the bad Eros in Pausanias' speech. This is mere lust for self-gratification, a kind of love which deserves the universal hostility of all civilized society. And every society does, in fact, mark this love as Public Enemy Number One.

Well, almost every society. On the assumption that civilization-building love is invariably between males (as boy-girl love can only find its natural consummation in physical pleasure), Pausanias divides the Greek cities into three groups according to their different attitudes toward homosexuality. The merely backward states, like those in Elis and Boeotia, approve of all male love without discerning how bad the one kind is. States under savage dictatorships, on the other hand, as in the cities under Persian rule in Ionia, try to stamp out male love in any form because they know that the good kind is a powerful threat to tyranny. Only in Athens and Sparta, above all in Athens,[26] is there an ambiguity in the attitude toward friendships among men, revealing thereby a half-understood awareness that love can be both the best and the worst thing for the state. On the one hand Athens had made a cult out of the love which inspired Harmodius and Aristogiton, and Athenians still condoned the most extraordinary self-debasing actions in suitors trying to win the favor of their boy loves; on the other hand, these same men loathed the thought that older men might be hanging around their tender sons hoping for sexual pleasure by them. The kind of love which is approved, Pausanias points out, is never one which could find fulfillment solely in physical pleasures; it is never directed toward unformed boys or toward any but the most intelligent and generous souls, and, although physical beauty in the younger man is undeniably important, such beauty is neither an indispensable requirement nor ever an end in itself. The relation is ideally that of student and teacher, each inexplicably inspired to think and act on a level neither had thought himself capable of before. The bond should be lifelong, however, and weaken not at all when the younger man matures and loses his good looks.

Eventually we shall have to come to grips with this ideal and try out on it the more sensational vocabulary of the Freudians. For the present, notice how, both in the rhetoric[27] and in the characterization of the speaker, Plato has taken pains to make us uncomfortable about Pausanias' essential honesty even while he says things we are unable quite to deny.

Before we leave Pausanias, there is one more feature of his speech which I should like to draw your attention to. The approved method of pursuing a boy love, as Pausanias describes it,[28] turns out to be remarkably like the extravagant behavior expected of a young man courting a girl in Hellenistic or Roman literature—and indeed in Courtly Love and the "Romantic" novel. The *erastae*, according to Pausanias, put prayers and supplications in their entreaties, swear oaths, lie on their loved one's doorstep, and willingly submit to slavery such as no slave would endure. These same men, he points out, if they did these things for money, office, or power, would be stopped by friends and enemies alike, the latter casting "flattery" and "servility" in their teeth, the former showing embarrassment for their sakes and trying to bring them to their senses. Yet when a *lover* does all these things, he says, it lends him charm (*χάρις*); and custom (*νόμος*) allows him to act in this way without a single reproach, there being a tacit assumption that what he is doing is entirely noble. What is most astonishing of all, Pausanias says, is that even the gods, so people say, forgive lovers when they break their oaths.

Now, when we compare this description with the honest, personal awareness of the violence of love, say, in Sappho,[29] we notice the large element of conventionality in Pausanias' ideal. He describes specific conventions, moreover, which, as we have seen, survive remarkably intact in the Romantic tradition of the following centuries.[30] Apparently these conventions are actually hardier than such details as, for instance, which sex a man should pursue! We might be tempted to suggest, like La Rochefoucauld, that indeed, if it were not for all this talk and these specific rules of behavior, most people would never fall in love at all. Perhaps it is all an illusion. "Men have died from time to time, and worms have eaten them, but not for love!" Strangely enough, however, the awareness of this artificiality in our modes of feeling and showing love has itself become a persistent feature in the Romantic tradition. Anthropologists (that most Romantic race) often assume without giving it a thought that when they go to primitive communities not touched by our ideas they will find sex aplenty, but never love.[31] *That*, they are convinced, is the invention of Western Civilization. But this observation is not usually made in a tone of disparagement. As any Frenchman will tell you, the awareness that it is all a game is the very secret of enjoying the life of love. This is the love which holds up Don Giovanni, rather than Romeo, as the ideal. Anacreon sometimes sounds this note.[32] In our dialogue it is best represented by Aristophanes' contribution.

The next speaker, according to the seating order, ought to have been Aristophanes. Unfortunately he has the hiccoughs. There is a doctor in the house, however, one Eryximachus, whose name, by the way, *means* Hiccough-fighter. He not only tells Aristophanes how to stop his hiccoughs but also obligingly takes his turn in the speaking order to give him time to recover.[33]

Eryximachus complains that while Pausanias had started out all right, he had ended incorrectly. That is, what he had said was perfectly correct, but he spoke of love as though it were found only in the longings of human *psyches* for the handsome. As any scientist, especially a doctor, knows, love is also the principle behind all bodily phenomena—not only the bodies of plants and animals but the very elements themselves, and indeed everything in the universe. What is medicine, for instance, if not the art of reconciling the desires of opposing elements, such as the cold with the hot, the bitter with the sweet, the dry with the moist, and so on?[34] The sick, Eryximachus points out, have a different class of desires from those which the healthy have. Whereas the desires of the healthy work in harmony and lead to happiness, those of the sick tend to destroy the well-being of the whole person. The doctor's task, therefore, is to diagnose all bodily desires and transform the warring kind into the other. When Pausanias distinguished two kinds of love, this is what he *really* meant. The sign of the good Eros is health, that of the other Eros sickness.

Turning away from human bodies, Eryximachus says, you will find the same principle to hold in gymnastics, farming, music, meteorology, astronomy, and religion. Each of these arts is, first of all, the study of a complex of independent but interacting desires. The universal study of all scientific investigation, therefore, is love. But each of these arts also is obliged to try so far as it can to produce a situation in which the love of each of the constituent elements cooperates to form a higher order of phenomena: healthy plants and animals, harmonic consonance, appropriate preparation for the seasons, and activities in accord with the desires of the gods. The good kind of love, therefore, really is the author of everything which makes life possible, beautiful, and worth while.

This is an extremely important argument. To make love the principle of all things is to give a thoroughgoing teleological explanation for all phenomena. By "teleology" I mean explaining events not by antecedent events but by goals apparently being striven for—not by efficient causes, in other words, but by final causes. It is the principle behind the vision of Aristotle, Aquinas, Dante, and Spinoza. Today, of course, teleology is recognized as the enemy of scientific explanation, in fact the very essence of unscientific naïveté. It is understandable, therefore, that when Eryximachus broadens the idea of love to include the dynamics even of inanimate things, the modern reader is likely to find himself alienated. He is relieved to find that in the next speech the concept is narrowed down again to human feelings. But notice, we do not ourselves limit love only to beings consciously pursuing some object. Animals, for instance, love, we think. And, if Freud is right, that which we are conscious of as being desirable accounts for only the smallest fraction of our real loves. (Freud, by the way, was a thoroughgoing teleologist within the realm of human phenomena: no slip of tongue, no dream, no irrational behavior, he maintained, was explicable in any terms but the goals being striven for on one level or another.) How far downward *do* we extend the notion of love? Of the love of children and of dogs we are certain. But apparently we draw a line somewhere about the level of the oyster. We seem to feel that there is some correlation between love and locomotion. That plants should be capable of love would never occur to us. If a compound can move itself in a manner *not* accounted for by the simple mechanics of classical physics, then we may assume final causation—love, if you will. But where the motions are *only* those which the physicist studies, then teleology, an explanation on the principle of love, seems out of the question.

Eryximachus is right, however, that an ancient scientist would have had no such reaction to his suggestion. We have already been reminded by the earlier speakers of the rôle which Love plays in Hesiod and Parmenides. Eryximachus now adds a reference to Heraclitus, specifically to his stunning idea that all harmonious and effective things are the products of tensions between irreconcilable drives.[35] He also reminds us of the medical writers, some of whom studied Heraclitus very closely.[36] But even more important to medical theory was the system of Empedocles, who made love the principle of union into higher compounds wherever that happened in the universe. Eryximachus does not mention Empedocles by name, but Empedocles was so famous that the Greek reader, we are forced to assume, must have thought of his theory throughout Eryximachus' speech. In fact, Aristophanes, who is the next speaker, apparently parodies Empedocles at several points.[37] Why, then, did Eryximachus not actually mention this famous physicist of love? There are two reasons, I think. For one thing, Empedocles called love Aphrodite, the Cyprian, Joy, Friendship, and Harmony, but never, so far as we know, Eros. For another thing, Empedocles saw nature as the product of two opposite tendencies, only one being Love of any kind, the other being Strife (on one occasion even called by its Hesiodic name, Eris).[38] Eryximachus, on the other hand, is at great pains to suggest that even when things are pulling apart or at odds to one another the same *kind* of explanation must be given. Every case of repulsion can be reduced to two attractions that happen to be for contrary things.

(Notice that Plato could easily have made Eryximachus expound a version of Empedocles' theory if all he had wanted to do was to collect and sweep aside current false beliefs on love. But his purpose was more complex. As we shall see later, Plato was presenting here, as in all of these speeches in the first half of the dialogue, a familiar idea, but in a version which he will be able to build on, rather than be forced to reject. We are nevertheless made aware of the fact that Eryximachus understands little of the philosophical complexities involved in what he is saying. This is achieved above all by his ludicrously bare and pedantic manner of talking. Eryximachus has as little taste for rhetoric or feeling as he does for wine.[39] What could he understand about love, we ask.)

Suddenly the pace livens as the great comic dramatist, Aristophanes, recovered from his hiccoughs, takes his turn.[40] He invents a wonderful, outrageous myth.[41] Mankind, he says, was once much happier and stronger, long, long ago. There were three sexes then, one all male, the children of the sun, one all female, the children of the earth, and one half male half female, the children of the moon. Each was vaguely spherical in shape, having four legs, four arms, two heads, and two sets of sexual organs. We were not reduced to walking forward, as we are now, he says; we could move in any direction. And when great speed was required, we could roll like a ball, limb over limb. Zeus feared, however, that we might be strong enough to take over heaven itself. He therefore cut us in half (as easily as one cuts an egg with a hair)[42] in order to weaken and humiliate us. (In fact, there is some reason to fear that he may cut us again if we are bad!) After the operation, Apollo healed the wound and drew the skin together on the cut side at what we now call the navel. He then moulded our breast and belly with a tool like a leather-worker's, but left the navel as the one reminder of our former state. Our heads he turned about so that we could see where we were going. At first, however, the two halves clung to each other in their longing to be reunited. The desire to return to our earlier wholeness was indeed so intense and incapable of fulfillment that nothing else could be thought of, and men died like flies. When one of a pair collapsed, the other would search out and embrace a stranger of the appropriate qualifications and languish in his arms. In pity, Zeus had our genitals turned around to the belly side and arranged for the seed to be spilled, not on the ground, as with grasshoppers,[43] but inside the female. This had the effect of making us express our longing for wholeness in sexual coupling.

As a result, we can now achieve periodic satisfactions which allow us to rest, look about us, and go on with the business of life. The sex of the person who can give us this release depends on the sex of our original other half. (Aristophanes gently teases Agathon and Pausanias[44] by suggesting that men who are not attracted to women but to others of their own sex are really the most masculine men, as is proved by the fact that most of our politicians seem to come from this class!) But whatever our tastes, what we all want is that person who will heal our wound, correct our lonely insufficiency, and make us whole once more. Once we find him, our desires all take the form of striving to become one person with him, separated neither in body nor in soul.

This is a much loved passage and one which has haunted many readers. I am not sure that its influence has been entirely good, however. The theory that people are born already polarized toward their own or the opposite sex must have done untold harm before it was suggested that this was not so.[45] And what about the idea, so dear to the Romantics, that there is some one person somewhere who is our perfect mate? "Somebody loves me, I wonder who, I wonder who she can be." How many marriages do you think have been wrecked by that idea, lodged in the heads of sentimental ladies who find themselves no longer very enchanted by their husbands? Nevertheless, the myth must draw some of its vividness and power from the fact that it touches something which we earnestly believe to be true. What moves us, essentially, is the definition of love as "the desire and the pursuit of wholeness."[46]

This idea might perhaps remind us of Kierkegaard, or psychologists like Otto Rank and Erich Fromm, who brood about universal "separation-anxiety," whether they mean separation from God, the womb, or the security of childhood. But these men do not agree with Aristophanes in making sexual union the primal, oldest way to overcome this pain. Freud does, however. Freud cites this speech by Aristophanes on a couple of occasions with great enthusiasm. Once he offers it, hesitantly but in all seriousness, as a clue to the truth about sexual desire.[47] By the observation in his patients of a compulsion to repeat, Freud had been driven to the conclusion that all basic drives were of a regressive character. In introducing the myth from the *Symposium*, therefore, he says, "I should not venture to produce it here were it not that it fulfills precisely the one condition whose fulfillment we desire. For it traces the origin of an instinct to *a need to restore an earlier state of things*."[48] He then repeats the myth. Afterwards he asks, "Shall we follow the hint given us by the poet-philosopher, and venture upon the hypothesis that living substance at the time of its coming to life was torn apart into small particles, which ever since have endeavored to reunite through the sexual instincts?" After life had evolved to a multicellular condition, he explains, it then "transferred the instinct for reuniting, in the most highly concentrated form, to the germ-cells."

At the beginning of his speech, Aristophanes had suggested that, unlike Eryximachus, he was not able really to build on what his predecessor had said; he was making a fresh start.[49] This is clearly true in that he does not continue the progression which we noticed in the first three speeches. Plato is in effect begging us to follow Aristophanes without feeling that we must reject what has been accomplished so far. Phaedrus began by identifying the desire which leads to procreation with the desire which leads to noble, selfless acts. Pausanias added the necessary observation that, nevertheless, desire was good only if it was desire for good things. Then Eryximachus tried to identify this desire for good as the urge toward growth, health, strength, and splendor, wherever that is found in nature. But the last two speeches before Socrates, Agathon's as well as Aristophanes', are apparently designed to awaken personal rather than theoretical and historical associations. Aristophanes reminds us of our profound conviction that love is the pursuit of a cure for an old wound which has left us helpless. And Agathon reminds us of what we had almost lost sight of: you cannot talk about love without talking about beauty.[50]

A talk about beauty at this point might have been embarrassing. A silly talk or a sound talk would have been equally unwelcome. Plato solves the problem with a magnificent turn: he presents a purring, catlike self-praise by the most beautiful person at the party. Not only is Agathon (whose name means "the Good") as lovely as a young girl,[51] he also has every conceivable charm and grace of speech and sentiment. He is an ancient Felix Krull, one of those happy creatures in whom the knowledge that they arouse delight wherever they go brings out neither contempt nor a desire for power, merely warm gratitude and a wish to be infinitely obliging. He cannot think but that the god of love must be just like himself, happy, beautiful and good. Love must be young, not old, as the others had said. It must have been Necessity, not Eros, who ruled Olympus in the early days, because love has no part in violence. He is soft as the softest part of the softest men, where alone he will be found. And do not the scent and coloring of flowers have a very special connection with love? As for Love's goodness, being the very essence of desire how could he ever work *against* anyone's desire and therefore unjustly? He is the master of all pleasures, and therefore maturity itself, the master of all aggression, therefore courage itself, and his touch can make the dullest wit into a poet, therefore he must be the master of all of the arts. Love is he who drains away all querulous tempers and fills men with the ability to delight in each other's company—especially at feasts like this, and at all dances and ceremonies. He dispels unkindness, discourtesy, thoughtlessness, selfishness, and opens our eyes to the wonders which we somehow inexplicably forget: the lovely, the tender, the musical, the delicate, the dreamy, the gay. It is not that happiness would be incomplete without love; happiness *is* love.

Agathon's procedure is perfectly legitimate. As we know what Ares is like by the way we feel when we are filled with the desire to kill, and Dionysus by the way we feel when we are drunk, so Love must be characterized by all that happens to us when we are in love. This can be done in two ways, however. We can either concentrate on those features of our own behavior which we only take on when in love, or we can concentrate on those qualities which love opens our eyes to in the person whom we love. Yet the difficulty we would have in deciding as to which Agathon is doing suggests that in his case the two procedures would amount to the same thing. In other words, he is, Narcissus-like, in love with his own reflection. Socrates will object to Agathon's picture of Love, but not because of his Narcissism. On the contrary, Socrates will substitute a portrait of Love which will be magnificently echoed by Alcibiades when he portrays Socrates himself. Nor will Socrates really reject Agathon's contribution, especially what he has to say about love's role in the creation of justice and art. The real objection is simply that Agathon's myth is a dead end for reflection. Because it does not separate beauty itself from the desire for beauty, it leaves love in the realm of exquisite sensual self-satisfaction. It rests at the dead center of all our memories of the most wonderful civilizing joys we have felt, without offering any clue as to the precise connection between these joys and the rest of life. For that we shall need a new myth, using as its central figure not the most beautiful of the company, but the ugliest.

This ends Plato's selective gathering-in of popular ideas on love in his time. A number of ideas important to us in the twentieth century do not appear in Plato's survey, and there are a few moments when the speakers in the *Symposium* clearly speak of prejudices which we today do not entirely share with them. Yet the agreement is much more important than the differences. It is great enough so that when we follow Socrates in the second half of the dialogue and find him asserting such unimaginable things as the identity of love and philosophy, passion and rationality, beauty and science, we cannot take refuge in the assumption that Plato did not mean by love what we mean. The first five speeches of the dialogue, designed to enlist the sympathy of the Greek reader and excite his memories and associations in the most constructive possible way, should still have much the same effect on the modern reader today.

# CHAPTER 3

## *The Discourse by Diotima in the* Symposium.

LOVE, IT IS BELIEVED, can intoxicate a man, rob him of his judgment, lead him to conclude false things about the world, and draw him to his own undoing. As the chorus says in the *Antigone*,[1] Eros wrests aside the understanding even of the just, making them act unjustly to their own ruin. Behind this idea is the assumption that love is a kind of fever, an enchantment, something which temporarily paralyzes all our instincts toward self-preservation. Love, in other words, is the very opposite of clear thinking, rationality, and prudent self-control. Nor is the noble lover any better off than the baser sort. In true love the illusion inspires one to do noble rather than base deeds, but even the noble lover is mad insofar as he is in love. This is a conviction which was just as common in antiquity as it is today. If Plato had not taken it into consideration, we would not listen to him, and neither would the Greeks have done so.

On the other hand, Plato is going to try to persuade us that this idea is basically mistaken. He will try to extend love to include all desire, including the desire to get things straight and to find where our true well-being lies. If love is the key to happiness, he argues, it must be the pursuit of that which really will make us happy. The only valid distinction between true and false love, therefore, is this: the true actually does lead us to happiness, while the false fails to do so. If we think of rationality not, in the Romantic fashion, as heartless calculation used to justify and achieve what the heart desires, but, in the Greek fashion, as enthusiasm based on an understanding of what is really important in life,[2] then it follows that true love and true rationality are actually the same thing. Both turn out to mean "the most efficient possible pursuit of what is most worth having." It is obviously impossible, therefore, that love correctly understood could ever be in opposition to reason or to the pursuit of one's true well-being. Love, as Plato understands it, is the essence, not of irrationality, but of rationality!

Plato works up to this revelation rather obliquely. As the first five speakers in the *Symposium* are set the task of praising Eros, Plato allows them merely to condemn the supposed irrational and self-destructive tendencies in love and identify these as manifestations of a different, false Eros, not the true one. But the problem of blind, misleading passions could not really be dismissed so easily. What Plato does is to broaden the idea of irrationality itself, precisely as he does the idea of love, far beyond the example of sexual infatuation. Now, the god of irrationality as such is Dionysus, not Eros. It is not surprising, therefore, to discover that the redefinition of Dionysus is almost as important in the *Symposium* as the redefinition of Eros.

Friedrich Nietzsche popularized the exciting notion that there was once a great, fruitful tension between Dionysus and Apollo.[3] Apollo, he maintained, stood for rational control, science, awareness of the lines which can be drawn between things—above all the line which separates the observer from the observed—and, in general, the knowledge needed in order to manipulate the world around us and avoid catastrophes of every sort. Dionysus, on the other hand, stood for the desire to forget who or where one was, to break down the line separating subject and object, to melt into the world—uniting either with another person, a group, nature, a god, or the universe. The realms of Apollo, therefore, included science, philosophy, politics, business, and those of the arts which revealed order in the world about us. But Dionysus was invoked by drink, sex, religious ecstasy, and the wilder sorts of music and dance. Apollo's instrument was the lyre, capable as it was of only a limited number of tones at any tuning. The flute, however, capable of wild chromatic music, belonged to Dionysus. Since wisdom and foreknowledge can be of either kind, reasoned or mystical, both Apollo and Dionysus were gods of prophecy. (In fact, they shared the same oracle, that at Delphi, Dionysus taking over from Apollo during the three winter months of every year. This, no doubt, preserves the memory of an ancient rivalry.) Attic tragedy, Nietzsche maintained, resulted from a marvelous tension between the two divinities. The plot, the dialogues, and the arias (accompanied by the lyre) were Apollonian. The wilder poetry of the choruses and the spectacular dances (accompanied by the flute) were Dionysian. Our pleasure at triumphant *dénouements* is obviously Apollonian. The darker joy at the death of the protagonist, with whom we usually identify to some extent, is a victory of Dionysus.

To speak of Apollo and Dionysus is to risk accusations of dilettantism from most scholars today.[4] Certainly the clarity and ubiquity of the opposition, so far as the Greeks were concerned, was very much exaggerated by Nietzsche. Plato himself, while an Apollonian in Nietzsche's sense, is not especially aware of Apollo as his deity (even though the rôle of Apollo's oracle in the legend of Socrates gave him a marvelous opportunity, had he wanted one); and as for Dionysus, Plato generally speaks of him with respect.[5] The closest he comes to Nietzsche's distinction is when he accepts Apollo's instrument and musical modes for his ideal state and rejects those associated with Dionysus.[6] What Plato will do in the *Symposium*, however, is reinterpret Dionysus. As we shall see, he concludes that if Dionysus really is a god, a bringer of good, he must possess all the splendors which Nietzsche reserved for Apollo, even while retaining the essentially ecstatic quality which tradition gave to the darker god.

What Plato started with, the people's Dionysus, *that* Nietzsche did not get wrong.[7] As Plutarch tells us, he was first of all the god of all liquids:[8] not only of wine, but also blood, sap, honey, milk, semen, all that gives us life, strength, and joy. We know (above all from the *Bacchae* of Euripides) that ecstasy, superhuman power, and release from all strains were among his gifts. Women are more susceptible than men, but Dionysus can come to anyone. His coming is usually preceded by a stubborn resistance, the denial of his divinity. His revenge is hysteria.[9] Euripides pictures him as a beautiful, effeminate stranger with long hair and an unearthly calm. More often he is represented as a splendid, happy young man, drunk, and crowned with fillets and with vines of grape or ivy.

There is a natural assumption that Dionysus and love must be closely associated.[10] After all, lechery, obscenity, and strong male potency are prominent in many Dionysian rites[11]—also in Dionysus' choice of animals (which include the leopard, the snake, the goat, and the bull) and in his followers, especially the various kinds of satyrs. Near the beginning of our dialogue, Socrates suggests that Aristophanes will be glad to praise Eros, "for his whole concern is with Dionysus and Aphrodite."[12] In fact, Plato goes out of his way to make us feel the presence of Dionysus from the beginning of the *Symposium* to the end.[13] The party as a whole, remember, is in celebration of Agathon's victory in the tragic competition—a competition which is held in honor of Dionysus, in the theater named for that god. And the party is in turn conducted as a kind of tragic competition. Remember, too, that the dialogue closes with a quiet but effective scene showing Socrates trying to persuade Agathon and Aristophanes, the tragedian and the comic dramatist, that the same gifts are needed for both of their arts.[14] But after all, what is a symposium anyhow if not a celebration among friends at which Dionysus is consumed by the cup? At the beginning of our party, there is a lot of talk about drinking. Pausanias points out that he, like most of the company, is still suffering from a hangover caused by the drinking of the previous evening.[15] At the suggestion of Eryximachus, therefore, measures are taken to keep the drinking down to a sane pace.[16] He deliberately excludes Socrates from his advice, however.[17] Socrates, as Alcibiades explains later, has never been seen drunk by any man, no matter how much he drinks.[18] His sober survival at the end of the party is vivid proof of this power of his.[19]

Late in the evening, as Socrates finishes his long speech on love, young Alcibiades bursts in. He is flushed with wine, supported by a flute girl, surrounded by his followers, and crowned with fillets, violets, and ivy.[20] He is almost Dionysus himself. He appoints himself master of the drinking, and moderation is banished. Soon a band of revelers swarms through the door, and everyone drinks until he drops. At the beginning of the evening, Socrates had told Agathon that Dionysus would have to be the judge as to which of the two was wiser.[21] And now Alcibiades takes that rôle upon himself! At first he gives Agathon his fillets, but then, on finding to his dismay that Socrates is also of the company, he takes some back and puts them on Socrates' head.[22] But just as we have begun to feel the presence of Dionysus in Alcibiades, Plato deliberately confounds our confidence in this identification. In a eulogy of Socrates himself, Alcibiades likens him to Marsyas[23] and Silenus.[24] These are Phrygian deities who are closely associated with Dionysus. Marsyas, himself one of the *silenoi* (elderly, but still lecherous, satyrs), invented the flute, or at least competed with a flute against Apollo's lyre. Another, named simply Silenus, was Dionysus' stepfather, and taught him winemaking. Like Dionysus himself, he had the gift of prophecy, was never seen without a wineskin and a crown of ivy, and was often shown supported by satyrs. But *Silenoi* were also small, snub-nosed, potbellied, bald little men—just like Socrates! Alcibiades says. And status of *silenoi* could be purchased which opened up and revealed lovely things inside their gross exteriors. Clearly, the spirit of Dionysus is at the party, but in whom does it live more truly, the wild, intoxicated Alcibiades or Socrates, whom no one had ever seen drunk or at a loss?

Closely akin to Socrates' imperviousness to Dionysus in the liquid form were his powers of endurance and his marvelous ability to concentrate regardless of his surroundings. These are brought home to us very vividly at the beginning of the evening when Socrates goes into deep concentration;[25] again later in various anecdotes which Alcibiades recalls to the company.[26] Most impressive of all, of course, is the shameful story of Alcibiades' attempt to seduce Socrates.[27] Socrates, you remember, was unmoved by the young man's famous beauty and fell immediately to sleep. Whatever the historical Socrates was like,[28] in the *Symposium* he is deliberately depicted as having been totally without sensual desire. When he pretends to be attracted to Agathon, or in love with Alcibiades, he is being ironical and merely playing along with the others. To a Greek this is a truly exquisite paradox: the beautiful Alcibiades loves the ugly Socrates, but his love is not requited! Whom *does* Socrates love? Nobody. And yet, as he tells us himself when the subject first comes up, he knows about love and nothing else.[29] The god of love is present at this party, too, but who is more brilliantly filled with him—he to whom one man means more, almost, than his whole life, or he who is apparently heartlessly impartial?

The evening gets wilder and wilder as it goes along. Even before the serious drinking begins, the recollections of love begin to reach a crescendo of intensity. Gaiety, warm friendship, and some deeper attachments charge the air. After the entrance of Alcibiades and the revelers, indeed, all hell breaks loose. Yet, through all of this, there is the remarkable, outrageous Socrates, absolutely unmoved. He is just the same at the end as he was at the beginning. The great lover indeed, we say! What can we do with a man like that? Not only did Socrates almost forget to come into the house at the beginning of the evening, but he could not even remember the rules of the game once he had joined the party. When Aristophanes finished his speech, for instance, but before Agathon started his, Socrates drifted imperceptibly into a cross-examination of poor Agathon, as though they had just met in the market place and were not in the middle of an elaborate celebration.[30] Agathon had professed stage fright. Socrates showed surprise, inasmuch as Agathon had appeared before thousands in the theater just two days before. Agathon says, innocently enough, that he is more frightened before a few who are discerning than a great crowd of fools. Ah, then you would be afraid to do something shameful before the few who were wise? Yes, says Agathon. But you would not be ashamed to do the same thing before the many? Don't answer him! shouts Phaedrus. If you do, we shall never get back to our party.

Again, when Agathon finishes his speech and the thunderous applause dies down, what does Socrates say?[31] Oh dear, how foolish I was. When I agreed to participate in your praises of Love, I naïvely thought you meant that we should tell the truth about him. But you just meant that we should say anything nice about him. I am terribly sorry; I shan't be able to participate in that game, as I have no invention of that sort.

Luckily, we know our Socrates, and it is not long before he is persuaded to tell the truth about Love.

Socrates must have aroused great curiosity when he stated at the beginning of the evening that love was the one thing which he did have knowledge of, because he was famous for his insistence that the only knowledge he had was that he had no knowledge.[32] Also, the prospect of any set speech from Socrates must have seemed irreconcilable with his well-known profession to be able only to cross-examine others. This latter difficulty is soon solved, however. Socrates begins (with the kind permission of Phaedrus this time) by cross-examining Agathon;[33] and then, when that becomes a little humiliating for his accommodating host, Socrates retells a conversation which he had had long ago with a priestess named Diotima.[34]

From Agathon, first of all, he draws the admission that love must be love *of* something, as a father is necessarily father of a child. Furthermore, love must be the desire for something of which the lover is in want, he argues. In the *Lysis*[35] this point is offered as a stumbling block, and in the *Gorgias*[36] and *Eryxias*[37] as a proof that desires are bad things. Here, however, the observation is offered merely as a paradoxical way to introduce a necessary distinction. That love is a desire (ἐπιθυμία) was assumed by all of the earlier speakers. That it entails the consciousness of incompleteness and imperfection was dramatically emphasized especially by Aristophanes. But what was not understood before was the peculiar relation which this implies between desire and the desirable: love is not the possession of desirable things, but the awareness that there are things which it would be desirable to possess, but which one does not yet possess. (To the quibble that some people desire only what they already have, Socrates replies that what they desire is continued possession of these things in the future.) More important is the question *what* is desirable. Anything which is in fact desired, such as money, strength, power, food, and the like, is in one sense capable of being desired and so "desirable"; but, in a stricter sense, we desire only those things which would prove to be worth having if we did gain possession of them. There is, of course, notorious disagreement as to what these things might be. But let us just agree to refer to them, whatever they are, as the *truly* beautiful and good things, that which is *really* desirable (τὸ τῷ ὄντι φίλον).[38] Love, then, is not well characterized as being all things splendid and fine; on the contrary, he can exist only in the awareness of the absence of these possessions.

Socrates gracefully covers Agathon's confusion at this point by saying that the priestess Diotima had once drawn *him* out in precisely the same way. At the youthful Socrates' shocked conclusion that Love, therefore, could not be divine if he was wanting in all that made one splendid and happy, Diotima had replied: as there is something between ignorance and knowledge, namely right opinion,[39] so there is something between us wretched mortals and the blessed immortals, namely the *daemons* who communicate between the two. Love is one of these intermediate *daemons*.

The equation of love with the mean between ignorance and knowledge is, of course, not merely an illustrative comparison. We begin to see why Socrates could say that love was the only thing he had knowledge of. Correctly understood, it amounts precisely to the same thing as his more characteristic profession of radical ignorance. As philosophy is not simple ignorance, but the awareness of the desirability of knowledge, so love is not merely the absence of all good things, it is the awareness of what they are, that they *are* absent, and that they would indeed be desirable. Really to understand one's ignorance and what that implies is thus to understand all about the *daemon* love.

The problem of Plato's literal belief in *daemons* is a famous one.[40] He speaks of them frequently, in different contexts, but with no very great consistency. There was a tendency among the Platonists of the later part of antiquity to construct dogmatic demonologies out of the dialogues, but these attempts only demonstrate the more clearly how wrong-headed we would be to try that. This does not necessarily mean that Plato completely disbelieved in the existence of *daemons*, of course. (Was Socrates himself not put to death for introducing *καινὰ δαιμόνια*?)[41] The frequent descriptions of *daemons* in Plato's eschatological myths have an authentic ring to them. Much more interesting than this problem, however, is the particular reason which Plato gives in the *Symposium* for calling Love a *daemon*. Love must be a *daemon*, he says, because it binds together heaven and earth and the whole cosmos. Now this *is* an idea which is repeated with real clarity and consistency in Plato's writing. In the *Gorgias*, for instance, he speaks of "geometrical equality" (*ἰσότης γεωμετρική*) which holds together heaven and earth and gods and men, in the form of communion, friendship, order, control, and justice (*κοινωνία, φιλία, κοσμότης, σωφροσύνη* and *δικαιότης*).[42] In the *Phaedo* he speaks of the good and the obligatory which binds and holds together (with a pun on *τὸ δέον* and *συνδεῖν*).[43] Again in the *Republic*, he speaks of that which binds together and makes a single whole, a thing which is the greatest benefit to any community, just as it is in the human body.[44] Finally, in the *Timaeus*, it is explained that the very elements of the cosmos were proportioned according to a strict order, and that they therefore have a friendship (*φιλία*) built into them which makes the universe indissoluble except by its maker.[45] The *Symposium*, like the *Gorgias*, emphasizes especially Love's role in making possible some harmony and communication between men and gods. Notice that Eryximachus had already demonstrated this,[46] as he had also the marvelous benefits of higher organic unity of every sort. It is, then, the specific aspect of *daemons* as guides, messengers, and interpreters, that made the identification of Love as a *daemon* right. Love, Socrates wishes to emphasize, is not perfection, it is the energy *toward* perfection, not divinity, but our longing for it.

What does this *daemon* look like? Like the truest and most perfect lover, of course. People tend to think of him as beautiful because he desires beauty, says Diotima; but that gets us nowhere.[47] Think of him rather as a philosopher, because the philosopher is the fairest lover of them all, the lover of the fairest thing: *σοφία*—that is, insight, understanding, profundity. Knowing its worth but never possessing it (for only a god can have that), he is bold, clever, inventive, brilliant, yet shoeless, penniless, homeless, harsh. He is unkempt, insatiable, no sooner full but he is empty again, flourishing at one moment, dead the next. His father was Resourcefulness, son of Knowhow, but his mother was Poverty. He was conceived on Aphrodite's birthday, in Zeus' garden. Resourcefulness, it seems, had drunk a great deal of nectar at the birthday party and had gone out to sleep it off among the flowers. Poverty saw her chance to improve her circumstances, and—well, that is how it happened.

If you are tempted to interpret this playful fable as a minutely worked out allegory, by the way, may I recommend that you look at the attempts by Plutarch[48] and Plotinus.[49] That will most certainly change your mind. The myth is offered by Socrates as a correction of the pictures suggested by the earlier speakers, especially Agathon, but its value is not really appreciated, as most modern critics have seen,[50] until Alcibiades comes in and gives an unconscious parody of it in his eulogy of Socrates himself. Without hammering it in too brutally, Plato leads us gradually to the conviction that Socrates really was the greatest lover of them all.

If Plato had stopped his dialogue at this point, we should have come away feeling that we had been in the presence of a wise man and a great artist, but we should hardly have been forced to change the idea of love which we had had when we picked up the book. Suddenly, however, Diotima's questioning becomes sharper, and we are alerted to the possibility that there is something implied in all this which is truly surprising.[51]

Love is of the beautiful. Agreed. But that is not the answer; that is the puzzle. What do people want when they desire the beautiful? It seems so mad, this strange fever which comes over us when we suddenly decide that we are in the presence of beauty. What we want is to possess the beautiful, to make it somehow our own. But why? Because we are convinced, for some reason, that this possession will make us happy. But why should that be? The beautiful, Diotima suggests, is but a special, electrifying example of the good—that which, when possessed, will make us happy. *Happiness* we may take to mean that which we all really want, the true alternative to misery, failure, disappointment, or settling for less than the best. "Good" is what we call things like health, leisure, freedom, or friends, which we suppose will lead us to this happiness. (If experiment shows us that one of these things does not bring happiness, we withdraw the label "good".) What is being suggested here is that the special all-consuming desire which comes over us when we see beauty is perhaps only an unusually intense example of the desire for happiness which motivates us all, all through our lives. Somehow beauty is, as it were, a sudden vision of what would really make us happy. If we desire only happiness, in other words, and agree to call "good" only those things which strike us as things the possession of which would bring us happiness, then perhaps that special quickening of desire which we call falling in love is but the result of a peculiarly clear glimpse of happiness, and "beauty" but the special name which we give to "good" under these circumstances. The real innovation here, as Diotima is quick to point out, is the suggestion that insofar as we ever want anything at all, we want the same thing as that which we desire when we are in love. In reality, we are all lovers all of the time. The popular habit of reserving the word "love" for special occurrences only is to be deprecated, as it suggests a difference in kind where there is only a difference in intensity. Ordinary usage not infrequently muddies our understanding in this way, she says.

Love, then, is defined as desire to possess the good, and good is the name which we give to things which, when possessed, will bring us happiness. This is the end of the chain, however. We cannot ask why we want happiness, Diotima says.[52] Happiness is what we want, no matter how mistaken most of us may be most of the time in our manner of pursuing it. Even when a man gives his life for another or simply kills himself in despair, he is assuming that there is no alternative course which would really be more rewarding. Now, this is a way of talking which, though easily reconciled with Romantic and Freudian ideas, is most annoying to some Christians. They call it Pagan "eudaemonism" and dismiss it as patently selfish. On the other hand, it seems to be ultimately inescapable. Even the Christians are told that if you live a selfless life, "your reward shall be in Heaven." This is a famous puzzle: look hard enough at any act of altruism and it seems to be merely a very devious, self-deceptive but socially constructive, path towards one's own self-esteem and well-being. Plato, therefore, has the advantage over the Christians (as do Aristotle, Spinoza, Hobbes, Schopenhauer, and Freud) in that he is proof against the attack of cynics. Plato's point is that even when men are perfectly clear that it is their own happiness which they are seeking, happiness rarely does come to them. Nor is the problem usually one of physical or social restrictions; it is one of intelligence. The crucial problem is how to discern a genuinely desirable goal among all of the activities and possessions which may appear to be desirable. We experience desires for many things, some of which turn out to be not really desirable at all; but in a sense we have only one *real* desire, to find and possess that which would be, not only not disappointing, but better than anything else we could have pursued if we had known and understood them all. What the Christians have really done, of course, is merely to identify one special vision of life as the answer to our quest for real happiness in the fullness of time. Their vision may be right, to be sure. If it is, we shall each of us know for certain after we die.

So then, being in love is just a special manifestation of that desire for happiness which never leaves us, and beauty is what we call any sudden, inexplicable vision of what we pursue in all our activities. What can happiness look like if that is indeed a correct explanation of beauty and of falling in love? The Freudians, we saw, identify the pursuit of happiness as a sexual nostalgia for a state never quite recovered since birth or shortly after birth. The trouble with this explanation is that in itself it suggests very strange advice to the adult in pursuit of his best interests. Plato's analysis is fortunately rather broader. He agrees with Freud in taking the phenomenon of being in love as the most valuable evidence as to what we are really after, but then argues that pleasure, pure and simple, is not necessarily always our goal, even in sexuality.[53] What we apparently really want, he thinks, is to avoid or conquer death. And this means not only keeping a tight grip on life and its pleasures so long as they last, but quite literally circumventing death. If it is a boy and a girl, they seem to want to survive in a child. If it is men, they seem to want to survive in achievements of the mind and spirit.

But the rôle of beauty is still a problem. Both Plato and Freud put special emphasis on the connection between beauty and sexual attraction. In the most "Freudian" passage in all his works Plato speaks of that which is full and ready to give birth as "pouring forth" in joy at the approach of beauty, but at the approach of ugliness, "shrinking" and "curling up" (*ἀνείλλεται* and *συσπειρᾶται*).[54] Apparently sexual excitement appeals to both philosophers as a kind of model for all enthusiasm in the presence of beauty. But there is an important difference between the two on this point. Freud would say that all consciousness of beauty is disguised response to sexual desire; Plato would say that sexual desire was only one of a number of responses to the awareness of beauty. It is the most common of the intense responses, perhaps, but neither the clearest nor the strongest one possible.

What *do* we make of the rôle which beauty plays in sexual excitement? Freud suggests that visual pleasure—even in the preparatory stages of love-making itself—is, as it were, a perversion.[55] For various reasons, personal and social, we are made to feel afraid or ashamed of our originally exclusive interest in the genitalia of our "love-object." As a result, he says, we develop a greater and greater tendency to linger over the preparatory activities, and finally fool ourselves into believing that it is the color, texture, and lines of our loved one's body that really draw us. In the end, we may even think that we are attracted by colors and sounds in such bizarre things as hills, trees, birds, the concert hall, and the art gallery!

This much can be said for Plato's analysis of beauty: it is at least no further from our ordinary awareness than Freud's is. Plato seizes on the rather obvious connection between the awareness of beauty and activity which leads to reproduction. What we really desire in sexual excitement, he concludes, is to reproduce in a beautiful medium, *τόκος ἐν καλῷ*. Beauty, in other words, is a vision which sets up in us longings to create. Now, Plato obviously cannot mean that what we consciously yearn for when we are sexually aroused is to conceive children. The actual conception of a child may, for one reason or another, be the last thing which we look forward to as we pursue our pleasure. Our restlessness is normally stilled, not by birth or the discovery of pregnancy, but by the sexual act itself. Indeed, it has been suggested that some primitive societies may have survived for generations without observing that there was any connection at all between copulation and pregnancy. That is, in any case, a fair description of the situation among animals; they surely have no thought of offspring when they are sexually aroused. What Plato must have meant is that the desire to create, although it is not conscious, is somehow the *real* nature of sexual desire.

It might be argued, as some anthropologists have done,[56] that the existence of a parental instinct in animals points to a family instinct existing in us also, and that sexual phenomena are therefore *really* a part of this more complicated mechanism. In evolution, in any case, sexuality would obviously function as a survival factor solely because of its connection with propagation. But Plato could not concern himself with sexuality in evolution. He would want to point, rather, to the inner history of individuals. His point is that, for all creatures destined to die, the desire for happiness, whatever form it takes, is at heart always a longing to overcome failure and death. The nature of an organism being what it is, however, this desire for survival, permanence, and perfection can express itself only in acts of creation. That, he suggests, is the real key to all our confused responses to beauty. It may be that most men successfully divorce their pursuit of erotic pleasure from any conscious urge to survive, but can they boast that their erotic activities have then provided them with all that they could want out of life? There are many kinds of creation to which a glimpse of beauty can inspire a man, and the best is not necessarily the commonest, the most obvious, or the one which occurs earliest in life. The best is the one which really does lead to happiness. Perhaps the common inability to imagine anything better to do in the presence of beauty than to act as though we wanted children, even when we do not, is at the heart of much unhappiness.

Diotima spoke of these things, not once, says Socrates,[57] but several times. On one occasion she began by directing his attention to the blind yearning to conceive and then to protect the young, observable even in the birds and the beasts. What can this be, she asked, if not a universal desire to achieve immortality—even if only by a serial succession (*εἰ τῷ ἐφεξῆς*), as Aristotle says?[58] But does that mean that men and animals are pursuing perfection only in that fraction of their lives which they give to their young? Certainly not. Look even at a man's own body. In one sense, she says, he is the same man at seventy that he was at seven—there is a unity there all right—but how was that precious unity maintained? Notice that his body does not remain unchanged, nor is it even made of the same material throughout his life. There is a constant flow of stuff both in and out, and, not only hair and nails, but flesh and bones themselves preserve their characteristic structures only by a constant, though of course unconscious, effort. We somehow manage to arrange a never-ending sequence of foreign materials into structures resembling or improving on the old tissues and organs which are always in the process of dying. And is there not an identical process in our character, mind, emotions, memory, and knowledge, the unity of which down through the years is even more important to us than the things which can be located in specific cells? A conception or an attitude drifts away as inevitably as the matter in any part of our body, and continuity with our past selves can be kept only by a constant effort. This process is clearly exemplified on the conscious level by recollection after a lapse of memory, says Diotima.[59] What is this insatiable appetite toward survival, health, growth, and perfection on every level, both in our bodies and our minds, if not our old friend, the insatiable vagabond, the *daemon* Love? Constantly, consciously and unconsciously, physically and mentally, we conquer death by continuous regeneration of all our structures from the simplest to the most complex.

Plato accomplishes in this remarkable passage what Freud so longed to be able to do: to trace love back to the very essence of the struggle of individual cells to survive, and forward again to the highest strivings of man. (We have here also, by the way, the sublime ancestor of that most stupid of all the vulgar things which are ever said about love—that it is all just "chemistry.")

A man with limited gifts, or even a gifted man in a wretched society, might be content, as most animals are, to aim for a full-grown and well-functioning body, a plentiful supply of food for the future, and a periodic spawning of more young. Since for such men the ultimate expression of their fight against death is in the production of children to survive them, it is not surprising that they should see beauty only in women and exquisite contentment only in sexual intercourse. Such men, says Diotima,[60] are pregnant only in their bodies. Far more interesting in the long run, she says, are the men for whom this is not nearly enough. Consider what made Homer write the *Iliad* and the *Odyssey*, or Hesiod, Lycurgus, or Solon their great works. In their attempts to realize higher structures, they were not content to create children or families, they gave order and splendor to whole states and civilizations, they uncovered justice and symmetry, and brought citizens by the thousands to excellence of character and understanding. And in the process did they not conquer death—not only in their fame but also in the lasting changes which they brought about? Can we not say that these men were pregnant in soul, as most are in body only? Freud calls this kind of ambition sublimated love, but he does not mean this in the literal sense of that word, he means "frustrated in a peculiarly fortunate way."[61] But who, Diotima asks, would not far prefer to have the children of Homer and

Hesiod rather than ordinary human children?[62] And if that is so, which is the frustrated instinct, the drive for immortality in human children, or the drive for immortality in this far more effective manner?

Plato now presents a portrait of the truest lover of all. Unfortunately, he is nowhere farther from our way of thinking than he is in his description of the truest lover. This gifted person, he says, is already pregnant with ideas of civilization and justice in his youth.[63] When he is older, he wants to father and conceive. Just like the common lover, he goes about in search of beauty in which he may bring forth his child—for he will never do it in ugliness. Quite understandably, beauty even of the body elicits more tenderness from him than ugliness, but he is more especially responsive to the beautiful soul. He looks for a young man who is naturally noble and is splendidly endowed in mind and character. If these qualities are found in a body which is also beautiful, of course, he welcomes the combination as best of all. In the presence of such a youth, he will find himself eloquent on the noblest ideals of character and achievement. In short, he will try to educate his younger friend. In contact with his friend's beauty, and in its company he engenders and brings forth the things with which he has so long been pregnant. Together the two become the parents of splendid visions, profound understanding, and high standards of conduct and achievement. They tend their offspring over the years, exploring, understanding, creating. Such a friendship, says Diotima, is as much greater than that based on the production of human children as the children of these friends are nobler and more truly deathless than children of flesh and blood.

Modern readers are often understandably suspicious of Plato's objectivity here. His ideal seems to be too patly in agreement with his own far from universal proclivities, and with the tastes of the Athenian gentleman of the fifth and fourth centuries. We suspect that Freud is probably right in describing such relations as the result of partially suppressed libidinal desire, finding expression in an activity which the super-ego will not be too horrified at. The arrogance of the teacher who maintains that only in teaching is a man entirely noble and successful! And the naïveté of the man who confesses that to teach good looking young men is more exciting for him than teaching others! We would sack him on the spot. Yet no reader of Plato can be entirely happy about condemning any of his suggestions as merely naïve or provincial, and, as the point is by no means a side issue but a very central one indeed, let us see what sense can be made of Plato's attitude.

People often gloss over the problem here, by the way. They speak of "the lover" and "the beloved," as though one could substitute specific genders according to one's own tastes. In particular it is hoped that Plato may be saying something which might be easily converted to modern ideals of boy-girl or conjugal love. This is probably a mistake, however. Plato has gone out of his way to say that love between the sexes finds its natural fulfillment in a relation which is basically sexual and which leads to the formation of a family. The idea that a good wife ought also to be able to inspire her husband to great achievements in art, music, science, and public service can probably be traced to the admixture of Platonic love in our Romantic tradition, but in this form it is more Romantic than Platonic. Peace, companionship, release from sexual frustration, a sense of order and decency, and a heightened pleasure in all activities are no doubt common rewards of marriage, but the will to write novels or symphonies would have to have been there before marriage and might just as well have been realized in celibacy, to judge from historical examples. That inspiration to great works often comes in the form of *das ewig Weibliche* cannot be denied, but are we so sure that Beatrice, for instance, would have played that role in Dante's life had Dante actually married her? Plato assumed that love between the sexes, because its natural issue was in sexual pleasure and the birth of children, was really but an elementary try at something far better which occurred only in a man's world. If we have any hope of understanding Plato, we had better not distort him on this point.

Actually, it could be argued that the world today is just as much a man's world as it was in Plato's time. Artistic, scientific, and civilizing activities are still carried on, on the highest level, almost entirely by men. In all this time there has still not appeared a great woman philosopher, mathematician, painter, composer, tragedian, or physicist—and poets, novelists, and scholars only of the second order. Nor can muscular inferiority or time lost in pregnancy and suckling really explain this fact in modern times. We must probably assume that there is some additional difference between men and women. It need not be a difference in intellectual ability, to be sure—there is no evidence for that—but there must be something which causes men to develop a more compelling sense than women usually do of an urgency in abstract standards—an urgency which can at times cause personal feelings to fade by comparison. Freud, as we have seen, has an interesting theory on this development.[64] Many otherwise orthodox Freudians, however, part company with him on this one point. But then, all theories on this phenomenon are unpopular, for the very recognition of the problem offends our liberal and democratic feelings.

Granted that the most splendid achievements are realized in masculine society, where does love come into this? Obviously only a fraction of the world's activities are the work of homosexual lovers: the theories of Phaedrus and Pausanias were far too simple. The rôle of love must be more hidden. Now, like Plato, Freud also traced the most splendid achievements to masculine love, but, again like Plato, assumed that this love was not ordinarily sexual in the obvious sense.[65] Sexual energy is in itself amazingly indiscriminate, he thought, but people do come to suppress from their own consciousness the sexual nature of their interest in many persons—their parents, for instance, or their children. The result is usually a bond of loyalty, often charged with warmth and protectiveness. When men suppress the sexuality of their pleasure in other men, a similar thing happens, he believed. Indeed, the business of the world could not be carried on if it were not for this phenomenon. Now add to this the peculiarly masculine tendency to identify with the abstract standards of one's culture and you have a possible source for great deeds and noble achievements.

Once more, the difference between Freud and Plato is instructive. For one thing, Freud dismissed out of hand the specific relation which Plato admired most, where the older man is drawn by the physical beauty of the younger.[66] This was a confusion as to which sex was really attractive, he thought, for the blushing boy was really admired for his girl-like qualities. In other words, the basic sexuality of the situation was insufficiently repressed for Freud's tastes. And yet, perhaps this is more of a difference in degree. After all, Freud, too, would not want the sexual element destroyed altogether, for then there would be no strong ties of the productive sort. His ideal, apparently, would be the man who would become aware of sexuality in his feelings for other men only after psychoanalysis. Plato, living in a society which was slightly less repressive in this one particular, seems to have expected even many of the unsophisticated to be aware of such inclinations. But the more important difference is in the theory. Freud assumed that the process was one of deflecting a desire which was in reality purely sexual. Plato supposed that sexuality itself was in certain conditions the deflection—that is, when a man was capable of more satisfying creations, but held blindly to a sexual routine instead.

In what she describes as the greater and more secret initiation,[67] Diotima hints as to just how one should use one's love to rise to great heights of achievement. The first step after falling in love, she says, is to realize that the more general vision which this brings is more important than the particular. That is, when we fall in love, not only the loved person, but the whole world is more beautiful than it had been before; trees, sky, people, music, all unlock their secrets to the lover. Surprising as it seems, this new beauty which our eyes are opened to around us is apparently the direct result of the strangely exciting qualities which we suddenly noticed in this one person. But we must accept this new awareness as greater clarity, not as befuddlement. The crucial decision here is that the new vision is closer to, not farther away from, the real world. For if we value the vision more than any sexual act which we can imagine, we are on our way to true wonders.

The second step is to realize the infinite superiority of beauty in intangible things, like nobility of character and fineness of mind, to anything which we admire solely through our senses. Once more this opens our eyes to unsuspected marvels all around us. If things go well, we come to value profound intelligence, real understanding, splendor of soul, and actually quite forget the individual who first quickened our awareness of these things. But even this is not the end. We go on from the admiration for brave decisions and just deeds to enthusiasm for order and justice themselves; from there to the knowledge and vision which push back chaos and make that order possible; and at last to a comprehension of the beauty which makes that order worth pursuing. At this point Plato's prose is itself dazzling and very moving, but he can communicate his ecstatic vision of a sea of beauty and beauty itself only in negatives: it is not limited, not local, not dependent, not conditional.

As we shall see when we come to consider the central books of the *Republic*, Plato has something very precise in mind even when his language is most like that of a mystic. In the *Symposium*, however, he merely teases us with hints and signs. Most of us have had some taste of love; Plato is telling us to recall what life was like at that happy moment, to go back to it as a crack in the envelope of darkness which usually surrounds us, and take it as a true indication of what we really want. It is a glimpse of the happiness which we are all pursuing. If we only know how to use it, love is the greatest help we shall ever have.

We have defined happiness as that which is more worth having than anything else, that which, if we could experience it, together with the knowledge of all of the other things which we might have been experiencing, would satisfy us most completely. The well-known difficulty which most of us have in discerning how this happiness should be won can probably be traced to the nature of the desires which we conceive along the way. A desire takes flame—as, for instance, the desire for money, comfort, or sensual pleasure—whenever an object or activity begins to look to us like the missing prerequisite for happiness. We have been fooled by these desires too many times, however, and above all by that peculiarly compelling kind which we associate with the beauty of persons. We waver, therefore, between the conviction that happiness can only be conceived of as the strongest possible desires together with the means to requite them, and the more desperate feeling that the only rational procedure is to rid ourselves of all desires. To this dilemma Plato offers a brilliantly simple solution. The instantaneous intensity of a desire may or may not be a sign of the true desirability of the object desired. How, then, can we be sure that we are actually on to the real thing? For this end, says Socrates,[68] one could not easily find a greater ally to human nature than Eros. Do not contemn the desire to speak noble thoughts and build lofty structures which comes on you at the sight of true beauty. Hard as it is to describe happiness, two things at least are known about it: it must be a permanent possession, a victory over death, and it must be a deep satisfying pleasure in the world as a whole and everything in it, including ourselves. If the realization that there is beauty in at least one place in the world can be used to lead us to the realization that the world is beautiful, then that is surely the most direct possible way to happiness.

Where is Dionysus now? If he lives in Alcibiades, then he is a dangerous god. After all, if rationality means the desire for what will bring us true happiness, then irrationality must mean action on desires which will lead to misery. But perhaps Dionysus lives rather in Socrates. If Socrates really is the greatest lover, then he must burn with the hottest flame. Not only is he not without the gifts of the god of enthusiasm, but his days must be full of a truly ecstatic power such as few others ever know. For all the advantages which Alcibiades had, which of us would not rather see the world as Socrates sees it? He is so at home in the universe that even wine only makes him more like himself. As Alcibiades says, Socrates was the only man who could really enjoy himself at a party.[69] He delighted in the presence of the fair (if their comeliness was really an expression of their inward beauty),[70] but look what he did in this delight: the happy energy which these meetings generated produced moral understanding so profound that our civilization is still benefiting from it. Not that we could picture ourselves as *being* Socrates. As Alcibiades points out,[71] Socrates is absolutely unlike any other human being past or present. He is not beauty, he is merely the personification of the love of beauty; not the desirable, but the *daemon* Desire at its best. Alcibiades has made a near tragic mistake in thinking that it was Socrates he loved. Agathon, too, has gotten it ludicrously wrong when he suggests that by touching, wisdom might flow from Socrates to himself, like water from the fuller to the emptier vessel.[72] Alcibiades is closer to the truth when he compares the touch of Socrates to a serpent's bite.[73] It is a sting meant to awaken us from the dream of desire to the dream of the desirable.

# CHAPTER 4

*The Connection between the Platonic Theory of Love and the Habitual Activities of Socrates—The* Apology, Lysis, *and* Gorgias. *The* Phaedo*: Love, Teleology, and the Forms as Causes.*

ONLY IN THE *Apology* itself is the subject of a Platonic dialogue more inextricably bound up with a portrait of Socrates than it is in the *Symposium*. Even in the *Crito* and the *Phaedo*, large parts of the discussion are carried on on an abstract level, and the presence of Socrates, while moving and exciting, is not really the essence of the argument in quite the same way. But in the *Symposium*, as we have seen, Socrates turns out to be himself the very personification of the phenomenon which the company is trying to understand. Love, says Socrates, is the key to everything he has ever done. It is the only subject which he has ever pretended to have knowledge of. Correctly understood, love is the same as philosophy, which is not so much the profession to which Socrates belongs, as a name for his way of life, and his only, in the whole history of mankind.

The other dialogues, from the earliest to the latest in which he still appears, present very palpably the same Socrates as the one so vividly characterized in the *Symposium*. Only occasionally,[1] however, is he represented as the great expert on love—and then usually in playful jest at his supposed preference for handsome young men. But, to be sure, when Socrates announces to the company in the *Symposium* that love has always been his only theme, it is in the tone of a paradox, and some of his friends apparently have no idea what he is talking about. But this is not the important thing. Even if the real Socrates did speak of love only on occasion, Plato—and this is the real point—nevertheless interpreted this talk of love as a special distillation of what was really involved in all of Socrates' habitual activities and concerns. As the heart of all Socratic philosophy, he suggests, there is this one concern, to clarify the true objects of desire, to make people strong and happy, in other words, by turning them from false loves to true. It should be interesting for us at this point, therefore, to examine Socrates at his more characteristic activities and see to what extent this is indeed an illuminating interpretation of his mission.

Philosophy to Plato *meant* conversations with Socrates. When readers find Plato reproducing a Socratic argument in the *Phaedrus*[2] proving that no man should ever put much trust in written works, they often think that they have caught him in a monstrous inconsistency, for did not Plato himself commit his lifeblood to writing? But, of course, what Plato did was to invent conversations, and conversations among people who are very much alive and with whom we can involve ourselves very vividly. More specifically, what Plato did is to make the effect of conversation with one special, extraordinary man a living experience even for those who never knew him in the flesh.

Now, in assuming that serious thinking was best done in conversation of some sort, Plato was, as usual, in the direct tradition of the earliest Greeks. Thought, to a Greek, was always best advanced by asking and answering questions: proposing alternatives, raising objections, predicting consequences, and comparing the consequences of alternative courses of action. In the *Sophist*[3] Plato actually defines thinking as an internal dialogue. But behind even this very sophisticated idea was an old habit. Remember how in the *Iliad*, for instance, in Book XXII, while Achilles is bearing down on Hector, Hector poses the alternatives open to him, giving the reasons why he ought to run and the reasons why he ought to stand his ground. When he has done this he says to himself: "Yet still. Why has the heart within me debated these things (*ταῦτα . . . διαλέξατο*)?"[4] More often, of course, debates were carried on aloud, between two men—in the epics just as in the histories and the tragedies, indeed, in the very places where democratic decisions were made. Socrates did add one new thing to this habit, however. He did not wait for a problem to arise or for the appearance of a conflict in opinions; he deliberately sought out the complacent and asked them questions which would destroy their peace of mind.

Of course, not all conversations, even of this sort, are good philosophy. We are all too familiar with talk which goes nowhere, or which gives each man the chance to expound his prejudice and exercise his sense of importance and which ends with no one even remotely inclined to change his views. The conversation needs, alas, a Socrates. It needs a man whom no one can suspect of merely trying to gain a reputation or win followers, who apparently urges no theory of his own, and rarely, if ever, demands of his interlocutors that they be mere listeners; a man whose only motive is to become clear himself and make others clear also about the most important things in life; a man whose intellectual abilities are equal to his energy and generosity, and whose life and death do not fall short of the implications of his cross-examinations. Only with such a man does conversation become philosophy. Socrates was undoubtedly the only person whom Plato had ever met—indeed, he was surely one of an extremely small group in all history—who was able actually to change a man's life by the purity of his motives, the clarity and profundity of his thought, and the power of his personality. According to his own boast, the incorrigible Alcibiades himself came within an ace of being made into a good man by Socrates.[5] Philosophy could not be a "Socratic" conversation; it had to be a conversation with Socrates.

The dialogue as such has many advantages over the philosophical treatise. Consider the bravery with which Plato can tackle vast problems in the briefest encounters. How ineffective even a Plato would have been if he had tried to write a fifteen-page essay on the connection between morality and religion (instead of writing the *Euthyphro*), a twelve-page essay on what a man owes to a state after it has treated him unjustly (instead of writing the *Crito*), or even a book on whether the good man or the unscrupulous man gets the most worthwhile thing life has to offer (instead of giving us the *Gorgias* and the *Republic*)! And it would be a mistake to think that the advantage of the dialogue lay merely, or even chiefly, in its ability to engage and persuade people who would never voluntarily read any philosophical essay. There are things which can be achieved in the dialogue which are simply beyond the reach of an essay. Think of the complexity of any of the questions which Plato treats—the nature of human happiness, for example. How could one begin to do justice to the thousands of questions, some unanswerable, some hardly answerable, which are involved in this problem? If the author's advice is new or uncomfortable, each reader of the essay will find some step in the reasoning which he can call incomplete, oversimplified, or unproved, and so reject the conclusion without further consideration. A conversation, on the other hand, if handled with extreme skill, can shift from point to point, break off, start again, and seem to go around and around. Hints can be thrown out, whether they are picked up or not; subtle things can be implied by the tone, the drama, little stories, or the backgrounds of the speakers. The talk can be guided seemingly only by the moods and idiosyncrasies of the interlocutors themselves—while the sequence of arguments may actually be superbly direct, more direct than one could justify or achieve in a single logical exposition. And yet, although many first-rate philosophers, from Aristotle to Santayana, have been inspired by Plato to try their hand at philosophical dialogues, there is not one of these latter-day dialogues which does not have the museum smell. Or if, like Shakespeare or Tolstoy, our writers have lacked nothing in the skill to reproduce brilliant and dramatic talk, they have not cared to go directly and openly to the most important questions and discuss them point-blank. We are convinced that philosophical talk must always be stilted and unreal. There was only one person in whose presence this was never so: Socrates. Even Plato's dialogues grew stiff and dreary when Socrates was no longer the central figure.

In Plato's version of the *Apology of Socrates* we have our single most valuable record of the manners and qualities of Socrates which aroused such feverish devotion in some of his countrymen, yet, at the same time, enough fury in others to lead to his public execution. Whether it is almost a literal transcript of what Socrates actually said at his trial or Plato's imaginative distillation of what was really going on does not matter. If we had our choice, it would be hard to decide whether we would prefer Plato to have been merely a clerk on that day or an artist and interpreter as well, for he obviously had a profound understanding of his master's mission. As many people have noted, if Xenophon's version of the trial is closer to a stenographic account than Plato's, he still fails so miserably to understand the real impact of Socrates on his friends and enemies that we are left without an explanation of either the philosophical revolution which Socrates started or the fear which caused his fellow citizens to vote his death.

The initial prejudice which Socrates had to try to overcome at his trial, according to Plato, was one which arose from a popular confusion according to which Socrates was identified with other teachers of wisdom. Not that he would not be delighted to be able to teach wisdom, says Socrates.[6] But he has no wisdom to sell. He does, to be sure, have a unique, strictly human wisdom of his own,[7] but that consists merely of the awareness that neither he nor any other man is really wise or has true knowledge. If he is wiser than all other men it is in this one respect: only he knows that men can know nothing.[8] He gives a vivid narrative of his daily activities.[9] His days were spent, apparently, going from one respected citizen to another —statesman, poet, artisan—and demonstrating by relentless questioning that their lives were obviously foolishly conducted because they had made the completely unwarranted assumption that they knew something. The most obvious result of a procedure like Socrates', if it is done with wit and brilliance, is to unnerve and depress capable adults and suggest a shallow nihilism to the young. By Socrates' own admission this is indeed precisely what happened on many occasions, and, together with his dubious political ties and his eerie claim to have a private voice, it is almost enough to account for his execution. But this is not exactly the result which Socrates was after, of course. He had great zest for his special way of life; indeed, he equated this activity with happiness itself.[10] He believed, moreover, that he had been divinely appointed to stir up the Athenians in this way.[11] Quite obviously he assumed that he was doing his fellow citizens a great good.[12] His questions, it seems, were designed to do much more than shake the complacent. Socrates did not aim merely at a man's satisfaction with the place he had made in society and public esteem; his target was a far more sensitive point: the man's satisfaction with the manner in which he had figured out what was needed in order to achieve his own personal happiness. He did not merely have it in for all famous and confident men, but only if they happened also to be people who had, in his opinion, made disastrous miscalculations as to where their true well-being lay. In particular, nobody was safe from Socrates' ironical queries who thought that money, comfort, power, and reputation were more important for his happiness than understanding, generosity, courage, and harmony with himself.[13] In fact, it turns out that practically the whole of mankind yearns for the wrong things. Socrates' mission was to make people fall out of love with the things which they habitually pursued and realize that there were other things far worthier of their zeal.

Here, then, is the reason why Socrates could say in the *Symposium* that love was the only thing which he ever professed to understand. He had a unique vision of the disastrous inadequacy of the understanding on which most men base their desires. Unhappiness is (by definition) that which we do not want, yet here we are, most of us, driving straight toward it like lemmings to the sea. The crucial flaw, as Socrates saw it, was the way men satisfied themselves with bad thinking and counterfeit wisdom. But by "bad thinking" Socrates meant corrupt desires. The correction of knowledge is valued so highly by Socrates because he does not expect from it merely shrewder calculation in the pursuit of one's desires; he expects new understanding of what is really desirable, and therefore new desires. Success comes when one covets only those things which really will bring happiness.

To be sure, the first step in the process is uncomfortable. The most common reaction to the first suspicions that what we have labored for is really worthless, and that we are therefore headed straight toward our own undoing, is fury at whatever awakened us from our comfortable illusion. Nevertheless, we could never have a better friend than the man who would risk that unpopularity and upset us in just this way, for only he has our real desires at heart. Socrates describes himself as a gadfly sent by the gods to awaken the great sleepy horse which is the Athenian citizenry.[14] He knows that his own contemporaries will arouse themselves only enough to slap him dead, but he is content in the knowledge that he is really doing them good, and that his fellow citizens will certainly realize that someday. As for the apparent waste and injustice of his own death, Socrates simply finds it incredible that men who do not understand what is really valuable could know enough to take that away from men who do understand.[15] His death at seventy, therefore, cannot in itself be an evil. (The strength and happiness with which Socrates faced his death are in fact startling indications that perhaps he really did understand what was valuable. It is impossible not to be moved by his behavior. Perhaps he really was the one who loved the truest thing, the truest lover, the *φιλό-σοφος*, "lover of wisdom.")

Socrates' two favorite devices for knocking people off balance and shocking them into new desires were irony and paradox. The two had basically the same effect, they made people wonder if their whole language was not an absurd tissue of meaningless words. Irony, in the Socratic sense, is a faintly dishonest profession of ignorance. Most typically, Socrates pretends that he can only understand people literally, refusing to enter into what then appears to be a universal conspiracy to find sense in verbal nonsense. In his paradoxes (as in the famous ones: no bad man is happy, virtue is knowledge, no one willingly does evil) Socrates annoys and bewilders his interlocutors by stating what is actually the conclusion of a very sophisticated train of thought in the form of a flat-footed announcement which seems at first sight to be simply false.

We are shy of paradoxes in philosophy today. For one thing, modern theologians often use the word for what is really a very un-Socratic procedure. By paradox they sometimes mean an absurdity offered as profound wisdom, an absurdity which, moreover, has the special merit of being beyond discussion, even, let alone proof. But Socrates' paradoxes can always be translated into other words, words which do not violate any of the rules of ordinary usage. "Virtue is knowledge," for instance, makes perfectly good sense if you realize that a brand new meaning is being stipulated for both "virtue" and "knowledge." New associations are forced on one in the process of translation, but not really new rules for the use of language. Many modern philosophers feel that this is a cheap trick, however, and a procedure, moreover, which, by encouraging us to contemn our inherited language, may well lead us straight to nonsense. I doubt if this would have impressed Socrates. He seems to have been much more worried about the way our language, most especially when it appears to make sense to all of us, prevents us from breaking through our satisfaction with our own understanding. It is typical of more than one school of philosophy in England and America today that the traditional duty of the philosopher to point out problems where none were felt to exist before is not only shied away from but actually condemned. But as Diotima said, the horrible thing about real ignorance is that it is invariably accompanied by a complete absence of desire for anything better.[16] It is the essence of Socrates' mission to make us desire something ever better, so that we may avoid disaster and achieve happiness. But you probably cannot change a man's mind about anything really important without forcing him to change his associations with at least one word—to accept, that is, what must at first invariably appear to be a paradox. In fact, a philosophical judgment which does not infuriate you at first, is probably bound to be nothing but a restatement of something you already believed.

The *Lysis* shows Socrates at his habitual task, and is, moreover, of special interest to us because the subject of the conversation is Friendship (*φιλία*).[17] The boy after whom the dialogue is named is represented as having every possible good quality of mind and body. He has a doting older would-be lover, however, who is a fool, and a spirited friend of his own age who is rather too fond of clever argument for its own sake. Friendship, says Socrates, is really quite the most wonderful thing a man could have, but have you ever considered its strange nature?[18] You would think, would you not, that friendship could exist even if only one of a pair liked the other? But there is something odd in that. It would seem to imply that we can love something alien and unrelated to us. On the other hand, if we assume that what we love must be akin to our souls, then it is hard to understand how this kindred thing could fail to see its kinship, and so return our warmth. Besides, the naturalists' principle of "like to like"[19] cannot really apply to friends, because even bad men are not drawn to other bad men. Perhaps, then, all love the good. That is easy to understand in the case of the bad men: the poor man has need of the rich, and the sick man haunts the doorstep of the physician—just as the dry yearns for moisture, and the cold for heat.[20] But "unlike to unlike" will not work as a principle of friendship, either, because such relationships are not usually mutual. Most excruciating of all; if a desire indicates a lack, what could a perfectly good man ever desire from another whether he be like *or* unlike? Here is a real paradox. It would seem that a perfectly good man would be incapable of love.[21] But that need not mean that only the bad can love; perhaps, as neither the perfectly ignorant nor the perfectly wise will yearn for wisdom, so neither the totally corrupt nor the divinely perfect can experience love and friendship.[22] What is loved, then, may be the good and the beautiful, but it is loved because of the presence of some element of evil. The ultimate object of all love is that which is without qualification desirable,[23] yet desire is possible only if some good is wanting.[24] But does that mean that if all evil were suddenly eradicated, we would cease to feel any desires, appetites, or loves at all? Surely that does not sound right, either. Perhaps we would still have our good desires. But what makes a desire good if not the fact that it is a desire for something really right and congenial for us? But that brings us around again to our original puzzle about the love of similars or dissimilars.

As we know from Plato's development of them in the *Symposium*, some of the problems posed in the *Lysis* are both more delicate and more constructive than one might suspect from the earlier dialogue. (Even the end of this little work is like a pale hint of the greater one, for the conversation, apparently far from finished, is broken up by an unruly group which has been drinking so much that it cannot be reasoned with.)[25] Socrates has accomplished one thing which he set out to do, however: he has demonstrated to Lysis' fatuous lover a way to talk to his boy which, unlike the indiscriminate praise and unimaginative commonplaces with which he usually woos him, would actually be a benefit to the young man. In the meantime, he has planted seeds of doubt in the minds of all of his hearers. In fact, like many of the earlier dialogues, the *Lysis* ends up with more doubts than concrete suggestions. But doubt is the prerequisite for desire for clarity, as desire for clarity is the prerequisite for the improvement of our understanding—and as that, in turn, is necessary if we are to have a shot at happiness. The particular uncertainties raised here about the nature of friendship, far from being haphazard and purely negative, are obviously the fruits of Socrates' habitual concern with the nature of desire itself. But quite as important as any single suggestion is the task of puzzling and infuriating us with paradoxical statements, so that we may be awakened from our thoughtless contentment and alerted to the desirability of acquiring a better understanding of so important a matter.

There is one distinction in the *Lysis*, made carefully but rather casually, which is repeated many times in Plato's subsequent Socratic dialogues. This is the distinction between what we desire at any given time and what we really desire in the long run.[26] The distinction is put most clearly in the *Gorgias*. In that dialogue, one of Plato's very best, Socrates challenges three well-known rhetoricians in their confidence that their art is worth pursuing, or even that it is an art at all.[27] The attraction of rhetoric, of course, especially in a democracy like that of Athens, is that it gives a man power—power to satisfy his appetites and power to prevent unpleasant treatment by his enemies. But Socrates, in his most paradoxical manner,[28] denies that rhetoric brings a man any power at all.[29] Not if power is a good thing to its possessor, anyhow. Once more we are stung by the apparently willful absurdity of Socrates' position. What could he mean? There is a crucial difference, he suggests, between doing what seems to you to be to your advantage at any given time, and doing what you truly desire for yourself in the long run. The true object of your desire is actual advantage, real good, happiness, your ultimate good, your *summum bonum*, and this may or may not be served by yielding to a momentary desire, however clamorous.[30] But it is for the sake of your real desire that you ought to find anything at all desirable.[31] Now, Rhetoric, he points out, is the art of flattery.[32] Its effectiveness is not judged by the ability to give people what they really desire, only what they think they want. Notice that it never seeks to make people *alter* their momentary desires, as Socrates, for instance, does, and as every true statesman must.[33] Socrates then tries to show that the orator himself does not reap any benefit from his trade, either. He is really unhappy, whatever he may say of himself. This is because it is precisely the people who have never seen the distinction between experiencing a desire and desiring what is truly desirable who are attracted to this sorry profession. For the life of the demagogue is clearly based on the assumption that happiness can only be realized when one has a large number of powerful desires—*any* desires—together with adequate means to satisfy them completely.[34] All other lives seem no better to these men than the life of a slave or of a stone, Socrates' argument against this view of things is that not only does it lead to a disastrous course of action, but it cannot even be pursued consistently. Even the rankest hedonist makes unconscious distinctions between more and less degrading appetites—and this implies a standard more ultimate than pleasure pure and simple.[35] Then Socrates tries to make his adversaries feel what a nightmare their notion of happiness would be if it were fully realized.[36] Finally, he tries to drag up from the depths of their souls a latent yearning for order and sef-respect.[37]

Plato, like Freud, is quite clear that our *psyches*, if only because of the complexity of our bodily needs, drive toward several goals at the same time, and that sanity, maturity, and success in the pursuit of happiness are largely a matter of harmonizing these desires, one with another, and respecting each in proportion to the real desirability of its aim.[38] In this he is quite "modern." Plato does not begin to leave his modern readers behind until he starts talking about *the* Good which *all* men desire. This is the language of religious and political fanatics, we say, and we all know what damage they have done down through the centuries since Plato's time. Surely our experience shows that it is better to assume that different people, even within the same culture and state, will have to find different compromises with life. Laws should be tolerated only to the point where they protect us from bigots and from the harsher demands of nature, and teachers and psychiatrists should be brought in only for the unformed or for those who cry for help. If a man says that he is happy, then he probably is. He is the sole judge of that. If he has a breakdown later on, his unhappiness dates from the day of his breakdown. It is simple prudence to watch for and avoid such breakdowns, of course, but what nonsense it seems to speak of being *really* unhappy even while we are still aware only of a zest for all the things we have. If Socrates had proved that all men who live the lives of public power and private pleasure invariably spend the last thirty years of their lives in despair, or that a large part of their good years are given over to needless anxiety—*if*, that is, he could have proved that this was in fact the case—we might have listened. But this talk of the Good and the *summun bonum* seems to imply something rather different, something quite foreign to our way of thinking. It seems to imply, first, that there is one and only one state of affairs which could be called happiness; second, that this state of affairs would be identical for each of us; third, that the crucial problem is an intellectual one—to figure out how to imagine that state; and finally, that successful intellectual comprehension of what is truly desirable is identical with experiencing a desire solely for that. What Plato does not seem to have realized, we feel, is that we are forced to make our lives within a world that is a jumble of forces which do not take us into account, that we ourselves are a jumble of more or less ineradicable drives, some of them of extraordinary antiquity and crudeness, and that we are bound to give the name "happiness" to any situation in which we manage to enjoy ourselves without bringing down on our heads the wrath either of the outside world or of any of our own instinctive appetites. Go straight for that mythical perfection, the Highest Good, the Truly Desirable, and you will probably miss what is under your nose: family, friends, nice possessions, travel, and the esteem of your colleagues and townsmen.

Now, what is it exactly that we object to in the Socratic way of thinking? We do not disagree, most of us, that the important thing is to train our desires so that they will harmonize with each other and with the world. Nor do we disagree that this requires an appreciation both of the nature of our own desires and of the relevant features of reality. The next step is the crucial one. Does this process of coming to grips with reality amount, on the one hand, merely to "realistic" calculation and manipulation, with the aim of allowing as unfrustrated a play as possible of those desires which mean most to us and have the best chance of being fulfilled? Or is progress in understanding what life is about inevitably accompanied by the replacement of old desires by new? If we concentrate on the historical growth of our desires, as Freud does, then we will come to the first description of rationality. If we determine the nature of a desire by its effective object only, as Plato does, then we will come to the second description. In other words, if we believe that desires are permanent, no matter how many disguises they wear, we will take rationality to be, not a separate desire, but an anxiety to avoid failure in these permanent appetites. But if we make Plato's distinction between our one true desire, the desire for real happiness, and individual desires for a specific satisfaction (which may or may not lead economically toward our true desire), then rationality becomes identical with the first, overall desire.

Intelligence, on either account, must be the ability to evaluate correctly what must be understood if we are to experience the most satisfactory things which it is in our power to experience. But according to what I have been taking to be a typically modern position, intelligence is still a servant of our permanent desires. Like Socrates' opponents in the *Gorgias*, we assume that our desires are all we have, and that it would be pretty silly to try to kill them. According to Socrates, however, intelligence *is* the desire for the best, whatever that may be. After all, do we not judge a man's intelligence by the correctness of his evaluations as to what pursuits are more important than what others in life as a whole? And is this not indistinguishable from the assertion that the intelligent man desires what is really desirable while the fool desires shabby experiences which he will find quite unsatisfactory when he gets them? The difference between the ancient and the modern positions is not merely a verbal difference. The ancient way of thinking actually suggests changes in the way we should go about seeking satisfaction. In the first place, it turns our thoughts away from what we now *seem* to want. In the second place, it lifts our desire to be rational from its place of ill repute to the place of honor among our desires. Third, it suggests that we should think as far ahead as we can and go only for the highest prize. And finally, it gives us a new standard for correct thinking, as intelligence must automatically bring with it happiness. For any unhappiness must be proof that we have failed in our understanding (although a lack of dissatisfaction might, of course, also be the result of complete ignorance as well as of complete success).

Here we have, I believe, the explanation for the strong kinship which one feels to exist among Socrates' many paradoxes. Consider these: only good men are happy but all goodness is really knowledge; no man is willingly bad; a bad man does not have the knowledge to take what is truly valuable away from a good man; to have knowledge of what it is to be good is to *be* good; bad men are always unhappy, but most especially if they are never brought to justice; the ability to do whatever one wants may be worthless or disastrous; and the only desire which is for true happiness is the desire for knowledge—"philosophy." Behind every one of these paradoxes is the idea that intelligence *means* having the right desires. The only real object of all thought, reasoning, understanding, or knowing is our own true and unillusory well-being. You cannot be good at life if you cannot distinguish the important things from the rest. Stupidity is ignorance of what will be rewarding in the long run. (Total ignorance in this sense is madness.) If almost all men are unhappy, that is because they do not see that they are caught in a mire of desires which are infantile and which ought to be discarded. We spend so much time scheming to satisfy our old appetites that we never look up to see how our real desire, to be happy, is faring in the process. Amidst all our scheming we do not really think. It was Socrates' mission to awaken us out of this bad dream.

Let us see what this amounts to in more modern terms. The only criterion for deciding whether our analysis of any situation has been correct is to find out whether action based on this analysis is more rewarding or less rewarding than action based on alternative analyses. Descriptions of the world which cannot be verified in this way are arbitrary; descriptions which lead to anything but the best possible results in the pursuit of our happiness are simply false. A man who took self-destructive appetites for the pursuit of his true well-being would therefore be led to make false judgments about life and the world. The correction of his desires and the correction of his knowledge, then, are interlocked to some extent, especially when the problem is one of great importance to him. We may work out many things communally and over centuries—the physical sciences, for instance—and even a fool may be able to take these over and make them his own, inasmuch as the connection between these theories and his most clamorous desires is oblique; but ask the fool to choose among several patterns for conducting his life, and you will see a failure of head and a failure of heart which are one and the same thing. Ultimately, therefore, real intelligence comes down to a comprehension of what is actually to our benefit.

The *locus classicus* for the Socratic redefinition of intelligence is, of course, the *Phaedo*. This dialogue is also of great importance to us because it purports, by means of this discussion of intelligence, to make clear what the connection is between Socrates' habitual concerns and the more abstruse metaphysical ideas of the longer Platonic dialogues.

About halfway through the *Phaedo*, Socrates pauses to tell how as a young man he once studied the physicists.[39] He found their suggestions completely useless, he says, until he discovered one writer, Anaxagoras, who made Intelligence the cause of everything. What he had gone to the physicists in search of was a way of accounting for each and every thing in the universe, the correct explanation for its coming into being, for its passing away, and for its existence.[40] At first the physicists only aggravated his uncertainty, however, because they reduced everything to coming together and separation, and these, Socrates maintained, are *more* difficult to understand, not less, than growth, nourishment, and the other things which they were supposed to explain. When one is added to one, what is really the cause of the coming into being of two? The mere juxtaposition? But why should mere proximity bring into being duality where before there were merely two unrelated units? And is the appearance of two unrelated units in the place of duality after "subtraction" really to be explained by spacial separation? This cause would be the very opposite of the one offered in explanation of the coming into being of duality.[41] Socrates seemed no longer to have a single explanation[42] for the appearance, disappearance and existence of a thing—not according to physicists' procedure, at least, which he did not like at all, although he did have another rather haphazard method of his own which seemed to work.[43] Anaxagoras, on the other hand, by giving Mind as a cause, gave a cause after Socrates' own mind.[44] What could it mean to give Intelligence as the cause of everything, asks Socrates, if not that we should look in each event for the good being achieved in order to understand what has really happened?[45] Socrates instantly recognized his own way of thinking.

Socrates' reasoning at this point is not likely to be immediately obvious to a modern reader. Anaxagoras, like Empedocles, had assumed that, to account for the separations and combinations which bring about the orderly coming into being and passing away of individual compounds, one had to postulate, in addition to the original stuff of the universe, some other moving agent. Empedocles identified two opposing forces, Love and Hate. Anaxagoras thought that we needed only one, Intelligence (*νοῦς*).[46] Now, if Intelligence is the arranger and cause of all phenomena, Socrates argued, that can only mean that everything is ordered for the best. Anyone, therefore, who wants to explain the existence of anything, its coming into being, or its passing away, must find what the best thing was which could have happened, for each thing involved as well as for them all together.[47] Now, to understand why Socrates should interpret Anaxagoras' theory in this way, we need only remember the Socratic habit of defining intelligence as the most direct possible procedure toward one's true well-being. If a thing has been brought about by Intelligence, then by definition nothing better could have happened. Would one not prove a man's real intelligence by proving that everything he did was the best possible thing he could have done? If Anaxagoras is right, therefore, when he maintains that Intelligence is the cause of everything, then what we must do is show how each thing that happens is for the best.

The more difficult question is why Anaxagoras' idea seemed so immediately correct to Socrates. If someone wanted to know why Socrates himself was sitting there in prison at that moment, he says,[48] a truly informative answer could never be given in the form of an analysis of all of the requisite physical conditions, such as the structure of Socrates' joints and muscles—although you would think from the physicists that that was the thing one wanted to know. The only satisfactory answer would be to tell what Socrates thought was the best for him, what the jury thought was the best for themselves, and, presumably, what really was the best for each and for them all.[49]

So far we are still with Socrates. The next step, however, disturbs us. Socrates goes on to say that the same procedure ought to be followed when we try to give "the cause and the necessity" of such things as the shape and position of the earth, the movements of the heavenly bodies, and so on.[50] In each of these cases, too, he says, we must indicate why that state of affairs is good and, indeed, better than anything else could have been.[51] What is good and what is required, he says, have more power than any Atlas to hold the universe together.[52] Now, this takes us by surprise. What could Socrates be thinking of? It looks as though he had made a fairly primitive mistake: if natural phenomena are intelligible in some sense, then an intelligence must be governing them. Or, worse yet: if regularity, dependability, and admirable order are found in nature, all things which men must impose on their own lives by using their intelligence, then these states of affair in nature must be the product of intelligence, too. The statement that the world is prevented from falling apart by "what is required" (*τὸ δέον*) sounds as though it might be merely a very misleading way of observing that in the universe as a whole there is a vast, dynamic equilibrium. It is as though Socrates were surprised that things do not destroy each other quite so fast as one would expect.

But the best clue to Socrates' thinking is surely to be discovered once more in the idea which we found to be common to all of his paradoxes—the notion that true intelligence is really only the desire for one's true good. Somehow, fantastic as it seems to us, Socrates has tried to deduce something about the objects and processes around him from this description of correct thinking. Here is how it apparently works: the analysis of any natural event should be, first of all, an analysis of all of the natural tendencies discernible in the event. Natural elements strive toward goals no less than Socrates and his jurors do; the same type of explanation can therefore be given for either sort of event. What do we mean by a tendency, after all, if not an apparent striving toward a goal? It is true, is it not, that we assume all flames "naturally" to tend upward and all iron "naturally" to sink when placed in water? Now, these observations are of more than statistical interest. They are observations which it would be dangerous to be mistaken about. (If we find a flame which shoots downward or a piece of iron which floats, we do not rest until we have found other things which have, in the pursuit of their realization, interfered with the processes which we were counting on, and brought about the novel phenomena.) If we remember our common-sense expectations, therefore, instead of our very sophisticated physics, we can see the attraction of saying that to understand any happening even in inanimate nature, you must find the good each constituent is apparently aiming at. Now, to call this causation by intelligence is not really so odd as it sounds—*if* we define intelligence, in the Socratic manner, as efficient action toward a real advantage. The flame never misses a chance to go upward nor the iron to go down. All we have to do, really, is to abandon the prejudice that conscious calculation is a necessary requirement for intelligence. Action toward an end, not conscious scheming, is taken to be the important thing. After all, as Aristotle points out,[53] art does not have to deliberate to act with purpose; perhaps nature is like art.

Now comes the big step. As we have noted, the correctness of any theory about a natural event can be decided ultimately only by finding out whether or not that is the best possible assumption *we* could be making as we try to avoid disaster and succeed in our *own* lives. What can this mean if not that somehow there is a direct connection between our perception of good for ourselves and our perception of good for anything else? At least that is what Socrates seems to have thought!

But we shall have to wait until we turn to the *Republic* before we get any further light on this staggering paradox. In the *Phaedo*, Plato has Socrates say that neither Anaxagoras nor anybody else was able to show him how a consistent system could be worked out along these lines.[54] Instead, Socrates was forced to take a longer way around, he says, and develop a less direct method for explaining events.[55] This new method of explaining things he describes at first as "using *logoi*,"[56] then later he identifies it as an application of the theory of Forms.[57]

*Logoi* could mean "explanations," "rational accounts," "concepts," "theories," "general notions," "propositions," or "definitions." Working with *logoi* is here specifically contrasted with the physicists' procedure of trying to understand things in their sensible occurrences. It may well be, therefore, a reference to the familiar Socratic procedure of going straight for the universal on each occasion, digging out the concept involved, sharpening our definitions, and so on.[58] Socrates referred to his own method before, you will remember, as a rather haphazard one.[59] Here he says that he likes to take the strongest *logos* he can find about anything—about the nature of causation or the nature of anything else—and then keep everything which harmonizes with this and throw out everything which clashes with it.[60] When he goes on to explain this more clearly, however, he introduces, actually for the second time in the dialogue, the famous theory of Forms.

To remind us of what Forms are, Socrates gives us several examples: "what it is to be beautiful," "what it is to be good," "what it is to be large," "and the other things of that sort."[61] A Form, it turns out, is a special kind of *logos*: it is not only the definition of the concept exemplified by the phenomenon which we are trying to explain—that which this occurrence has in common with others, allowing us to give a common name to them all and making it possible for us to draw conclusions by comparing our separate experiences—it is a vision of what these occurrences would be if they were perfect examples of what it is to be that sort of thing. And since the mind, moreover, can draw far more precise conclusions about a Form than it can about any of its occurrences (about the Form "what it is to be equal," for instance, as compared with any so-called "equal" pairs of objects which we sense), the Forms, rather than the fleeting sensible resemblances to them, are presumed to be the real things. That is, when we fill out our knowledge, make the necessary connections, understand what must be understood, we find ourselves clarifying our comprehension of Forms every time, not of unique events. If knowledge is a correct grasp of things as they are, then things as they are, are Forms.

With the help of these Forms, Socrates is finally able to solve his original puzzle about what really is happening in addition and subtraction. The correct way to describe any of these events, he says, is to name the new Form which now informs the resulting product and describe its relation to the Form which is no longer exemplified.[62] Thus, in order to explain what happened in the addition of one to one to yield two, the main thing is to understand that the Form "what it is to be two" now informs what were previously two unrelated units. If you try to describe the event in any other way, Socrates maintains, you merely get into trouble. Eventually, of course, the philosopher will want to question the nature of Duality itself, he says, by positing yet higher things. But for the present, stick to this simple procedure. Later the philosopher will lead things back, however, back indeed until he has arrived at "something which requires nothing further."[63]

Now comes our most important problem, indeed the most intriguing question in the *Phaedo*. What are we to make of Plato's representation of the theory of Forms as just a more laborious method of explaining all things as the work of Intelligence? It will not do just to say that somehow in the process of going from Form to ever more general Form we shall eventually reach the Good, the true object of Intelligence. A more rewarding clue can be found in the way in which Plato described the Forms when they were first introduced earlier in the *Phaedo*.[64] His example was "what it is to be equal." As with all Forms, it is something about which we can achieve very precise knowledge and universal agreement, while we are yet unable to find a single perfect representative of it on the level of individual sensed objects. But what exactly is the relation between equality and a near-equal pair? Visible pairs which exemplify equality are not only just "wanting" (*ἐνδεῖ*), says Socrates, they are straining (*ὀρέγεται*) toward true equality, although they fail.[65] We are reminded of equality when we see the pair, he says,[66] but our eyes also tell us that the pair is only "straining toward what is equal" (*ὀρέγεται τοῦ ὅ ἔστιν ἴσον*), and succeeding but imperfectly. We must assume that we get our knowledge of "what it is to be truly equal" from some source other than our sense experiences, because our senses all tell us that a concrete pair can only "desire" (*προθυμεῖται*) to be equality but is condemned to be always "inferior" to it (*φαυλότερα*).[67]

The clear implication is that the Forms, the realities behind phenomena, are by nature all good, and things on the sensible level yearn only for their perfection. Now see how this feature of the theory of Forms allows it to be offered as a theory of causation in lieu of a more directly teleological theory. If one gives the new Form which appears after any process, such as "what it is to be two" after addition, one is really giving the cause of the phenomenon, because this new Form was somehow a goal being striven for. There is a catch in the word "somehow," of course, but then, if Socrates had been able to tell us exactly how this process worked, then he would not have had a second-best method of explaining phenomena—he would have had the best. Socrates here merely tries to demonstrate the usefulness of this procedure by applying it to several phenomena, such as freezing, burning, and "dying." The deductions which he draws from these examples, however, particularly concerning "dying,"[68] are maddeningly unsound. In fact, Plato never did do much more with this theory of causation. It was Aristotle, as we shall see later, who picked it up and made an effective system out of it.

What is of interest to us here is to see how the theory of Forms, for all its bizarre, controversial, and apparently un-Socratic consequences, really does appear to be, if not Socratic, at least a clear and direct development of a basically Socratic idea. The important connection to make is not between the Forms and Socrates' habit of sharpening definitions, as Aristotle does,[69] but the connection specifically made right here in the *Phaedo*, between Socrates' insistence that intelligence is desire for the good, and the clear consequence of the theory of Forms that reality correctly understood is entirely good.[70] Each thing, not merely a man, moves toward some realization, and if that is how we are going to define intelligence, then all of nature is governed by intelligence. The whole phenomenal world is seen as a series of doomed attempts to achieve perfection in each kind of thing. Or, looking at it exclusively from the point of view of man, if real intelligence in a man is simultaneously a correct grasp of reality and a comprehension of what is necessary for his own happiness, then intelligence must be the comprehension of what is good in reality. Or rather, as Plato has it, intelligence is the comprehension that reality is good! Reality is the Forms and the Forms are all beautiful, he maintains. And, after all, do not we ourselves mean *something* like this by happiness, a deep conviction that the whole world is wonderful? That is why Socrates insisted that the glimpse we get of the world when we are in love is a glimpse of the truth, not as most people maintain, an illusion.

If the Socrates of the *Phaedo* is in part an invention of Plato's,[71] therefore, at least he is an invention that grew out of piety and understanding. For behind even the wildest and most distressing of Plato's metaphysical suggestions, we may still find that dry, good-humored needling by Socrates, aimed at shaking us out of the morass of our daily desires for undesirable goals and revealing to us how infinitely more wonderful things are than we ever suspected.

# CHAPTER 5

*The Metaphysical and Political Implications of the Platonic Theory of Love: The* Republic. *The Sun, the Line, and the Cave.*

ACCORDING TO THE PLATONIC ARGUMENT, if a man believes that a sound understanding of things as they are brings happiness, then he must believe that things as they are, are wonderful. Here we have the sharpest possible difference between the Platonic and the Romantic positions. Schopenhauer, for instance, argues that the philosopher is the man who can bear to pursue the truth even though, like Oedipus, he has an overwhelming presentiment that the truth will be horrible.[1] Most people, he says, lacking the grim courage needed to be philosophers, take the part of Jocasta, who begged Oedipus for God's sake not to enquire further. A sound understanding of things as they are brings such an appalling vision that, if disgust or despair are not to follow, we must turn from it and create a world of our own making—out of a cultivated detachment, or out of tenderness and loyalty toward one another. Plato's quarrel with this conclusion would be that it implies an untenable definition for the phrase "reality" or "things as they really are." "Reality" must be what is "out there," what was there before we were born, all of the things which we are not at liberty to invent or interpret just as we wish. But we have only one way of finding out whether an assumption about reality is an arbitrary, incorrect interpretation of our own, or a true grasp of the way things are: we must see what happens when we act on the assumption. Yet what kind of result could confirm the correctness of a theory about the truth of some matter? Not a catastrophic result, certainly, but success, delight, contentment. We can learn by suffering, of course, but what we learn that way is that we have been wrong so far. The person who was right about reality all along is the person whose assumptions and attitudes when he acted on them brought him deeper and more lasting delight than any conceivable alternative assumption could have. The man who understands reality, then, must be the happiest of men. And so, if happiness means zest and keenness for things as they are, reality, things as they really are, must be wonderful. Here it is in a sort of syllogism: if (a) happiness is a lasting satisfaction with the way things are in the world, and (b) happiness is the only possible criterion for proving the truth of one's assumption about the world, then (c) the world correctly understood is beautiful and satisfying. The heightened vision of the lover, not the humdrum assumption of the non-lover, is the closer to the truth.

The example of Oedipus, however, is very disturbing. Surely in actual fact, even for the brightest, best informed, and best intentioned of men, the discovery of things as they are is almost always the discovery that things are much worse than they seemed. If we were truly honest to our experiences in life, the Romantic would argue, we would have to dismiss Plato's metaphysical talk about "reality" and "things as they really are" as patently false.

A Platonist could reply that *of course* the correction of a mistaken notion about life, the world, or oneself must always come in the form of unpleasant experiences. How else would we know that we had been mistaken? But notice: if Oedipus had had real knowledge from the beginning, he would not have killed his father or married his mother in the first place.

Ah, but there is the rub, says the Romantic. Life is short and art is long. Human limitations being what they are, the wisest person must actually be the one who has had the largest number of the most telling of those "corrective experiences." Fools are often happier than wise men, and everybody dies in the end. We would be better advised to leave philosophy alone and cherish whatever innocent pleasures come our way: work, friendship, and respectability. The best moments may be exhilarating, almost beatific visions, but these moments, so like those which can be purchased for opium or even alcohol, come as often to the man who lives for the day, who cherishes bright colors and bursts of laughter among friends, as to the restless searcher after the truth. Not only for the sake of progress in science, says the Romantic, but also in the name of simple prudence and maturity, we had better assume that the universe whirls through its paces, on every level from the spinning atom to the spinning galaxies, in total disregard for what would warm the cockles of your heart or mine. We cannot afford not to correct the infantile assumption that the world is in harmony with our true will. Even the laws of human society and the workings of our own unconscious minds, according to the Romantic, are mechanical and valueless until we create the value. We had better settle for the calmer pleasures of the detached scientific observer.[2] The man who can remain satisfied that the world is governed by an order which works for his personal benefit is not only hopelessly limited in his powers of observation, he is a menace to us all. Such men have no appreciation of the cruelty and waste which we must constantly battle against in the world as it *really* is. Such is the position of the Romantic.

There would seem to be this difficulty with any kind of idealistic philosophy: a conviction of the existence of a real world far more beautiful than the one which the ordinary man understands is apt to weaken one's detestation for cruelty, stupidity, and injustice. Aristotle, as we shall see, is liable to this charge. Neither Paul nor Dante is, however, nor is Plato. It is a fact that the great visionaries, men who, like Heraclitus, have called on their fellow men to wake up, to open their eyes to a brilliant world which they are missing in their private dreams, are also often the bitterest and most energetic opponents of the evils of the ordinary world. The man who believes in Paradise may also believe in Hell. Plato, as we have seen, assumed that the bright world of perfect Forms was the real world, and that the world which most men accepted as the real thing was a confused shadow of that world. It never occurred to him, however, that he could therefore turn his back on the ordinary man's concerns for politics and justice. On the contrary, he is far more concerned than the typical Romantic is with the details of everyday misery around him. The Romantic, convinced of the hopelessness and meaninglessness of the world as a whole, will often settle for the concrete gesture, a helping hand when his neighbor is in trouble, and the small, patient protest of the liberal democrat in the voting booth. Plato, consumed with fury at the forces of destruction everywhere,[3] tries to shake his fellow citizens out of their bad dream, and argues in detail for sweeping, revolutionary changes in every aspect of private and public life. Men think that they could cure themselves of their unhappiness if only they had the means to fulfill all of their current desires. But in fact, says Plato, they desire things which could bring them neither peace nor joy. Our habit of tolerating in our neighbor any desire which he may conceive so long as it does not interfere with other people in pursuit of *their* desires is actually very unkind. For the benefit of each person and of the whole community, people must be trained to desire the *right* thing. Nor can this ever be done while the men who have the greatest influence in our society are men other than those whose understanding is the most profound and complete. The philosopher, therefore, far from being a useless dreamer, must be enlisted into the highest office of the land.

This is the thesis of the *Republic*, Plato's greatest dialogue and perhaps the greatest single work of philosophy ever written. In this work Plato attempts to describe in detail how a state would be organized if it were governed completely by intelligence —that is, if everything were done for the true good of the whole community. In many details it is a distressing picture; it sometimes reminds us more of the worst horrors of modern Germany or Russia than of Paradise. But that is the key to the dialogue —it turns out that the rational state is necessarily based on the very principle which distinguishes all totalitarian states from democratic regimes: the assumption that the wiser must always be allowed to tell the less intelligent what he must do and what he must not do—that most men have to be told what is to their good, as, left to their own devices, they would not only contribute toward chaos and waste in the community as a whole, but in the process also fail to find any lasting satisfaction in their private lives.

Our own liberal tradition is based not so much on a denial of this principle as on a pessimism as to whether we may ever trust a man who claims to have this superior wisdom. In its most extreme form, however, democratic theory does assume that happiness, if it will come at all, will only come when interference from one's neighbor is limited to the most trivial and incidental regulations required by the mechanics of government, that men must not be allowed to help each other unless asked, as it is from liberty itself that all good things will follow.[4] But even this form of the idea is based not so much on any evidence that a significant number are capable of achieving happiness when left to themselves as on a vivid appreciation of the violence and stupidity that most governments have shown themselves capable of down through the centuries. Now, Plato's idea, in turn, is based not so much on any certainty that we could ever trust a man's claim to be the wisest as on a vivid appreciation of the incredible shortsightedness of most men's desires if they are not carefully educated by wiser men. It comes down to a difference in the definition of freedom. *We* feel that we are freest when we are least influenced by outside pressures of any kind. That way we can do just what we feel we desire. Plato asserts, on the contrary, that this in fact results in the worst kind of slavery unless we educate men to desire what will *really* bring them happiness. But education is interference —a deep, lasting interference which is the only path to true freedom.

The great problem, of course, is to figure out who the educator should be. Here Plato runs afoul of another of our democratic prejudices. We must accept as a fact, he says, a great inequality among men as regards their natural gifts and their ability to understand the important things.[5] Nor can the masses be allowed even to judge whom they believe to be the wisest among them, because they will always choose the man who promises to give them whatever they think that they desire at that moment, not the man who understands what the people really desire better than they themselves do.[6] The man who has the right to the position of greatest power in the state is the one who will guide things not according to what people think is for their happiness but according to what he knows is really for their happiness. Not that people will chafe under his orders, of course. On the contrary, that would be a sign of failure on his part. Given enough time, the citizens of the completely rational state would glow with enthusiasm in whatever role they were cast. But the educator must have absolute power to bring about this state of affairs and to maintain it; he must be a philosopher king.[7] We may shudder at the prospect of trying this experiment, but we must at least allow Plato the right to imagine so far as he can what this completely happy state would look like.[8] If a philosopher will not do that, others less objective certainly will!

The really dangerous rival of the philosopher king for the place of chief influence in society is not the simple power-hungry tyrant, as Plato sees it, nor even the unscrupulous demagogue, dangerous and detestable as these men are. The great rival, as he is depicted in the middle books of the *Republic*, is the cultured and educated man who is the ideal of most of Plato's intelligent readers, modern as well as ancient. He is gentle and bright, and is well indoctrinated in the traditional attitudes about what is just, what unjust, what is good, what foul.[9] He knows many things, appreciates art, and is quick to side with order and sense against any form of viciousness or stupidity. And yet, Plato argues, so long as this man, and not the true philosopher, is thought to be the highest development which men can reach, the rational community will never be realized.[10] The trouble with these so-called educated men is that, far from being able to achieve precise knowledge of the beautiful, the noble and the just, and being able to demonstrate the correctness of their knowledge to all challengers, they do not even believe that there is such a thing as absolute excellence, only excellence of various sorts in various concrete things.[11]

As we might have expected, Plato makes the distinction in terms of two different kinds of lovers.[12] As in the *Symposium*, the philosopher loves the good itself, the beautiful itself, the just itself, while the other kind of person is only part way up the ladder and is infatuated with good things, beautiful people, and just actions. If you even try to tell this second group that there is such a thing as the Just itself, the Form "what it is to be just," they are as disbelieving as is the man who is in love with a beautiful individual when you try to tell him that it is Beauty itself which he really loves, not this person whom he thinks he wants to embrace.[13] But the philosopher king will have to be interested in what is actually, essentially, really, universally involved in being just or good. Otherwise he has no claim to his position.

Plato's habit of characterizing men according to the nature of the things which they love most dearly seems sensible enough. We do it all of the time. The idea even has a degenerate descendant on Madison Avenue, called "motivational research." In the *Republic* he notes how a man who is identified as a lover of some one thing, such as sex, wine, worldly success, or knowledge, is a lover of everything within that class.[14] Plato is not denying that the connoisseur is finical in his taste, of course. We do not expect a true wine lover, for instance, to love just any Algerian wine which is set before him, and old Fyodor Karamazov is only showing himself to be a monster when he asserts that all women are beautiful if you only know how to look at them. But a man who loved only Wagner and not Mozart would not be essentially a lover of music, and one who loved only claret and not burgundy would not be a lover of wine. And when their loves become all-consuming, these lovers do approach the condition of the alcoholic, the compulsive jazz musician, and the sex maniac. A lover of sexual pleasures will find beauty, Socrates points out, in the most extraordinary variety of colors, sizes, figures, and expressions.[15] A man who is attracted only to women who have one special set of characteristics should not be called essentially a lover of women.

Now, the case is exactly the same, Socrates argues, with the true lover of knowledge.[16] He seems to be hungry for knowledge of all kinds, from his youth all through his life. This is the class of lovers from whom the rulers must be chosen. And actually there are a fair number of these men who thirst above everything to use their minds—if you include the men whom Plato calls "those who love to watch," the *φιλοθεάμονες*—people, that is, who are eager for the revelations which they experience in musical and dramatic performances and the like.[17] But, no matter how much more refined and closer to the truth these lovers of art and culture are than the lovers of sex, wine, or success, they are still a long way away from having the necessary qualifications for being the philosopher rulers. This is because they hunger only for the individual event which shows beauty and order, never for beauty itself and order itself.

There follows the familiar distinction between complete knowledge and mere right opinion.[18] The first is a correct understanding of the Form, what is really involved in being this or that; the second is a correct grasp of these things as they are exemplified in the world which we have contact with through our senses. Let us take an example. Our cultured gentlemen, the φιλοθεάμονες, while responding enthusiastically to beauty in its many varieties, will repudiate as boorish the idea that there is a single formula for beauty. There is no single beautiful sound, color, or shape which is not also ugly. (A note which is exquisite in one song might be hideous in another, or a color beautiful in an orchid might be appalling in someone's complexion.) And any given act that is just on one occasion, such as giving back to a man his own sword, might be unjust on another occasion, exactly as a number which is double another is only half of yet another number. One goes to concerts and the theater, talks to friends and reads the newspaper, and develops a kind of sense about these things. Beauty and Kindness and the like do not exist in the abstract any more than "double" or "half" do; they only exist in concrete experiences. The philosopher, on the other hand, will not take this for the truth of the matter. He will long for knowledge of what it really means to be beautiful or just, what the real reason is for their superiority to ugliness and injustice. If we are challenged to defend the judgment that some song is beautiful, there is no profit in pointing to notes or intervals that in themselves are no more beautiful than ugly. So also if we were challenged in a moral or political judgment, there would be no profit in pointing to procedures which in themselves were neither just nor unjust. The man who shies away from asking what the essence of justice is, is not the man to whom we should surrender our whole state. We must find a man who has a natural, insatiable thirst for the whole truth.[19]

If our man's amorous energy is all channeled toward learning the truth about everything, Plato argues,[20] then he will have none left for the distracting appetites of the body. He will therefore be mature, gentle, thoughtful and well-balanced. Of course, as things are now, this true philosopher's voice is far from evident or influential in the state. But that is because the things pursued are not the things he would pursue. It is no wonder, therefore, that he sounds ridiculous, unrealistic, and even subversive to the multitude.[21] And the situation is made even worse by the existence of a bunch of rogues who claim the title of philosophers, but are actually scandalous fools.[22] Also, as things are now it would be a miracle if the true philosopher were not hopelessly corrupted by the world by the time he reached adulthood, so dictatorial is the power of public opinion.[23] The man who does not conform to the tastes of the multitude is crushed.[24] Moreover, the gifted man is the special target of all of the most ambitious factions of society.[25] If he remains uncorrupted, by some chance thing, like a sickness which excuses him from the usual career, or a divine voice like that of Socrates, he will still be unable to move directly toward the improvement of the monstrous appetites of his fellow citizens; he will have to live like a man fallen among beasts, or one crouching by a wall in flight from the fury of a dust storm.[26]

Somehow, somewhere, if men are to rise above this maelstrom, there will have to be a state which is ruled so wisely that all those who are capable of becoming philosophers will be recognized and trained with the utmost care and intelligence to that end, and then given the power over the state when it comes their turn. Before the state will know enough to select its future rulers in this way, of course, the reigning ruler will himself have to be already a philosopher. But that we shall have to leave to chance and the infinite passing of time.[27] What we *can* do now, on the other hand, is to describe what the steps would be by which a man could, in ideal circumstances, rise above the useless relativism which so regularly satisfies the leaders of opinion in these corrupt societies of ours.

We begin with men naturally inclined to be lovers of truth and reality, *τοῦ ὄντος τε καὶ ἀληθείας ἐρασταί*.[28] These men have a nature which is akin (*οἰκεία*) to what is most excellent. That is because the Forms, the true nature of justice, beauty, and the rest, are permanent, splendid, ordered, and divine, and so he whose mind habitually moves on this level would be certain to take on these qualities by imitation if he did not have them already.[29] As he orders himself, his fellow men, and the state as a whole, he will look in both directions, Plato says,[30] up at the one perfect pattern for each excellence, then down again to the world he is molding. Here is where our friends the *φιλοθεάμονες* fall short: they love to use their minds and to savor and discover excellence, but they cannot be persuaded to look beyond the individual events. They have no passion for the essence of each thing. They do not go for the best, for they feel at home only on the level of daily happenings. A government under their control is a constant, fruitless series of makeshift proposals.

In the earlier books of the *Republic*, tests and training procedures are outlined by which the most gifted of the younger citizens would be detected and brought along. The last step, however, is the most difficult—the one which separates the true philosopher from the man who can never quite make it. Comprehension of such things as the division of the human *psyche* into three parts and the excellence appropriate to each and to the whole can be attained even by people of moderate intelligence. But the highest object of study, the *μέγιστον μάθημα*, that which converts all this from true opinion to knowledge, is open only to a few. What is this highest study? Socrates tells Adeimantus that he has heard the answer many times: it is "the Form of the Good" (*ἡ τοῦ ἀγαθοῦ ἰδέα*) "by the use of which just things and the rest come to be useful and helpful."[31] That is, even the ordinary man can learn from his experiences to draw certain conclusions, about, say, the general requirements which must be met before we can call someone mature or some decision the act of a just man. This is of little use, however, unless he understands the connection between the acquisition of these virtues and the attainment of happiness. Unless a man knows what makes a thing good—what does or does not lead to his happiness—how can he ever make anything but private and uncertain sense out of words like "good," "just," "noble," and their opposites?

If the true nature of the Good could be demonstrated to us, we would have a kind of knowledge not open to us yet. What, then, is the Good? But Plato cannot just tell us. As he says in a famous passage of the *Seventh Epistle*,[32] however much we want direct comprehension of reality, all our instruments of thought and communication only compare things; they tell us *τὸ ποῖόν τι*, not *τὸ τί*, what a thing is like, not what it is. Things in themselves he has never even attempted to discuss in writing, he says, and any man who thinks that he himself can do so is a fool. Let us take an example. Suppose we wanted to grasp the essence of justice. Everything which we could say about it would be in the form of *τὸ ποῖόν τι*, what it was like, how it resembled this, differed from that, how it was more evident here, less evident there, useful in this sort of thing, irrelevant in that sort, and so on. The only way in which we could convert this to direct and exact knowledge of *τὸ τί*, what it *is*, is to know what the Good is. That is, unless we had a complete understanding of what makes a thing good, we obviously could not have a perfect comprehension of what justice really amounts to. But it is the Good that Plato cannot talk about.

The Good is our true good, complete happiness, that for the sake of which we do everything we do.[33] The difficulty lies just here, however. We are each of us forced to assume that *the* good is the same as the highest criterion to which we do in fact appeal when we search our souls in making critical decisions. But this assumption, alas, cannot be scrutinized and criticized in the way that all other assumptions can. For how could we ever examine our ultimate criterion and discuss whether or not it is the conception of good which *should* be motivating us? For once, we have no higher criterion by which to compare alternatives. Suppose we dragged up out of ourselves, by psychoanalysis or some other drastic means, the complete honest truth about the things we value most and would never knowingly go against. If someone then asked us why we held these things supreme, we could only say that any description of happiness which contradicted these desires would be unthinkable. If we were not acting in a way which was entirely consistent with our highest criterion, then a friend could help us by a Socratic cross-examination. But if he tried to change our ultimate criterion itself, our conception of the Good, he would have no luck whatever. As Aristotle said,[34] we can deliberate about means but never about ends. If a man is wrong about the Good, then no single rational argument, however long and complicated, can ever demonstrate that to him. This is because to judge between two goals you have to have a higher criterion to judge them by. The highest criterion, then, must be *by definition* beyond judgment.

No description of ultimate success can suggest a plan of action, therefore. We can only give it a name. Anything informative which we attempted to add would be a description of the means to happiness, not happiness itself. When over the years men do change their understanding of life, they are changing above all their grasp of the Good; but this comes about slowly, indirectly, and as the result of habits and subtle influences of many kinds.

No wonder that so few, even of those who are capable of it, ever attain to a correct vision of the Good! In the *Symposium* Plato offered a way up by means of a correct use of personal love. In the *Seventh Epistle* (and the *Phaedrus*) he will describe a special relationship between a student and a teacher. But in the *Republic* he is attempting to find a way which could be institutionalized, written into the constitution, rather than depending on the caprices of personal friendships. In a way it is the most ambitious thing which Plato ever tried.

Plato suggests, by way of example, that there are two major conceptions as to the nature of the Good.[35] There are men who conceive of it as a kind of pleasure, and a finer sort who conceive of it as a kind of intellectual understanding (*φρόνησις*). Both demonstrate the same paradox. When asked if all pleasure or all kinds of intellectual understanding are equally productive of happiness, they are forced to say no. But that implies yet a higher criterion, by which some of the experiences which they equated with the good are judged better than others. They act, Plato says, as though we already understood what was meant by the word "good." Any formula which purports to be a description of happiness but which suggests anything really informative turns out actually to be a proposal as to the means to happiness, not a definition of happiness itself. We can only define happiness as that for which we do all that we do, that which makes any experience, be it pleasure or understanding, rewarding. It is that, as Plato puts it,[36] which nobody is satisfied to have only in appearance and not in reality. We may be content with the appearance of honesty, for instance, but never with the mere appearance of the really good.

Every *psyche* pursues the Good, says Socrates,[37] not merely the one which has understood it correctly. It is that for the sake of which a *psyche* does everything it does. Even the simplest *psyche*, therefore, must have an inkling that the Good must exist (*ἀπομαντευομένη τι εἶναι*). Yet, most of us are at a loss as to how to describe it; we do not have the same kind of confidence (*πίστις*) about it that we have about other things, and so we lose whatever good there may have been in these other things. As Socrates has put it so many times before, no one wills evil for himself, men do wrong only through a failure of understanding.

At this point Socrates is asked if he would himself identify the Good with knowledge, with pleasure, or what.[38] Then follows a curious interchange which is apparently meant to signify that what Socrates is about to say is not just one more opinion but an attempt to suggest a sort of revelation (*φανά τε καὶ καλά*). He would dearly love to be able to explain the Good in the way in which he explained Justice and the rest. He protests that he cannot do that, however. In his enthusiasm he would surely cut a ridiculous figure if he tried, he says. He begs permission of the company to dismiss the question of the Good. "Yet if you wish," he says, "I am willing to describe something which seems to me to be the offspring of the Good and very much like it—although if you would rather not, we can let it drop."[39] The interlocutors are, of course, extremely anxious that he continue, even if he cannot give them a complete account. Then follows the famous passage of the Sun, the Line, and the Cave.

Socrates, after warning his companions to be on their guard that he does not deceive them, starts in a familiar fashion.[40] He begs the company to recall the distinction which he had made earlier between the many individual things which could be called "fine" or "beautiful" and the reality of what it was to be fine or beautiful. The *φιλοθεάμονες*, remember, denied the existence of anything beyond the events which we actually see before us, while the philosopher, using not the eye but the mind, does not rest until he has collected the visual samples into a single Form (*μία ἰδέα*) and understood what is really involved. Now, as we might have expected, there is no small resemblance between what happens when we see with our bodily eye some example of loveliness and what happens when we see with our mind's eye what loveliness really amounts to. In both cases, in addition to the eye and the object, there must be a "third kind of thing" (*τρίτον γένος*); in the case of the bodily eye, this is light, or best of all, the sun. This, he says, is what he had in mind when he spoke of the offspring of the Good, that which has exactly the same position in the visible world as the Good has in the intelligible.

The sun, Socrates points out,[41] is not only the cause of vision but is also an object of vision. There is indeed nothing so clearly visible as the sun itself, however hard it is to look at directly. The Good, too, is not really remote to the mind, but blindingly clear and discernible wherever anything at all is discernible, however hard it is to apprehend directly. As an object is no longer visible when the light of the sun no longer falls on it, neither is anything intelligible when it no longer shines because of the Good—or, as he puts it, when the *psyche* is no longer fixed upon the region "where truth and what is shine over it."[42] That is, if a man cannot discern what it would be good for him to assume about something, there remains no other way for him to determine what the truth of the matter is; he has his mind fixed, says Plato,[43] on something mixed with shadow, which comes into being and passes away, on which he can only conjecture and stare without sight, changing his opinion back and forth, apparently quite without intelligence.

Then Plato gets a little more precise.[44] The Good is "that which bestows validity on the things which are known," also that which "gives to the knower the ability to know." It is therefore "the cause (*αἰτία*) of knowledge," and the cause "of truth so far as that is known." Yet it is itself something other than, and fairer than, knowledge and the truth. As light and vision are not the sun but like the sun, so knowledge and truth are not the Good but good-like (*ἀγαθοειδῆ*, a *ἅπαξ λεγόμενον*). The Good itself is to be prized even more than these.

More important yet, as the sun is the cause not only of the visibility of the visible world but also of all of the birth, growth, and nourishment within it, so the Good is the cause not only of the intelligibility of the intelligible world but also of its reality and existence. But as the sun is not itself that which comes into being, so the Good is not itself reality—it "rises beyond reality in venerableness and power."

Here it is in less picturesque language. Ultimately, the only criterion which we have for determining the validity of any assertion is our own true well-being. That is, a statement is declared to be true if, and only if, it can be assumed that action based on this suggestion will yield the best possible results. Everything depends, therefore, on whether or not we have understood what the best possible results would be. Furthermore, if it cannot be shown how it could ever make any difference whether or not we accept an assertion, then we have not made an assertion about reality. In a manner of speaking, then, our true good is the cause of reality as well as of our knowledge of it, for the real is that which we must assume to be true if we are to succeed in our search for happiness.

Suppose, for example, that I were trying to decide whether a proposed change in the laws would be equitable or not. In order for my judgment to be true, I shall have to make correct assumptions about, say, the present distribution of property, the changes which are physically and psychologically practicable, the real importance of this kind of property, the probable consequences of alternative proposals, and so on. And then I shall have to decide which of the alternatives is closer to a valid goal in the maintenance of justice. Not only this last step but every one of the preliminary decisions would be impossible to make if I had no idea of my true good, and would be wrong if my conception of true well-being were quite mistaken. Even assumptions about the physical situation, the belief, for instance, that under the new circumstances the citizens will act in this or that way, will be validated or disproved in a crude way by the consequences to me of believing that this is so. And in the higher question, the problem which made the matters of fact interesting in the first place, the importance of a correct understanding of true good is obviously very great and direct indeed. Our true well-being is not the same as reality and true knowledge, but as that on which these wholly depend, it is "beyond reality in venerableness and power." All men desire it. It is *defined* as that which all men really desire. But most men understand it incorrectly. The cost of this is failure, failure in grasping reality and in attaining happiness, both at the same time. It really is to the mind what the sun is to the eye.[45]

So far this all sounds like a riddle. That is because we have not yet been given much of a clue as to how we should change our lives and our thinking. To accomplish this, Plato substitutes for the image of the Sun a new, more complicated image, and then an allegory. The new image is the Divided Line.[46] Plato asks us to imagine a line. (Draw it vertically.) Divide it into two parts and then divide the parts again according to the same ratio.[47] Now, the basis of the division is clarity and obscurity, the top segment being completely clear, the bottom the murkiest of all. The line represents our attempt to understand reality, because reality is perceived, Plato maintains, on four different levels. At the lower two levels one is working with the visible world, at the upper two with the intelligible world.

Let us begin with the two ways of grasping the visible world. What is the difference between the bottom and the second to bottom segments? In the bottom one, says Socrates, we are not in direct contact even with the objects of sense themselves, but only indirectly through images. In the upper one we are looking at the objects directly. As he puts it, in the upper of the two segments we are beholding individual plants and animals as they come into being and pass away around us, but in the lower we see only the shadows and reflections of these.

Now let us look at the difference between the upper two segments, the realm of intelligence. The difference here is not worked out on quite the same principle. The important thing this time is that in the lower of the two we are still forced to assume the correctness of the true nature of things without being able to demonstrate this. Also, we are forced constantly to check our assumptions by reference to the objects of the visible world. In the topmost segment, on the other hand, we are freed altogether of our dependence on the visible world and are able to derive our knowledge of the essence of each thing from "the first principle of the whole" (*τοῦ παντὸς ἀρχή*),[48] a principle not itself derived from anything (*ἀρχὴ ἀνυπόθετος*).[49] (Later we discover that this first principle is the Good.[50]) In the top but one, the procedure is like that "of the so-called arts" (*τῶν τεχνῶν καλουμένων*),[51] of those who work in "geometry, calculation, and subjects like that."[52] In these "sciences," men are working with intelligibles, to be sure, not tangibles, but they cannot seem to get away from tests and models on the visible level, nor can they ever prove the validity of their basic axioms. On the topmost level, however, we are able to do what Socrates said in the *Phaedo* that he could not do: to show how everything was dependent on the Good. At this level, our knowledge of reality is validated by the only true method, and so checks on the level of phenomena are never necessary.

Unfortunately, this simple line is not quite adequate to express so complex a vision. There are several details which have misled scholars and readers time and again. First there is the odd-sounding suggestion that at the bottom we are examining visible phenomena through shadows and reflections —in water and on other shiny surfaces. While the criterion for the subdivision in the upper half of the line can be interpreted more or less literally, that in the lower half surely cannot. To begin with, notice that Plato implies that most people never rise above that bottom level. His name for the state of mind which it represents is *εἰκασία*, comprehension of things through images only. What could he have in mind? Now, the only examples which Plato gives of the kind of thing which might be apprehended on each of the four different levels are the beautiful, the just, and the good,[53] especially the just.[54] That is, beautiful objects and just acts on the visible level, and the nature of beauty and justice on the intelligible level. Obviously, the comprehension of particular just acts, decisions, situations, etc., which does not even rise to the level of sensed phenomena could not be comprehension derived from physical shadows and reflections. What Plato must have in mind is the grasp which one might have of such things if one were dependent on the way these matters are represented to us by others, and did not observe them for oneself. The state of mind at the second step up, where we are looking at the sensed world itself, is called *πίστις*, a feeling of confidence. By this Plato surely means the state of mind which we achieve when we have seen through the newspapers, the novels, the opinion setters, the "images" created by the publicity and public relations men, and have made contact with the world of affairs itself.[55] Why, then, did Plato speak of shadows and reflections, we may ask. Well, for one thing, his equation of the Good with the sun forced him to this. He needed an image for visible reality only indirectly illuminated by the sun. But a better reason for the mention of shadows will be clear when we come to the allegory of the cave. As for his emphasis on reflections, that was surely made in a conscious effort to connect what is being said here with a number of other important discussions in the *Republic*. For the same metaphor recurs in several passages. The most significant is in the description of the training of small children by means of music and stories.[56] A glance back at that discussion reminds us of something very important: Images, *εἰκόνες*, can be either good *or* bad, true *or* false. Even the philosopher, when he is a child, must be shown the ways of the world through images, says Socrates. Only they ought to be *good* images. That is, they ought to be the kind of representations which will prepare the child, when he reaches the age of reason, to welcome the reality as an old friend.[57] In our corrupt societies we are not often so lucky.

Another misleading detail is the mention of geometry and arithmetic as the sole examples of the level which is second from the highest. Many have concluded from this that the object of this third state of mind was mathematical entities—a kind of reality intermediate between Forms and particulars. The trouble is that, according to Aristotle,[58] Plato eventually did develop a theory of this sort. And his famous lecture *On the Good* is said to have involved mathematics somehow.[59] But the way in which the top two segments are distinguished clearly suggests that both deal with the same intelligible realities of things, Justice and the like. Of course, there is a remote possibility that, like the Pythagoreans, Plato supposed each thing like Beauty and Justice to have a mathematical formula.[60] But as a description of a stage between the comprehension of just acts and comprehension of the true nature of Justice, this would be more than unhelpful, it would be bizarre in the extreme. It is far more likely that Plato is giving geometry, mathematics, and the so-called *τέχναι* as merely the best examples in his day of the scientific state of mind. His word for this is *διάνοια*, "using one's mind." His point is that this is not the ultimate achievement. The highest level of understanding he calls *νόησις*, direct and complete intellectual comprehension. At both of these levels we deal with universals, what it is to be just rather than just actions, but at the lower of the two we are dependent on concrete examples and can see no way to derive our formulations from a premise that does not itself need proof. In the language used in describing the lower subdivision, the man in *διάνοια* is not seeing things illuminated directly by the light of the Good. The mathematical sciences are obvious examples of *διάνοια*, because they are quite clearly concerned with intelligibles, not particulars, and yet, as a matter of fact, never do defend their basic axioms. Nor could a mathematician ever tell you why mathematics is right or good, or why it is more than a sophisticated pastime or a humble aid to merchants, engineers, and physical scientists. To be sure, inasmuch as mathematicians do not *as mathematicians* try to reason out the nature of justice, Plato did seriously risk misunderstanding in using them as his example. He took that risk, however, probably in order to prepare us for what he will say shortly about the real uses of mathematics.[61] Mathematics, he will point out, provides an excellent way to train a young man to see the intelligible patterns behind phenomena. But mathematics is also, he will say, one vital step away from the highest level of understanding, which he calls dialectic. To reach this highest stage we have to see how everything fits with everything else, what is more important than what, how each thing is related to everything else and all are derived from the truly good.

Finally, Plato recasts this whole scheme in the form of an allegory.[62] The level of *εἰκασία*, contact with the world through "images" only, is represented by a scene deep in a cave, where men are chained along one wall, watching shadows on the opposite wall. This is the pitiful state of most men, for they do not understand the realities even of the visible world except as they are represented to them in the words, opinions, stories, prejudices—right or wrong—of other men. The next step up, the state of *πίστις*, confidence, is arrived at when a prisoner is unchained and made to turn around and see the original artefacts, the things which threw those shadows which he formerly took for reality. He will be blinded by the fire at first and refuse to accept the new revelation, but eventually he will see how much more right these objects have to be called real. This is the painful disillusionment with the opinions of the world which a man must go through if he is ever to understand what really goes on in the world of affairs. The next step, *διάνοια*, abstract thinking, is achieved by a long, arduous training, mostly in the exact sciences, to get him to have confidence in the superior power, splendor, and reality of intelligible things. This is represented by a long climb out of the cave, a journey which a man will have to be forced to undertake against his will. At the top, once more he will deny that the objects he now beholds, the originals of the artefacts which he knew before, are real, for once more he will be blinded by the light. Slowly, however, he will be able to see the objects as they appear in shadows and reflections or at night, although he will not yet be able to look at them in the full light of the sun. The last stage, νόησις, complete comprehension, is the final ecstatic awareness of things as they really are, in their natural place, illuminated by a brilliant sun. Eventually he will even be able to look at the sun itself, the Good, and he will know that that is what has given reality to everything he sees, and also what has given him the power to behold these things directly in their true nature.

This is the truly happy man, not only because he can do nothing that does not lead—more directly than anything else he could do—to a deep lasting excitement, but also because he has found that reality itself is infinitely more beautiful than that which men take to be the real world. He will, therefore, dwell in deep contentment in that vision. And yet, since he is also the only man with the knowledge needed to be able to govern society—and since, moreover, society was in part responsible for liberating him in this way—he will eventually have to descend back into the cave for awhile and take his turn as educator-ruler. Incidentally, when he gets down there he will be unable to see anything in the dark for awhile. He may well be an object of ridicule and scorn, therefore. But eventually, when he gets used to the murky world of the masses, he will be better than any of them in their quarrels over the shadows of just events, for he has seen Justice itself.[63]

Education, it seems, is not well-characterized as the placing of knowledge into a mind; it is quite literally the conversion, the turning around of the whole *psyche*.[64] This is just as we might have expected from the *Symposium*. In the Allegory of the Cave, however, the process is described as though it were always resisted by the student. How are we to reconcile this with the idea in the *Symposium* that Love is the greatest of all helpers in the climb toward happiness, or with the assertions in the *Republic* itself that no man can become a philosopher who is not by nature already a lover of intelligible reality? Perhaps there are just these two different ways of reaching the same end. The ideal state would force all of its young to see the truth so far as they were able; but if a man finds the special friendship described in the *Symposium*, he may attain the same heights even in our dismal and confused societies. On the other hand, remember how even Alcibiades struggled painfully all the way against the glorious revelations given him by Socrates. Alcibiades did not make the final grade, of course. But probably there is always a certain amount of terror and disbelief in this process. How could there not be, when the essence of what is happening is the realization that what one has always desired most is not what is really desirable at all?

# CHAPTER 6

*Rational* vs. *Irrational Love: The* Phaedrus.

LOVE, ACCORDING TO PLATO, is the universal longing for happiness. The intense joy of love at its best, therefore, is not a problem. The problem is how to account for unhappy love, what Pausanias identified as Eros Pandemus, Vulgar Love. If all men yearn only for their true good, and if that is the only principle at work in the dynamics of the soul, how is it that men conceive desires for things which will destroy them? The philosopher, Plato says, is not merely the only man whose desires are for things which will bring him the best possible rewards, he is the only man to see what is desirable for *every* man. But unintelligence, a failure to see how one could live happily, is not a state of apathy; it has a dynamic of its own. Indeed, most people reserve the name "love" for the irrational excitement of the unintelligent (in the Socratic sense of the word) and can only think that the completely reasonable man must be without passion altogether.

Unhappy love is easily identified by the Christian as animal appetites which naturally pull a man this way and that if he has not seen how infinite the peace is which one gets from the knowledge of God's love for him. There is just no connection between God's love or our imitation of that and our carnal desires. The Romantic, on the other hand, feels that unhappiness is probably an essential part even of love at its best. The lover seems to know that failure, misery, and death are themselves somehow a part of his desire. But the Freudian would say that unhappy love is rather a drive toward pleasure which has gone wrong. It may have gone wrong in one of two ways: either through a failure to appreciate reality, or through a failure of reality (that is, civilization) to appreciate our drive toward pleasure. In extreme cases, the very opposite of love, a desire for release from strain in death, may be confused with love itself.

But for Plato, none of these descriptions can be right. The Christians, he would say, deny what is obvious: that a lasting, glowing peace is not a denial of desires but the ultimate refinement of them. The Romantics, on the other hand, do not leave themselves any very clear criterion for distinguishing between better and worse loves. And the Freudians, Plato would say, when they identify success with bodily pleasure, oversimplify what is required for happiness. They also overlook the fact, as the others do, too, that only the man who finds lasting pleasure in reality has a right to claim that his understanding of reality is correct. On the other hand, Plato's description of love had its special problem as well: if there is no conflict between pleasure and reality, why are most people unhappy most of the time?

On Plato's theory, happiness must be one and the same thing for every man. It would be reasonable to assume, after all, that two men who had each found an analysis of the world which never let them down would probably not have two totally different descriptions. This is obvious in every sane person's life insofar as we are all dealing with the same physical world. It is also necessary insofar as we are able to communicate and make predictions which others, not only ourselves, will find valid. But from here on there is a vital difference between the philosopher and the ordinary man. Most people can afford to make personal compromises with life, violently suppressing the desires which had led to painful disappointments, and arranging things around them for a reasonably adequate satisfaction of their more limited drives. But a philosopher, if he really does live at the top division of the Divided Line, must have understood what life is about as a whole and must, therefore, be able to work out consistently the connections between his vision of life and the correct analysis of each and every thing about him. That is, the non-philosopher, even the relatively contented non-philosopher, the mystic or the unimaginative man, may find solutions which are adequate only for himself; but the philosopher must take as evidence of error any discovery that his own assumptions will not work for all men. This, after all, is the reason why the philosopher, rather than the man with private tastes, should be teacher and ruler. He is presumed to be in a position to help any and every man to happiness, not just himself and others with his tastes. The man who is not able to think through his real desires, on the other hand, will be expected to allow the laws to be written and enforced by the more intelligent men.[1] Unfortunately—and this is our new problem—the men of more limited perception do not easily perceive the necessity to yield to direction from others. The nature of this stubbornness, the tenacity with which men cling to their unhappiness, is what we must consider now.

One step down from the philosophic vision is the man who sees the necessity to find universal laws and patterns but fails to see how these must be checked, not by phenomena, but by their consistency with the ultimate values of life. He may, like a mathematician, soar far above the purely sensible, but he is entirely unable to explain why he finds this activity enjoyable. If he is a student of jurisprudence, for instance, he might extract surprising and important principles, but he is forced to look always down, at actual laws and case histories, and only very dimly in the other direction, toward the criteria for judging among alternative ideals of justice and equity. A second step down and we have the men who find no pleasure in what they will call "abstracts." The palpable events of daily life are all the good and evil which these people care about. Somehow, dimly, there is implied in their judgments, a more basic standard of better and worse—they have an inkling, that is, of the final good. But they not only despair of working things out consistently, they attack as "unrealistic" those who even try. One final step down we find men who cannot even comprehend with any directness the palpable events of daily life around them. They are dependent on the way in which these things are represented to them—by public opinion and prejudice, art (both good and bad), and the very suggestions embodied in ordinary language. The perfectly rational state would be so arranged, of course, that, both in the daily facts and in the popular images of them, men incapable of anything more than groping would nevertheless be helped to the right conclusions as much of the time as possible. But in order for this state of affairs to be brought about (also, of course, for the sake of the gifted man himself) every person capable of climbing out of the cave must be forced to do so. Yet just here is the puzzle: men resist this enlightenment at every crucial point along the way. What is the explanation for this resistance?

At the end of the last lecture I suggested that, for one thing, this ruinous stubbornness was inevitable since each conversion was tantamount to the discovery that what one cared about most was really empty and vain. But at each conversion one is also presented with the originals, as it were, of the shadows one was satisfied with before. Resistance ought soon to be replaced by new enthusiasm. No man who had ever attained a higher vision should take pleasure in returning to the more shadowy level. There are, we are told,[2] no Forms of ugly and trivial things such as mud, hair, or dirt. And even ordinary things such as air or water,[3] or common artefacts,[4] take on a divine splendor at the level of the Forms. One is seeing them in their reality, illuminated by an understanding of what it is that makes anything valuable. Now, Plato is not the only man to have felt this. It is a fact, however, that very few men recognize this vision as a vision of reality and not an illusion.

Under the influence of certain drugs, cacti, or mushrooms, I have been told, even tables, shapes, positions, and squares of color take on unearthly rightness, eternity, and beauty. And yet, even if heroin did not have its appalling side effects and if mescalin did not cause a collapse of our will, would we be entirely happy about turning in our humdrum vision permanently for that new conviction? Others have told us, mystics, that they achieve this state without such mechanical aids, and therefore, usually, without side effects. We admire them more than the drug takers. But do we really envy them? What Plato is suggesting is that a similar visionary state can be reached by some people, systematically, by love and philosophy. If it is done in this way, he says, we will learn eventually to leave behind our misguided anxiety to hold on to the ugly, the petty, and the ever-changing, for we will have control even over the ordinary world and will know exactly what to make of it. In the *Symposium* he speaks of a way to philosophy through love, in the *Republic* of a way to love through philosophy. In the *Phaedrus* he speaks of the philosophic lover (*παιδεραστήσαντος μετὰ φιλοσοφίας*).[5]

Plato's final vision is like those of the mystics and the drug takers in that it tends to take away a man's pleasure in the unreal problems of his fellow men; but unlike the others, those who succeed in the Platonic course have a permanent hold on this beautiful world and can, moreover, bring their revelations to bear on the shadowy pursuits of everyday life. Thomas Aquinas, near the end of his great labor in theology, was simply incapacitated for further work as the result of a beatific vision. He went through his duties mechanically and died shortly afterwards. Apparently, what he saw in his vision was not anything which equipped him for his duties among men—just the reverse. William Blake provides a similar example. Although he was able to go at will in and out of a world where angels walked an earth of jewels, the connections which he made between the two worlds were not the sort which make us especially eager to put him at the head of our state. A well-known poet once convinced me that under the influence of heroin he could suddenly see order and connections in, say, a C´zanne, which he remembered and still believed after the symptoms of the drug withdrew—things which he could communicate intelligibly and with which, moreover, others never under the influence of the drug would agree enthusiastically. Yet I would no more expect this man to be able to write a just law than I would trust him to build a sturdy bridge. But Plato is suggesting that if the vision is not cheaply bought, if it is worked toward slowly, systematically and, in the correct sense of the word, rationally, then a few—a very few, but a few—will see reality illuminated in such a way that nobody else will be a better judge about anything important, even in the world of practical affairs.

But if the vision of the Good and of the Forms is a grasp of reality, not a private dream, if it is the world which all men live in, only more consistently delineated than they are able to do—if, in other words, it is what all men ought to see, not a fantasy to which one man escapes—then why is the light not instantly recognizable to us all? Why do we fail to recognize the shadows on the wall as shadows merely? If all men really long only to see the Forms in their clear reality, why do they consume their lives with ruinous passions for images of images of images of their true desire? Plato was not insensitive to this problem. In the dialogues which we have considered up to this point, there has been a general tendency, to be sure, to explain all human experiences as caused by the magic drawing power of the Good. The only ultimately satisfactory explanation for any event, says Socrates in the *Phaedo*, is the good being achieved; second best is to name the Form being realized. The Good, says Socrates in the *Republic*, is the cause not only of our knowledge but also of the reality of what is. But at the same time, Plato had far too deep a sense of the gap between this ultimate cause and the opinions and experiences of ordinary men to be able to stick to a thoroughly monistic system. He would obviously have had no stomach for a system which asserted that everything which happened in the practical world was for the best. Even in the *Phaedo* itself, therefore, where Socrates is presented as longing for a teleological theory of causation, he is also shown deeply moved by the horrors which result when one is dragged down by the body and its appetites.[6] He recognized the existence of evil, and he knew that he must try to explain its nature.

There was, to be sure, a kind of saintly optimism about Socrates. As the inventor of the notion that no bad man can be happy, that no good man can be unhappy, and that no man is capable of harming anyone but himself, he was above all a bringer of good news. The identification of stupidity with ignorance pointed toward pity and a desire to help as the proper attitudes toward any man who fails to live as he should. The sting is even taken out of punishment when that is redefined as a cure for the misled.[7] True, Socrates was not invariably gay and witty, teaching through laughter. He was not amused by Euthyphro, and there are moments of anger even in the *Apology*. But hatred for evil was not a prominent feature of his manner. He probably made no systematic attempts to impose new laws and constitutions on his fellow citizens. His notion of reform was to show as many individuals as he met how each could improve his lot, rather than to confront the state and criticize its existing laws.[8]

Socrates went to his death with a gay good-night. Plato, however, felt nothing but fury and despair that this could be allowed to happen.[9] He felt that there was such a thing as unregenerate evil, and that a good man should preserve in his heart a well of hatred for these hopelessly bad.[10] His two longest works are devoted to violent recommendations for destroying our societies at their roots and starting all over again. A comparison of the later of these two works with the earlier shows, indeed, that Plato's ability to detest evil grew rather than mellowed through his years. The problem of explaining the source of this evil became one of his chief concerns.

As we have seen, Plato approves only of the man who finds something kindred to his soul in the Forms; the enemy is the man who is at home only in the flux of the perceptible world. The first man has a passion to know; the second actually prefers opinions. The identification of evil must begin with this observation. Now, what is it about the perceptible world which makes it incapable of yielding the knowledge necessary to be happy and good? Above all, it is the disheartening way in which it fails to stand still, even from minute to minute. Intelligence discovers patterns, but the senses report only incessant motion.[11] Incessant motion, then, would seem to be the source of evil. On the other hand, Plato could not accept a theory which made corporeal nature as such the cause of corruption, because he was convinced that our failure to see through phenomena was a sin upon our own heads. Each *psyche* must stand trial after death for its success or failure to overcome the distracting qualities of bodily existence.[12] It must be, therefore, some quality within each *psyche* akin to bodily flux which is responsible. After all, motion as such cannot be evil. Soul, thought, life, and intelligence (*ψυχή, φρόνησις, ζωή, νοῦς*), says Plato in the *Sophist*,[13] all things which imply motion, are part of the splendor of reality. It will not do to recognize only the eternally motionless Forms. What is the *psyche* itself if not that which gives a live person his characteristic ability to move himself?[14] And what is love if not the motion of the *psyche* toward the Forms and the Good? Plato's inevitable conclusion, therefore, as we shall see, is that there must be two *kinds* of motion, both somehow native to the *psyche*, one toward the beauty of the motionless Forms, but one also which is somehow akin to the regrettable flux which characterizes particulars. There is something in us which ties us to our bodily appetites, not only to hunger and thirst but also to fear, anger, pleasure, pain, and all of the distracting emotions which characterize our life in the world of sensed objects.

The human *psyche*, left to itself, Plato says on many occasions,[15] will always exhibit only rational activity, motion toward its true good. Incarnation, on the other hand, necessarily forces us to divide our attention: between nutrition, moral inclinations, and intellectual understanding, all three at the same time.[16] On this point Plato's opinion did not remain entirely unchanged throughout his life, however. The problem, remember, was to explain the destructive capacities of the more trivial desires. When he wrote the *Republic*[17] he still suspected that the whole *psyche* must in its true essence be only rational, and that it was the experience of incarnation which forced on it this temporary division of interests. Later he seems to have concluded that our rational *psyches* suffer alien and not immortal kinds of *psyche* to be grafted on to them as we are born. These, he thought, were designed to get us through life in a corporeal state, but were also capable of destroying our better part.[18] But, as I say, he evidently never quite made up his mind on this.[19] The earlier theory, which assumed that the whole *psyche* was immortal, had the advantage of explaining how the *psyche* could sustain a damage during life which it could be punished for after death. The later version, tracing the regrettable tendencies to things not really native to the *psyche*, had the advantage of explaining better why a *psyche* could ever be dragged, against its own true desire, to illusory goods, and so fall short of the main prize.

Plato's tripartite division of the human *psyche*, for all the trouble that it gave him, is one of the most momentous and fruitful of his innovations. His description of the many-headed monster which lurks even in good men, expressing its desires openly only when he is asleep,[20] is as exciting as anything which Freud has said about the unconscious. And his analysis of the good man's fierce will to side with reason and order against the beast below—an idea reasonably close to Freud's *super-ego*—rings marvelously true. But it is the third element which is Plato's most characteristic suggestion. Like Freud's *ego*, it is the quintessential man, unlike the *ego*, however, it is a pure and unerring passion for the true good of the whole man. The name for its mode of action is rationality. In the *Republic*, Plato shows at some length how civilization, that is, a rationally ordered society, could train an ordinary man's spirited element so as to enable it to placate the beast and to move toward the whole man's true well-being. But this can only be done, he argues, if society is dominated by a few men who are themselves ruled not by a similar spirited element but by a higher, reasonable element. Everything depends on the possibility that in some men, at least, a clear, direct, and conscious energy for the true well-being of the whole man dominates completely. Rationality, in other words, is not thought of as calculation arising out of anxiety over the problem of fulfilling our desires; it is the master passion of the man who understands what the good of his whole person is.

The great mystery in Freudian philosophy is the nature of the *ego*. At one time Freud thought that this, rather than the *id*, was the great well of libidinal energy.[21] Later he changed his mind and decided that the *id*, that is, the many-headed monster of the unconscious, was the source of the *libido*.[22] His final position was one of bleak pessimism. "One can hardly go wrong," he says, "in regarding the *ego* as that part of the *id* which has been modified by its proximity to the external world and the influence that the latter has had on it." The *ego*, he says, "serves the purpose of receiving stimuli and protecting the organism from them, like the cortical layer with which a particle of living substance surrounds itself. . . . The *ego* has taken over the task of representing the external world for the *id*, and so of saving it; for the *id*, blindly striving to gratify its instincts in complete disregard of the superior strength of outside forces, could not otherwise escape annihilation. . . . On behalf of the *id*, the *ego* controls the path of access to mobility, but it interpolates between desire and action the procrastinating factor of thought, during which it makes use of the residues of experience stored up in memory."[23] Thus, according to Freud, the *ego* can synthesize, harmonize, and reconcile the conflicting drives and apprehensions, and even calculate for remote pleasures, and because of this it deserves the title of the true man and the very essence of the will to live—what Freud calls *eros*. But it gets its values from only one source, the many-headed monster which clamors blindly night and day. Anything in the outside world which tends to limit this mad energy, the *ego* is bound to declare evil and inimical.

Plato's conception of the true man at the core of our desires is also obscure and problematical, but perhaps not quite so seriously so as Freud's. For, according to Freud, the conflict between passion and reason is merely a conflict between a drive for pleasure which knows no sense of time, and a drive for the same pleasures confounded by a sense of the past, the future, and the laws of cause and effect. This suggests that reason itself has no value except as an element of prudence in arranging for the satisfaction of bodily desires. The life devoted to reason itself (as opposed to a "reasonable" life), the ideal of the most admirable men, becomes only an elaborate and peculiarly fortunate sublimation, an unusually satisfying fantasy which a few gifted men are capable of. Plato, on the other hand, accepts as the all-important fact of life, the necessity for the dominance of reason if there is to be happiness either in the individual or in society. Irrational desires, that is, desires which, if obeyed, would lead to something other than the good of the whole, can lose their hold on us, he argued, if we but train ourselves to see ever more rewarding goals. We must believe in our ability to alter our more infantile appetites. Freud was impressed by the extreme danger in ever denying a desire all expression whatever. Plato was more impressed by the way desires grew and grew when you gave them expression. Freud was satisfied that there were countless ways in which men could modify potentially bestial desires and thus suffer no serious consequences. He thought that there was no other source of energy. Plato was convinced that the forced subservience of desires to reason (which Freud also believed to be necessary, of course) was *not* the same as a prudential modification of these same desires. True happiness, Plato maintained, comes in the form of an intellectual vision which leaves bodily life far behind. The society which thought that pleasure in rationality was a matter of taste, Plato believed, was lost.

Plato's most extensive discussion of this problem is the *Phaedrus*. This dialogue seems to fall into two parts, because the question has two aspects. First, there is the question of the right way to understand the conflict between passion and reason. This is done in terms of a debate on the relative merits of two kinds of love, that which is the energy of the rational part of the *psyche* and that which is the energy of the irrational part. Second, there is the question of the practical consequences of this analysis, in art, politics, and morality. This is done in terms of a debate on the relative merits of rhetoric, which is the appeal to the irrational part of the *psyche*, as against those of philosophy, which is the appeal to the rational part. Some commentators have thought that the dialogue as a whole was a kind of amorous contest between rhetoric and philosophy for the soul of the young Phaedrus.[24] But this will not explain the change in tone and subject matter halfway through the work. One would do better, I think, to concentrate on the question of the two kinds of love. The great discovery which the discussion makes is that rationality is just as surely a love as irrationality is. Once this has been established, it is shown that this has important consequences in evaluating the art of persuasion. The art of persuasion is a kind of wooing of the *psyche* (*ψυχαγωγία*), but as there are two loves in every man, there will be two wooers. It is nothing less than all-important that we learn to distinguish between them.

The opening scene of the *Phaedrus* is one of the most famous in ancient literature. It is noontime in midsummer and we are outside the city walls. Socrates, in his usual high spirits, meets young Phaedrus, the same that was the "father of the idea" in the *Symposium*. Phaedrus, it seems, has spent the morning listening to Lysias, the greatest orator of the day, repeating a very clever speech which he had written. Phaedrus is about to walk in the country and find a place where he can practice this speech by Lysias, for he wants to commit it to memory. Socrates shows interest. As a matter of fact, says Phaedrus, the subject is one which is especially appropriate for his ears: love. The speech purports to be that of a man to a handsome boy, giving reasons why the boy should grant his favors to him. But the man is not in love with the boy. That, says Phaedrus, is the clever part. The speech sets out all of the advantages of yielding to the non-lover. How democratic, says Socrates. Would that he would add the advantages of yielding to the old rather than the young and the poor rather than the rich. Then Socrates would be sitting pretty. Phaedrus leads Socrates off to a beautiful spot under a plane tree by the river, where Phaedrus will read the speech. There is a mythological event associated with this spot, and Phaedrus asks Socrates if he believes such myths. Socrates replies that he is not interested in the modern preoccupation with rationalizing legends. He is more interested in trying to find out about himself—whether he is a monster more complex and intertwining (*πολυπλοκώτερον*)[25] than the Typhon, or a gentler and more unified being. When the two arrive at their spot under the tree, Socrates is astounded by the beauty of the place. Phaedrus taunts him on his passion for the city and his complete ignorance of the countryside. Socrates replies that he is a lover of learning (*φιλομαθής*),[26] that men, not trees and rural scenes, are his teachers. But Phaedrus knew how to get Socrates out into the country: he dangled a book before him as one dangles a bit of greenery before an animal.

The speech purporting to be by Lysias[27] is a common-sense description of the difference between passion and reason. It is assumed that if a man is in perfect possession of his wits and is not tempted to endanger any of his long-range good for an immediate pleasure, then he cannot be in love. The non-lover, therefore, has his own and the boy's well-being clearly before him and none of the well-known consequences of a passionate affair will follow. The lover, says the non-lover, is ill. He is aware himself that his fever is driving him to folly, but he cannot stop. Non-lovers, on the other hand, have control over themselves and prefer to do what is best rather than win someone's good opinion (*κρείττους αὑτῶν ὄντας, τὸ βέλτιστον ἀντὶ τῆς δόξης τῆς παρὰ τῶν ἀνθρώπων αἱρεῖσθαι*).[28] It is characteristic of the lover also that his passion has little connection with the boy's true merits, whereas the rational man will admire only true excellence. Furthermore, there is no reason why a firm friendship (*ἰσχυρὰ φιλία*) should be impossible just because there is no sexual passion. After all, the bonds which tie sons, fathers, mothers, and companions do not come from this kind of desire but from other cares (*οὐκ ἐξ ἐπιθυμίας τοιαύτης . . . ἀλλ' ἐξ ἑτέρων ἐπιτηδευμάτων*).[29]

What Phaedrus mainly admires in this speech, besides the boldness of the paradox and the artistic smoothness of the language, is the fact that Lysias has said absolutely everything that could be said on this subject. Socrates scoffs at this and says that even he, although not, of course, from his own invention, could do infinitely better than Lysias. Lysias did, to be sure, make the one indispensable point, that the lover is ill and driven to folly while the non-lover acts with wisdom, but he merely repeated this over and over again. The only really effective way to tackle a subject, says Socrates, is to define the true nature of whatever is being discussed (*ἡ οὐσία ἑκάστου*),[30] and then to say what kind of thing it is and what its effects are (*οἷόν τε ἔστι καὶ ἣν ἔχει δύναμιν*).[31]

Socrates begins his version of the wooer's speech by slyly changing the dramatic situation for the address in two important details. First, the boy is pictured as being a bit older, presumably one who can be expected to have more than merely physical charm.[32] Second, Socrates goes out of his way to say that the man who is to praise rationality is really in love, even though he has persuaded the younger man that he is not.[33] He then proceeds to define the essence of love in a careful analysis by genus and species. It is obvious to everyone, he says, that love is some kind of desire (*ἐπιθυμία τις ὁ ἔρως*).[34] The question is, what species of desire, for even non-lovers desire the beautiful (*ὅτι δ' αὖ καὶ μὴ ἐρῶντες ἐπιθυμοῦσι τῶν καλῶν, ἴσμεν*).[35] How are we to distinguish the lover from the non-lover? The first thing to understand, he says, is that there are two kinds of ruling or guiding things in each of us, two separate things whose lead we follow: one is a desire for pleasure which is ours from birth (*ἔμφυτος ἐπιθυμία ἡδονῶν*),[36] and the other is an acquired judgment which desires what is best (*ἐπίκτητος δόξα, ἐφιεμένη τοῦ ἀρίστου*).[37] Sometimes these two drives are in harmony, sometimes at civil war (*στασιάζετον*); sometimes one dominates, sometimes the other. When judgment leads us rationally (*λόγῳ*) toward what is best and that is in command, this command is called discretion (*σωφροσύνη*). When desire drags us irrationally (*ἀλόγως*) toward pleasure and that gains control over us, this control is called depravity (*ὕβρις*). We can further divide depravity into several species according to the particular pleasure, desire for which has conquered both our ability to calculate our true advantage and all other desires as well (*κρατοῦσα τοῦ λόγου τε τοῦ ἀρίστου καὶ τῶν ἄλλων ἐπιθυμιῶν*).[38] If it is pleasure in eating, then we call the man a glutton, if pleasure in drink, then he is an alcoholic, and so on. It is obviously here that we find the man who is in love. Love is the desire which irrationally overcomes the judgment which urges us toward true well-being whenever we are drawn instead to the pleasure of "beauty" (*ἡ . . . ἄνευ λόγου δόξης ἐπὶ τὸ ὀρθὸν ὁρμώσης κρατήσασα ἐπιθυμία πρὸς ἡδονὴν ἀχθεῖσα κάλλους . . . ἔρως ἐκλήθη*).[39]

Socrates pauses for a moment, remarking that he seems to be divinely inspired, so eloquent is he today.[40] The place seems to have a divine presence, as he is evidently possessed (*νυμφόληπτος*).[41] Phaedrus agrees enthusiastically. Socrates pretends to fear this influence, for, after all, he is at this moment pretending to despise all emotions.

The rest of Socrates' first speech is a brilliant portrait of the man who is in love, based carefully on his analysis of what love is. This speech is much more orderly than Lysias', and so is more convincing as a complete account of the matter.[42] Socrates begins with a catalogue of the harmful effects which a lover can have on the boy. First he gives the harmful effects on his mind, then on his body, finally to his possessions. Next he describes how the boy must feel toward a lover: first how he must feel while the love lasts, then how he must feel after the love has vanished. But far more important than the superior organization is the demonstrable advantage of having first defined the subject by genus and species. The love in question was identified as a species of depravity, and depravity was defined as a compulsion toward pleasure and a slavery to it.[43] Since this necessarily meant that the man must fail to pursue his true good,[44] the man can only be described as sick[45] or mad.[46] It follows that such a man will tolerate nothing which might endanger the boy's dependence on him. Consider, then, Socrates says, how very disagreeable for the boy must be this constant, anxious attention from the aging, possessive, and eternally jealous man (for it is assumed that the boy will have no love for his lover).[47] As for the boy's duties in gratifying his lover's sexual desires, these are too horrible even to talk about. And what a shock the boy will receive when his lover loses his passion and recovers his intelligence and discretion (*νοῦς καὶ σωφροσύνη*).[48] Being no longer the slave to immediate gratification, but able once again to look out for his long-range interests, he will find it prudent to side-step the boy once held so dear and find excuses for not honoring his extravagant promises. The boy finds that love is not an honest concern for the well-being of the loved one; it is a desire to gratify a hunger.[49]

Suddenly Socrates finds himself speaking in hexameters, so he breaks off abruptly and starts to get away from these nymphs, or whatever it is that is inspiring him. Phaedrus, of course, is disappointed, because he wanted to hear the other half of Socrates' speech, the arguments in praise of the non-lover, and because he then wanted to compare the art of the two speeches. Socrates satisfies him on the first point in one sentence: for every evil attributed to the lover there is a corresponding good to be expected from the non-lover.[50] But, as a matter of fact, Socrates will have to give Phaedrus a whole new speech, because his familiar daemonic sign came to him just as he was about to go away.[51] He knows what it means. (His *psyche* has a prophetic power.)[52] He understands that he must give a second speech recanting the first, a Palinode like that by Stesichorus, because he has monstrously misrepresented the truth. He had talked as though there never was a man of highborn and gentle character who had loved another of the same excellence,[53] as though Love were not a god or something divine.[54] His fault (*ἁμάρτημα*)[55] is grave for his account was truly extraordinary (*δεινὸς λόγος*).[56] He must therefore purify himself (*καθήρασθαι*).[57]

Now what is it really that was monstrous about Socrates' speech? We miss the point if we think of Socrates' wooer as a cold-blooded sensualist. It is precisely the quality of his love (for remember, he was said to be really a lover, although he denied it) which is the all-important puzzle that Socrates fails to make clear. All that we know about it, really, is that it is full of intelligence—that is, a genuine and enlightened care for the true happiness of both the lover and the boy. The grotesqueness of saying that such rational self-control was the absence of love is shown in two places. First, there is the qualification that the so-called non-lover must really be a lover in disguise. After all, why is all this care lavished on the other man if there is no desire of *any* kind? And then, later in the speech, when Socrates describes the lover falling out of love, his irony points up sharply what is wrong. He speaks as though the mere dying out of love brought with it a reign of intelligence and order.[58] The speech is otherwise perfectly within the Socratic manner.[59] But this one qualification was of extreme importance to Plato: intelligence and moral excellence are not the result of an absence of passion—they are themselves a passion of a different kind, a desire for the best.[60]

The first mistake, it seems, came at the beginning when we examined the genus of which love is a species. We had assumed that only depravity was madness, while desire for the best was not. What we had not realized was that madness (*μανία*) was not invariably bad. After all, are not prophetic visions, purificational rites, and poetic inspiration superior to sober calculation in these activities?[61] To understand this, we must go one step farther back. The right place to begin is with an examination of the nature of the human *psyche*.

First of all, we must understand that all *psyche* is immortal.[62] This follows from the fact that anything which is in eternal motion is eternally alive, and the kind of motion by which we identify the presence of *psyche* can be proved to be a kind which can by its nature never stop. For we may observe in the universe not one but two kinds of motion, self-generating and induced. Now, the self-generating kind rather than the induced must obviously be the first principle and cause of motion everywhere. If that is so, however, it means that there can never have been a time when this self-generating motion was not there, for then it would not be by its nature self-generating, but would be dependent on something else to have generated it. Furthermore, if it is its nature to be self-generating, then it can never cease moving; otherwise it would be departing from its essential nature (*ἀπολεῖπον ἑαυτό*).[63] And besides, if self-generating motion ceased to exist, all visible phenomena, this great flux which we call the world, would collapse and vanish into thin air. But what is our name for this self-generating motion if not *psyche* —that which distinguishes the animate from the inanimate? If a body can move itself we say it is alive.

Now imagine this immortal *psyche* as the combined effect (*σύμφυτος δύναμις*)[64] of a pair of winged horses and their winged charioteer.[65] In the case of the gods, the horses and their driver are of the finest stock, and we may think of them as flying round the heavenly courses, ordering the universe. For all *psyche* has under its care all that is inanimate; it traverses all space, taking on now one form, now another.[66] Zeus leads the way and the others take their appointed paths. (Jealousy has no place in the dance of the gods: *φθόνος γὰρ ἔξω θείου χοροῦ ἵσταται.*)[67] But in the case of the *psyches* of men, the horses often give them trouble, and if the drivers are not skilful they will be unable to drive their teams to the summit.

If it does reach the summit, a *psyche* may look out to a region beyond the heavens.[68] Here are the Forms themselves in all their beauty, not seen or touched, but beheld by intelligence, the pilot of the *psyche*. This is the *psyche's* proper food and the only thing which can content it: to see Justice itself, Self-respect, Knowledge (*αὐτὴ δικαιοσύνη, σωφροσύνη, ἐπιστήμη*).[69] The best of the human *psyches* are able to follow a god and raise the head of the charioteer into this region beyond. All desire to do so,[70] but some, because of some failure in the charioteer,[71] are unsuccessful in controlling the horses. The wings drop off and the *psyche* falls and is for a time encased in a body here on earth. Those who had the best view of reality are born as philosophers, also called lovers of beauty, followers of the Muses, lovers.[72] Those who got the second best look at reality are born as men of great practical understanding, strength and decision—natural leaders. Third in order are the businessmen and bureaucrats, those who keep order on a lower level. Fourth, those who understand only the human body, its health, development, and beauty. Fifth, the prophets and the priests of the mysteries. Sixth, the poets and other imitators. Seventh, the laborers in the fields and in the shops. Eighth, the men who are clever at argument and successful in persuading crowds. And ninth, those who saw least reality of all, the dictators. Not that any *psyche* which is ever born into the body of a man can be entirely without memory of the Forms. For this is the distinctive thing about mankind: man alone of all earthly creatures understands the world in terms of the Forms, gathering together a number of impressions and arriving that way at a recovery of the single idea.[73] But the only *psyche* which can so clarify the vision that it will eventually be able to escape recurrent incarnation is that of the man who has either loved wisdom and nothing else, or the man who has managed to combine his love for the young with love of wisdom, *ἡ τοῦ φιλοσοφήσαντος ἀδόλως ἢ παιδεραστήσαντος μετὰ φιλοσοφίας.*[74] His life is spent doing deftly and directly what all men really desire to do—to recall the Forms.

Philosophy, then, is a fourth kind of madness, the madness

of the lover of beauty.[75] This is by far the best madness, for it amounts to a desire for that which all men would desire if they could only see it. Nor is it grotesque to call true rationality a madness, because the true rationalist, when he sees beauty here on earth, is seized with a passionate memory of true beauty and begins to regrow his wings. In his single-mindedness and lack of concern for practical affairs, therefore, he will exhibit all the symptoms of the lover which the ordinary man finds so ridiculous. Our senses are dull, and it is hard to reach the point where likenesses of Justice and the rest thrill us with the memory of their true beauty. With beauty itself, however, it is different.[76] It shone the brightest in that fiery land,[77] indeed it was surely the pure light itself which bathed us when we were pure.[78] So also, in this shadowy world we live in, Beauty alone is instantly recognizable. (We are irresistibly reminded of the sun in the *Republic.* We are undoubtedly meant to equate Beauty here with the Form of the Good.)[79]

Even *psyches* born weak or corrupted by their way of life respond to beauty, but they do so in a hideous fashion: they surrender to pleasure and try to go in the manner of a four-footed animal and procreate—or they consort with depravity and have no fear or shame preventing them from chasing after pleasures which are contrary to nature (*παρὰ φύσιν*).[80] These are the men whom both of the first two speeches rightly condemned. They do indeed lose all sense of proportion in their judgments as to what is worth pursuing, for they have not understood what it is which they really desire. But the man who understands what is really going on when he is captured and drawn by beauty is not the man with cool worldly self-possession (*σωφροσύνη θνητή*),[81] as Lysias would have us believe. On the contrary, the man who understands what must be understood, when he sees a godlike face or a bodily form which mimics Beauty well, experiences a shudder of awe and reverences the presence of the divine. He sees the god on whom he had kept his eye as he climbed to that great vision. He reaches out for this god in his memory and is possessed by him.[82] He thus takes on the special virtues of his god. Because he holds the beautiful person responsible for this he loves him the more (*μᾶλλον ἀγαπῶσι*).[83] Like a worshiper of Dionysus, what the philosopher draws in from his god, who is Zeus, he pours over onto the one whom he loves, making him as much like Zeus as is possible.

For the climax of this extraordinary passage, Plato returns to the tripartite division of the *psyche* into a black horse, a white one, and a driver.[84] The white horse is the spirited element. It must take its directions from the intelligence, but it is naturally inclined to do the decent and orderly thing and is ashamed to do anything wrong. The black horse, on the other hand, is ugly, irregularly shaped, and shameless. When the *psyche* as a whole is first suffused with those sensations of heat and prickliness which mean that beauty has been sighted, the black horse violently drags the trio forward in a senseless attempt to leap on top of the carrier of this beauty. The white horse is horrified and draws back. The charioteer, in awe and reverence for the truth which he sees shining there, draws back on the reins for all he is worth. Certainly he will not allow the violent animal to drag him toward monstrous and forbidden acts (*δεινὰ καὶ παράνομα*).[85] But neither will he withdraw entirely, for it is no more possible for a good man not to be a friend of a good man than it is for a bad man ever to be a friend of a bad man.[86] He will first brutally suppress the dark beast,[87] with the full consent and aid of the lighter animal, and will then proceed to a companionship with the beautiful person which is based on a complete understanding of what it really means to be beautiful.

The reward for the younger man will be far more than instruction and protection in the usual sense. Although the older man is not presumed to be physically beautiful any more, his love will be, as it were, reflected from the younger man back to himself.[88] The younger man will see his own beauty in its effect upon his lover. If they are truly lovers of wisdom, the only intercourse which will appeal to them is rational exploration together, to be companions in adventures in the life of the mind. These are the creators of all great things in civilization. If, however, they are men of the second order, lovers of honor rather than of wisdom, their unruly animals will never be so surely under control at all times. Some day, when they are wrestling, it may be, or have been drinking wine, their constant proximity may be too much for them and they will find a sexual expression for their love.[89] If they do, their wings will fall off and they can never soar to the heights which the philosophic friends can reach. Being essentially good men, however, they will indulge in sexual pleasures only very rarely, understanding the regrettable effects which these have on the freedom of their minds in the search for the Forms. And they are not lost like the depraved. They are still eager for wings, and that, it is ordained, is the first step on the way to the heavenly vision.

We find here two differences from the theory as it was explained in the *Symposium* and the *Republic*. The first departure is the new decision that it is not necessary, or perhaps even possible, for the philosopher to fall out of love and cease to need his special friend. It is interesting to speculate on the reasons for this change. Did Plato feel, perhaps, that only Socrates was capable of the completely impersonal love?[90] Or did the development of a more precise and constructive dialectic require a steadier relationship than that usually realized in Socrates' habitual way of life?[91]

The other innovation was far more momentous, however, and was destined to complicate the Platonic theory of love and all but destroy it. This is the decision that the *psyche* itself was in essence self-generating motion and the only cause of all motion in the universe. Now, if this is so, it is difficult to see how the Good or the Beautiful could be the first cause even of intellectual energy. If *psyche* is defined as incessant self-generating motion, then the drawing power of the Good or the Beautiful, it would seem, is no longer needed. The doctrine of the Good is more mysterious than ever. A new effort will have to be made, therefore, to distinguish psychic energy when it is and when it is not directed accurately toward the highest good. It will have to be shown just *how* self-generating motion toward true good differs from self-generating motion directed at other things. Plato's tripartite division of the *psyche*, like Freud's also, is the product of an acute appreciation for the facts—the facts of men's misery and of unhappy love above all, but the facts of the rewards of intelligence as well—but Plato the metaphysician will not be satisfied until he has given a precise and consistent description of the motions represented in each *part* of the *psyche*: the unreasonable appetite of the black horse, the unthinking energy of the white one, and the dizzy vision of the charioteer.

# CHAPTER 7

*Plato's Theory of* psyche *as Self-caused Motion and his Theory of Evil: The* Timaeus *and* Laws. *The Eventual Eclipse of the Theory of Cosmic Love. The Difference Between Plato and Aristotle: The Similarity Between Aristotle's System and the Vision Implied in the* Phaedo.

ARISTOTLE SUMS UP THE DIFFERENCE between his analysis of the world and Plato's as follows.[1] Each saw the necessity for identifying three factors. First, there must be Form (*μορφή* or *εἶδος*), which is by nature divine, good, and desirable (*θεῖον, ἀγαθόν, ἐφετόν*).[2] Second, there must be something underlying perceptible phenomena which is co-cause (*συναιτία*) with Form of all that comes to be on the sensible level. This is what Plato called in the *Timaeus*[3] the Mother of that which comes to be as the Form is the Father, and Aristotle does not disapprove of the metaphor. Third, when one concentrates on that which is contrary to Form as the cause of evil (*τὸ κακοποιόν*),[4] the cause, that is, of the failure of the perceptible world to realize the excellence and full reality of the Forms which are recognized in it, then one sees the need to identify non-being in phenomena. These are the Form, Matter, and Privation of Aristotle's system. He complains, however, that Plato confused two of these, Matter and Privation. The underlying matter was in Plato's system simultaneously the co-cause of coming into being and also the cause of the failure to be completely real. But, says Aristotle, if the Forms are desirable, if they are the cause of motion as the patterns of perfection which are yearned for and striven for, there must be something which by its nature yearns and strives for this realization (*ὃ πέφυκεν ἐφίεσθαι καὶ ὀρέγεσθαι αὐτοῦ κατὰ τὴν αὐτοῦ φύσιν*).[5] In Plato's system what underlies Form, because it is also the cause of failure in phenomena to reach reality, in effect desires its own non-existence (*ὀρέγεσθαι τῆς αὐτοῦ φθορᾶς*).[6] Plato has nothing, therefore, which desires what is desirable. Form cannot desire itself, for it is not wanting in perfection (διὰ τὸ μὴ εἶναι ἐνδεές),[7] and that which is contrary to Form can only desire Form's destruction.

What Plato did not understand, says Aristotle, was that Matter by its very nature desires only Form. It contains no independent energy; it never obstructs the realization of the Forms. The ugly desires the beautiful, Aristotle suggests, and the female the male, but the desire is not felt by the defect itself, the ugliness or the femininity, it is felt by substratum temporarily characterized in this way.[8] Privation, the true opposite to the real Forms, is the degree to which a particular piece of informed matter is not a perfect realization of the Form in question. In a sense, therefore, it is pure non-existence; but non-being does not enter as active cause in the essential makeup of particulars. Privation turns out really to be merely a way of referring to the other Form or Forms, the influences of which hamper the realization of the Form expected at some particular time and place.[9] There is no separate factor of any sort actively causing evil, failure or non-reality.[10] In one way of looking at it, therefore, there are in nature only two things, Form and Matter, the first of these is perfection, the second that which by its nature desires this perfection.[11] The third thing, Privation, is not a third component but a shorthand way of referring to the degree to which some Form, because of the influence of yet other Forms, is not actualized, merely desired.

Aristotle is not unfair in this summary of his differences with Plato. He is giving a scrupulously careful account of Plato's later system, specifically the description of the world in the *Timaeus*. The surprising thing, however, is the striking similarity between the scheme which Aristotle opposes to Plato's and the scheme implied in Plato's own earlier dialogues, particularly the *Phaedo*.[12] There, as we saw, the perceptible world was described as yearning and striving toward the perfection of the Form patterns, and it was boldly maintained that when Forms were given as causes this was but a roundabout way of giving the good being realized as the true cause. In the *Republic*, too, we saw how the world was explicable only by finding the Forms, and the Forms were explicable only when it was seen how they were good. But it was Aristotle rather than Plato who worked out this idea in minute detail.

There are, of course, important differences between the nature and identity of the Forms in Plato's and in Aristotle's systems. We shall examine these differences later. Notice now this one very striking resemblance. In both philosophies, the Forms are causes as patterns of perfection being striven for, and the identification of these Forms, both philosophers maintained, provides the only satisfactory explanation for any event. In Aristotelian language, formal and final causes are ultimately identical.[13] If a house comes into being, you may name the housebuilder as the cause, but you can only explain why *he* was moved to build this structure by saying that he knew the Form "what it is to be a house." (This is the formal cause.) And you can only explain why knowledge of what it is to be a house set the man in motion if you include in this knowledge above all the good of a house, why anybody would want a house—its purpose. (This is the final cause, the end being striven for.) Nature, says Aristotle, is precisely the same as art except that the Form being striven for, instead of informing the mind of a human agent, informs directly the entity which is coming into being—as when an acorn strives to achieve the shape of an oak.[14] The Form of the full-grown oak must be there already in the acorn, pulling it to its realization. But this amounts precisely to what Socrates in the *Phaedo* longed to be able to do, to give always only the good being striven for as the cause of an event. One step down on the Divided Line and you can give only the Form; but at the top, the formal and the final causes become identical.

Now, Plato probably never abandoned the assumption that the Forms were "divine, good, and desirable." Aristotle himself seems to testify to that.[15] But the manner in which the world desired these patterns became ever more obscure in Plato's later writings. Aristotle, like Eryximachus, saw no real difficulty in making love the sole cause for all events in the universe. The first mover of the universe as a whole, he says, is the best and most beautiful thing of all and causes the whole to move by being the object of its love (*κινεῖ ὡς ἐρώμενον*).[16] And, in Aristotle's system, a complete explanation of any event within the world can always be given by naming the great hierarchy of Forms yearned for by the piece of substratum in question. But Plato was haunted by the conviction that there was irrational energy in the universe. He, therefore, had to bring in a divine Craftsman, the δημιουργός, who looked upward to the Forms, saw their goodness, then looked down again and made the particulars as like the Forms as possible.[17] It is the Craftsman, then, who is responsible for making the visible world as good as it could be (ἐπὶ τὸ βέλτιστον).[18] Left to itself, nature would *not* yearn for its own perfection.

The Craftsman's task, indeed, is a strenuous one, according to Plato. He effects his purpose in two ways: by imposing greater regularity on the atoms of the natural elements themselves,[19] and by creating a world *psyche* to guarantee orderly circular revolutions. This latter motion introduces a centripetal tendency and thus produces the heterogeneity necessary for perpetual motion of every kind.[20] To be sure, even before the divine Craftsman interfered, the world did have an innate source of energy, but it was energy entirely without intelligence.[21] It is not true that there was *no* trace of order before "creation," because the four elements, insofar as they were recognizable as the different elements, did bear traces of the Forms; but the world body as such—Aristotle was right about this—contained, according to Plato, no natural desire for perfection.

Aristotle mentioned neither the world soul nor the divine Craftsman in this summary of Plato's physical system. It is really hard to blame Aristotle, however. For one thing, he was criticizing specifically Plato's analysis of the relation between Form and substratum. For another, it is in any case very difficult indeed to know what to do with Plato's divinities. In the *Phaedo*, as we saw, Socrates rejoiced in the idea that Intelligence ruled the universe. (In this belief Plato probably never wavered.) But there are two rather different ways of understanding what the rule of Intelligence might really amount to. First, there is the explanation suggested in the *Symposium* and the *Republic*, that the true well-being of each thing and of the universe is the ultimate cause of all energy as the goal being striven for; and second, there is the more literal vision of an intelligent being thinking, planning, and working night and day to see that the world is well governed. Plato seems in effect to have shifted from the first, the more sophisticated explanation, to the second, the more primitive one, and Aristotle has returned to the more sophisticated version again.

To be sure, Plato may well have thought even of the Form of the Good as being somehow a live God,[22] but it makes no little difference whether you speak of the author of everything as the goodness and beauty which the world desires, or as a builder who struggles to superimpose on an unruly stuff the semblance of eternal Forms the beauty of which *he* admires. In the first version, the very nature of the world is to be moved by love; in the second version, only The Creator is so moved, really.

At the end of the last lecture I suggested what I think is the most probable reason for this important change of emphasis in Plato's philosophy. The explanation is to be found, in the first instance, in the new conception of the nature of *psyche*—the notion common to the *Phaedrus*, the *Timaeus*, and the *Laws*, that *psyche* is self-generating motion. And behind *this* development is Plato's refusal to deny the existence of evil and irrationality, in man or in the world.

Plato had obviously worried for a long time about the nature of *psyche*. In the *Phaedo*, for example, the difference between *psyche* and body turned out to be of crucial importance,[23] and yet Plato was forced also to recognize a gap between *psyche* and the pure unchanging Forms as well. *Psyche* is merely more like and more closely related (ὁμοιότερον and συγγενέστερον)[24] to Form than to body, he concluded. Somehow it was neither a Form nor a particular. Indeed, in the last proof of the immortality of *psyche* in the *Phaedo*,[25] it is just this ambiguity—as to whether an individual *psyche* might be a kind of particular, partaking somehow in the Form *psyche*, or whether *psyche* fails altogether to obey the rules of Forms and particulars—which makes the discussion so unsatisfactory. And, of course, always, the undependableness of man's psychic energy, the way in which a man can be fooled by "bodily" appetites and so lose his true desires, interested Plato deeply. What could the true nature of *psyche* be? The idea that the *psyche* was in its essence just self-generating motion must have seemed a brilliant one to Plato, a sensational suggestion, a "breakthrough," as we say. For one thing, this conception of the *psyche* was not really so very remote from commonly held ideas. One looked at a live person and at a corpse and summed up the essential difference as the key to the nature of the *psyche*. Surely far better than warmth or breath—the qualities usually taken to be most significant, is the ability of the live body to move itself. The secret of life is the ability to originate motion and not to be dependent on outside movers. Some Presocratics had already thought along these lines.[26] But even more important was the elegant proof—so Plato thought—of the immortality of *psyche* if it is defined as self-generating motion. We have already seen in the *Phaedrus* how this argument works. Plato had tried many arguments to support his conviction that the human *psyche* survived its separation from the body at death, but he discarded them all until he found this one.[27] Clearly, the idea that *psyche* was energy itself deserved careful consideration.

But this new definition of *psyche* also brought with it some problems. First, if *psyche* is by definition ceaseless self-caused motion, then it is difficult to see how the Good is the cause of its motions at all. The intelligent motions of any *psyche* must still be identified as those which are directed toward true good, but the Good cannot be the cause of the motion as such. Plato apparently never abandoned the idea of the primacy of the Good, but the role of the Good became very obscure. In the *Sophist*, for instance, he gives a hierarchy of universals; the top, all-inclusive universal, however, which he calls Reality, is not described in terms even remotely reminiscent of the Form of the Good in the *Republic*. It is known, also, that Plato lectured late in life on the Good. At this time he seems to have spoken of the Good somehow as unity and opposed it to the indefinite great and small.[28] This, no doubt, was a development of the idea which we noted in the earlier dialogues that the Good is a binding force and the cause of higher organization in all forms of life.[29] It is also related to the idea, found especially prominently in the *Philebus*[30] as well as the *Timaeus*,[31] that a thing is good insofar as it is exact, definable, and ordered.[32] It is an entirely Platonic way of describing that which makes the Forms "divine, good, and desirable." It does not, however, offer much help in the problem as to how either the Forms or their goodness are the causes of events. The human *psyche*, Plato could once say, derived its very energy from the glimpses it got of the excellence of the real world. That is the essence of the Platonic theory of love, and it did offer a way of explaining how the Good, and therefore Intelligence, functioned in the world. But what can we make of purposive action now—now that *psyche* is defined as self-generating motion and the cause of all other motion? If there would be energy whether a good were being striven for or not, then in what sense can good be a cause at all? Plato's lecture on the Good, in any case, is known to have disappointed and mystified his audience.

Nor did this new definition of *psyche* offer Plato much help in his old problem of explaining waste, disappointment, and destruction—in human lives or in the world as a whole. You would think that Plato would have to choose one of these three possibilities: either (1) *psyche* was the cause of all motion and all motion was intelligent—directed, that is, toward the true good, or (2) *psyche* was the cause of all motion, some of which was directed toward true good, some not, or (3) *psyche* was the cause of motion toward true good only, and something else caused all other motion. The first possibility was ruled out by Plato's belief that not everything men do is the best thing which they could have done, the conviction that there is such a thing as blind stupidity, both in men's actions and in the world at large. The choice was between the other two possibilities, that *psyche* caused all action good and bad, or that *psyche* caused good action and something else caused the bad. Now, Plato's long-standing conviction that there were irrational as well as rational potencies in our psychic energy would favor the second hypothesis, that *psyche* could cause both good and bad actions. And, after all, this is the most consistent position if you are going to insist that, as the only self-generating motion, *psyche* is the cause of all movement everywhere. On the other hand, by raising the nature of *psyche* as the cause of motion to a universal principle, the problem of giving an exact description of the sources of evil becomes excruciating. If *psyche* is just the name for the ceaseless energy which is the ultimate source of all motion, good or bad, then it loses the honorific status which Plato, like Socrates, always assumed it had. It is not too surprising, therefore, to find Plato in the *Timaeus* trying the third possibility—that there were two sources of motion, *psyche* and another, even after he had defined *psyche* as the only eternal cause of motion anywhere.

Disorderly motion, Plato suggests, motion not directed invariably toward the good, is caused not by *psyche*, the seat of Intelligence, but by Necessity. He defines Necessity as motion which is not self-generated, like *psyche*, but induced from without.[33] He further characterizes this induced motion as invariably rectilinear—the six wandering motions, as he calls them, up, down, forward, backward, right, and left.[34] These have no essential tendency toward order. But the self-generating motion of *psyche* does, for it is circular. This is the *δίνη* of the Presocratics, the whirling motion of the heavens which keeps the earth in the center like the flotsam in a whirlpool.[35]

A new problem has been raised by this idea, however. If the disorderly motion which characterizes induced motion can be traced ultimately only to *psyche* and Intelligence, then how does the quality of disorderliness creep in at all? (Intelligence, remember, is defined as motion directed toward true good.) Space itself, in which things come to be on the perceptible level, is described as undifferentiated.[36] What differentiation there is, is due entirely to the perfect Forms. And the interaction between the particles thus variously differentiated is guaranteed by the intelligent *psyche* itself.[37] Yet the result is random motion, which the divine Creator is unable to reduce entirely to order. How can this be? Plato does offer an explanation, although at the cost of consistency. Before the addition of intelligent energy, he suggests, the world body was not inert, but displayed already a restless motion of its own. This motion is described as a jiggling motion, like that of a winnowing basket, presumably rectilinear motion only. It had no tendency toward order, except insofar as particles thus jiggled tend to get sorted out in layers by a mechanical principle of "like to like." On this the divine Craftsman had to superimpose a circular motion in order to insure the order which we observe in the universe.[38] (Although this circular motion was said to have been added to the world just *before* the *psyche* was housed in it, it is impossible not to assume that it is the *psyche* which by its natural tendency carries the universe around in this way.)[39] Without the *psyche*, Plato says,[40] the constant jiggling of that which underlies perceptible reality would separate the elements completely, in concentric shells—earth in the center, water next, and so on. But the result of this would be that the heterogeneity of the kind needed to perpetuate motion would cease to exist, and perceptible reality would therefore cease to move.

This description of the world, besides being bizarre, contains, as I say, a glaring inconsistency. If *psyche* is self-generating motion[41] and thus the first cause of all motion,[42] how can the world body be in some motion, however irregular, before the *psyche* is housed in it? And if *psyche* is needed to guarantee heterogeneity and thus rectilinear motion, how was it that the world body had not stopped long before creation? (Nor will a redefinition of time really help with this problem!) Some of Plato's followers later suggested that the narrative of the creation in the *Timaeus* was not intended to be taken literally, that it was an expository device, like a construction in a geometrical demonstration. (Aristotle, with some cogency, refused to accept this explanation. Some modern scholars have sided with Aristotle, others with the Academy.)[43] Notice, however, that the suggestion by the Academy does not really solve the most important problem. Even if the cosmogonic myth was not meant literally, we must still explain why Plato chose to describe the pre-cosmic world body as being in ceaseless motion before the cause of all motion was added to it. Why could he not say that all was still before the creation?[44]

Surely the answer to this question is fairly obvious. First of all, Plato, as we have seen, always assumed that there was inherent in the perceptible world a kind of flux which was the very essence of its inferiority. This must somehow be divorced from Intelligence, however true it is that that, too, is a motion. There must, then, be energy which does not owe its existence to Intelligence. How absurd to think that the world had the still permanence of the Forms themselves before Intelligence introduced confusion! Consider what this pre-cosmic state of affairs would amount to. Why would the world not be as perfect as it could be if it were a motionless reflection of true reality? Second, there is the related question of the bodily appetites within men, the irrational parts of the *psyche*. These, says Plato,[45] have motions of their own, different from the revolutions of the rational *psyche*. He also says that they are, unlike the rational soul, mortal.[46] Although he does not explain this further, by a process of elimination we must assume that the motions which are characteristic of the irrational parts of the *psyche*, like that of the world body, are rectilinear, not circular, (or their motions would be indistinguishable from rationality) and induced, not self-generating (or they would be eternal, not mortal). But the idea that irrational passions could really be only induced motions is even more grotesque than the suggestion that the world body might have been motionless until Intelligence introduced the flux. The irrational parts of our *psyches* are the origin of blind passions, emotions, fear, pleasure, and so on—sources, in other words, of restless energy. And so, like the source of wandering motions in the world as a whole, the mortal parts of the *psyche*, the bodily appetites, could not, when it came right down to it, be described as induced or secondary. Plato was stuck, therefore, with an inconsistency in the *Timaeus* which he made no real effort to hide: the rational *psyche* might be the source of all energy, but there was some energy which did not owe its existence to this *psyche*.

In the tenth book of the *Laws*, or so I would maintain, Plato corrects this inconsistency by the obvious, though rather desperate, expedient of declaring that there are two kinds of *psyche*. One is self-generating circular motion, like all of *psyche* but the "mortal parts" in the *Timaeus*, and the other is self-generating rectilinear motion, characterizing both the tendencies of bodily nature as such and the irrational parts of human and animal *psyches*. This astonishing idea is the extreme, but logical, development of Plato's later thought. It brought with it, however, among other things, a serious obfuscation of his theory of love. Let us see how it worked.

The problem, remember, is the origin of evil, the reason why things in the perceptible world inevitably fall short of the patterns which can be recognized in them.[47] Now, there are three basic ways by which evil could be accounted for. It could be maintained that it is to the benefit of the whole that one level of reality be imperfect, or that there is a Devil at work in the universe who plots against the tendency toward good, or that it is somehow in the nature of corporeality to be incapable of reaching perfection. The first of these is hinted at on one occasion by Plato,[48] but it is not his characteristic approach. The second, the assumption of a Devil, is entirely contrary to his way of thinking and is never entertained by him. (It is clear that Plato never wavered in his conviction that the universe was ruled by a divinity incapable of anything but good.[49] And, after all, if intelligence is defined as activity toward true well-being, it would be difficult to imagine what "evil intelligence" could mean.) Plato's characteristic answer is the third, that although the ruling intelligence is all good, it is not omnipotent[50] and can never entirely overmaster the materials with which it must work. Moreover, Plato habitually pictured this resistance to intelligence not as a static intractability but as a tendency to move in directions other than toward the true good. And, then, after coming to believe that *psyche* was self-generating motion, the idea was forced on him that somehow *psyche*, though surely not Intelligence, must be held to be ultimately responsible for this unfortunate flux. Plato's explanation of evil must therefore fulfill the following requirements: (1) it is the opposite of intelligence, (2) it is not itself a divine plot, (3) it is a result of the inability of the divine ruler to reduce his material entirely to order, (4) it takes the form, not of sluggish resistance, but of a tendency to move in a random and sometimes destructive manner, and (5) these motions, like all motion, have their origin in *psyche*.

The tenth book of the *Laws*, Plato's final and most detailed discussion of this problem, has as its main purpose the outline of the rational arguments which could be presented to a reasonable young atheist in order to prove to him that the gods do exist, that they rule the universe, and that they are truly excellent. The heart of this proof is the demonstration that Intelligence is the dominant power in the cosmos. First it is shown that *psyche* is prior to corporeal reality—that there had to be *psyche* first before visible events could have begun; and then it is shown that of the two kinds of *psyche*, that which is intelligent and that which is capable of causing harm, the first rather than the second is in control of the universe as a whole.

The Athenian, the leader of the discussion throughout the *Laws* (for Socrates does not appear in this grim dialogue), says that he would begin the conversion of the youthful atheist by pointing out that the universe about him was not standing still, but full of motion. He then launches, quite surprisingly, into a long and technical classification of motion into ten categories.[51] It is not really an exhaustive enumeration, nor yet the orderly division by genus and species which we might have expected from the author of the *Sophist* and the *Politicus*.[52] Rather it is a list of five different dichotomies on five different principles. First, all motions can be divided into two classes by determining whether the motion is in one place (*ἕδρα*) or in more than one.[53] Next, the motion of an object which suffers collision without changing its state (*ἕξις*) can be classified according to whether it results in the division of that object (when it collides with a single stationary object) or combines with other objects (when it gets between two, coming from different directions). Third, the combining process of the previous dichotomy can be looked upon as increase, and can be contrasted, not with the possible splitting of one of the colliding objects, but with divergent motion, resulting in decrease. Fourth, any change of state (*ἕξις*) involves destruction,[54] and thus can be set in opposition to coming into being.[55] And finally, a fifth dichotomy can be made according to whether a motion is self-generated or whether the motion of the object is induced from without.

What Plato has apparently done is to reproduce all of the approaches to classifying motion which he knows, both those which were already familiar to the Presocratics and some which probably appeared for the first time in his own later dialogues. All of these principles of division have appeared before in Plato's writings, and, with one exception,[56] all those which he has used in previous works appear again here. He presents the results as a straight list of ten kinds of motion, however, and arranges them in the order of their importance. Primary among the ten, as we might have expected from the *Phaedrus* and the *Timaeus*, is one of the motions resulting from the last dichotomy, namely self-generating motion—that which is the cause of all other motion because it is its nature to move itself. But self-caused motion, says the Athenian, is the very definition (*λόγος*) of life or *psyche*.[57] Without *psyche*, therefore, the visible world would have no source of motion. *Psyche* and Intelligence, therefore, cannot be products of bodily processes, for *psyche* is prior to and the source of all visible events.

The modern analysis of motion forbids us to distinguish between self-generating and induced motion except on a crude level. We cannot accept the suggestion that there could be no motion of any kind whatever if there were no life. There is not a whit less real motion in a helpless corpse, we say, than there is in a live person. Before Newton and Galileo, however, the world looked very different. A man can walk, but a stone must be thrown or otherwise moved from without, the Greeks observed. *We* know that the stone, when it leaves the hand of the live man, would hurtle on forever at the same speed and in the same direction if it were not for other influences. But Plato was worried as to why the stone did not stop dead the instant it lost contact with a live source of energy.[58] Looking around him, the Greek was amazed at the continual motion of fire, wind, and the sea. As often as not, he concluded that the very universe must be alive.

And yet, Plato testifies to the fact that there were those in his time who considered bodily phenomena almost as we do—as a ceaseless mechanical activity of corporeal stuff which needed no life or *psyche* to explain its motion. He identifies this idea as the very source (*πηγή*) of atheism, because it involves the belief that *psyche*, and thus art and intelligence, are accidental side effects of valueless processes.[59] The first thing he had to do, therefore, was to re-establish the common-sense assumption that if a thing is in motion, it either contains its own source of motion—which must mean that it is alive—has a *psyche*—or it was moved from without by something which *was* alive.

It soon becomes apparent, however, why a single dichotomy of motion will not do. If *psyche* is the ultimate cause of *all* activity, says the Athenian,[60] then it must be the cause (*αἰτία*) not only of all good, beautiful, and just achievements, but also—and he does not hedge—of all evil, shameful, and unjust things as well (*κακά, αἰσχρά*, and *ἄδικα*). This is an inescapable consequence, he says (*ὁμολογεῖν ἀναγκαῖον*). That *psyche* controls the world (*διοικεῖν*) has been established, therefore, but it is clear that this will not make any man a believer in the gods unless a further division of *psyche* can be made, between the kind which accomplishes good (*εὐεργέτις*) and the kind which is capable of bringing about the opposite (*τἀναντία δυναμένη ἐξεργάζεσθαι*). Then it must be demonstrated that the former, not the latter, rules the heavens.[61]

Plato's talk of evil *psyche* has caused a great deal of trouble to his readers.[62] But notice that he cannot mean either a diabolical counterpart to the world's *psyche*, or purely evil creatures inhabiting the world. He is talking about two different *kinds* of *psyche*;[63] and the kind called evil is not said to plot against good—it is merely capable (*δυναμένη*) of causing destruction. It does not necessarily work *for* good. We think inevitably of Necessity, the "wandering cause" (*πλανωμένη αἰτία*) in the *Timaeus*, and of the unpredictable but not invariably bad activities of the lower two parts of the human *psyche*.

The Athenian spells out the unflattering names which we give to some of the motions by which *psyche* drives (*ἄγειν*) all things in the heavens, on land, and in the sea. They include the making of false judgments (*δοξάζειν ἐψευσμένως*) as well as grieving, fearing, and hating motions (*λυπουμένη*, *φοβουμένη*, and *μισοῦσα κίνησις*). These are all primary motions (*πρωτουργοί*), he says, not induced. They take on (or receive, *παραλαμβάνειν*) the secondary motions of bodies (*δευτερουργοὶ κινήσεις σωμάτων*) and drive all things to increase and decrease, separation and combination (four of our original ten motions, by the way), and ultimately to heat, cold, heaviness, lightness, hard, soft, white, black, bitter, and sweet.[64] In manipulating (*χρῆσθαι*) these qualities, *psyche* manages things so that they are right and fortunate (*ὀρθὰ καὶ εὐδαίμονα παιδαγωγεῖν*) only if it also takes on intelligence (*νοῦν προσλαμβάνειν*). If it associates with unreason (*ἀνοίᾳ συγγίγνεσθαι*) it may produce the very opposite effect.

The fact is, says the Athenian, there are at least two kinds (*γένη*) of *psyche*, one wise and full of excellence (*φρόνιμον καὶ ἀρετῆς πλῆρες*), the other possessing neither of these qualities. Both, as *psyche*, must be self-generating motion, but there must be some way to distinguish between the self-caused energy which works only toward true good, and the self-caused energy which is undirected. Back to the list he goes, to find a suitable criterion for this all-important subdivision. There, he recalls, he had given special prominence to one principle for the dichotomy of motion and had elaborated it at some length.[65] The distinction was between things which move in one place (*ἕδρα*) and things which move in more than one. By motion in one place he means circular motion about a fixed center. The Athenian marvels at the fact that in such cases the same motion is imparted to all parts, but not with the same velocity. The center has no motion at all, and the velocity of the circle which is described at any given point is directly proportional to its distance from the center. Because of the perfect proportion (λόγος) and harmony (ὁμολογεῖν) discernible in the distribution of velocity, this kind of motion is the source of all wonders (τῶν θαυματῶν ἁπάντων πηγή). One might have expected this condition to be impossible (ἀδύνατον ἄν τις ἐλπίσειε γίγνεσθαι πάθος).

The next step is to point out that the kind of *psyche* that is dominant (ἐγκρατές) in the revolution of the heavens (περίοδος) is circular, not rectilinear.[66] Then it must be shown that this is the mark of *psyche* when it is acting intelligently, toward true good, not of the other kind of *psyche*. If bad *psyche* (κακή) ruled, the world would move in a frenetic and disorderly way (μανικῶς τε καὶ ἀτάκτως). But as a matter of fact, the Athenian points out, the circular motion of the heavens is the very essence of order.[67] It is a motion proper and similar to the turning (περίοδος) of reason. What do circular motion and rationality have in common? Both move steadily, consistently, with order and due proportion (κατὰ ταὐτά, ὡσαύτως, ἐν τῷ αὐτῷ, περὶ τὰ αὐτά, and ‹καθ'› ἕνα λόγον[68] and τάξιν μίαν). But the motion related to the absence of all intelligence (ἀνοίας ἁπάσης συγγενής) is rectilinear; that is, it does not move with a single reference point, with order, arrangement, or proportion.

If (a) all *psyche* is self-generating, as opposed to secondary, motion, and (b) there are two kinds of *psyche*, distinguished according to whether the tendency is circular or rectilinear, and (c) self-generating *circular* motion is identified as the good and intelligent kind of *psyche*, then *psyche* which is the source of frenetic and planless motion can only be self-generating rectilinear motion.[69] What can Plato have in mind? It would appear from his assignment of human emotions—fearing, grieving, and the like—to this inferior kind of *psyche*, that the irrational parts of the human *psyche* are at least primary manifestations, even if not necessarily the sole instances, of this kind of energy. Now, going back to the list of ten motions, we find motion in more than one place described as follows: "things which move by locomotion (φορᾷ), always changing their positions from one place to another; and this happens both when they have single points of support (literally, the support of one point—that is, when the same side of the object touches the ground or floor throughout the movement, as in sliding), and when they have more than one (point), by rolling around (*περικυλινδεῖσθαι*)."[70] There is, it would seem, a further subdivision of self-generating rectilinear motion into simple change of place, and change of place combined with some circular motion.[71] Was Plato perhaps attempting to find a way to distinguish between the irrational *psyche* which was nevertheless a natural ally of Intelligence, and that which was totally without intelligence—between the white horse and the black?

But the irrational emotions of human beings are hardly the only source of disorderly motion in the universe. The six "wandering motions" of the *Timaeus*, rectilinear energy, that is—the tendencies to go up, down, forward, backward, right, and left—were found also to be somehow innate in the world stuff. Now, when Plato comes to describe how the guiding divinity of the world handles the bad kind of *psyche*, he leaves a deliberate and provocative ambiguity as to whether he is talking about the source of irrational energy within human character, or that in the world at large.[72] In both cases the inferior parts are "housed" and "settled" in "locations" where the intelligent *psyche* can dominate so far as possible.[73] On the human level, this means that our irrational *psyches* are so "housed" within us that we have no excuse for failing to subordinate these to intelligence.[74] In the macrocosm it means that the divinity will, like a player of checkers, move individual *psyches* (compounded of both the intelligent and unintelligent kinds of energy) up and down, from the stars to the beasts, according to the excellence or foulness of each as an effective unit. In this way the heavenly intelligences, here called *daemons*, are able most of the time to win the battle against the unintelligent tendencies—the tendencies, that is, which cause natural catastrophes (as we call them), such as pestilence (*λοιμός*).[75] This battle against irrational tendencies within the cosmos is never ending and requires a wonderful watchfulness, says the Athenian,[76] "for we have agreed among ourselves that the universe (*οὐρανός*) is full of many good things and also of things of the opposite sort, but of more of the things which are not (good)."

Suppose that we, like the Greeks, took the apparent revolutions of the sky as real. If we then looked up one day and asked ourselves what would happen if all circular motion were taken away and only rectilinear motion left, would there not follow a vision of all things falling apart? There would be no orderly sequence by which one could tell time, no night and day, no seasons. The very generation of life as we know it would cease in this nightmare. Furthermore, when you stop a whirlpool the heavier flotsam no longer has a tendency toward the center, or the lighter for the periphery. If the *δίνη* were subtracted from the universe, therefore, surely the earth would not stay at the center, and we could not depend on air and fire to rise toward the periphery. All the things which we count on to keep our sanity and to plan for our happiness would vanish instantly in this rectilinear hell. If we then believed in a divine Intelligence in charge of the whole, would we not be severely tempted to see the primary manifestation of his goodness in the orderly return of the sun, the stars, the tides, the seasons—that which caused the very pull of the earth and the buoyancy of the air we breath?

That Plato believed the equation of intelligence and circular motion is beyond question. Aristotle, although he came to deny self-generating motion as the right description of *psyche*, never lost his enthusiasm for the extraordinary properties of circular motion.[77] Of all of Plato's later ideas,[78] this was one of the most influential in the succeeding centuries. Indeed, it was not until Newton and Galileo reinstated the primacy of rectilinear motion—after Kepler had discovered that the planets do not in fact move in a circle at all, let alone move about the earth—that modern physics could begin. What persuaded Plato of this extraordinary idea? Surprisingly enough, the Presocratic vision of the cosmic ordering powers of circular motion, although it is part of the effectiveness of Plato's cosmology, is not offered as a specific argument in favor of the theory. In the *Timaeus*, as we have seen, the world *psyche* is said to squeeze the world in order to guarantee a continual heterogeneity, but the tendency to separate into layers, the tendency which guarantees that rocks will fall toward the center and flames will shoot toward the periphery, that is pictured as present even before circular motion was added! The true beauty of circularity is said to be its appropriateness to divinity, a moving image of eternity.[79] It is also, perhaps, a compromise between motion and rest, and thus a mean between the motionless Forms and the flux of the sensed world.[80] Also, Plato may have had the Greek geometer's respect for the purity of the circle. For Greek mathematicians attempted habitually to limit their mechanical tools to the compass and the straightedge, as though rectilinear and circular lines were the chief and natural species of all things in two dimensions.[81] But surely, most important of all, was the prior decision to equate *psyche* as a whole with self-generating motion. This brought with it the necessity to find yet another subdivision of this motion, or risk making Intelligence responsible for the flux of the perceptible world and for the unreasonable passions within men's souls. From there it was a bold, but not entirely incomprehensible, step to the equation of circularity with Intelligence. This is ludicrous, to be sure, when Plato presses it to the point where even the minds of men (housed in craniums which reproduce in miniature the shape of the heavens!) are pictured as literally moving in circles like those in the sky;[82] but when we look up and consider the apparent role of circular motion in the universe as a whole, the idea is not entirely unworthy of Plato's imagination.

In this way, then, did the identification of *psyche* as self-caused motion lead Plato to a fantastically physical description of the rôle of intelligence and good in the dynamics of events. But such a description necessarily put an end to the hope that the world could be explained with any clarity as the product of love. You might believe that there was that within men and within the universe itself which strove for good, and that this was what you must always look for when you tried to make sense of nature and life; but then you had better not identify this striving for excellence with any particular direction or figure! Plato still insisted that the eternal patterns were good, and that it was their goodness which motivated the creator in all that he did; then, however, instead of showing *how* all things in the world were caused to strive for their perfection, Plato spoke of the universe as being caused by the divine intelligence to spin on its axis!

This last development of Plato's philosophy has its own brilliance and fantastic boldness, to be sure, but, dependent as it is on a queer physics, as well as on a private faith in guarding deities and in our personal survival after death, it fails to kindle the modern reader in the way in which the earlier vision still can. The fate of Plato's later system was much the same in antiquity, also. Aristotle, as we shall see, introduced changes which did away with most of Plato's later innovations and in effect re-established the idea of the *Phaedo*. What Aristotle did was to abandon the notion of self-motion in favor of a system based once more on desire for good. Even a failure, he thought, could be explained as the result of *something* pursuing its good. Nothing is really irrational anywhere; we need assume no source of planless energy. It is, then, this system which Aristotle constructed from Plato's theory of love which dominated in the history of philosophy right up until modern times. It became, indeed, a kind of orthodox world-view. Even some of those who called themselves Platonists were likely to find themselves describing systems closer to Aristotle's than to the *Timaeus* and *Laws*.

Aristotle's all-important decision was to abandon Plato's last innovation, the idea that *psyche* was motion itself—whether one meant the *psyche* which was the source of human energy only, or the *psyche* which was the seat of the intelligence which turned the world and guaranteed all orderly process. Forms—and *psyche*, Aristotle suggested, is merely the name which we give to the Forms informing live organic beings—are by nature "divine, good, and desirable," and the substratum of the world is animated only by desire for these. A man's *psyche*, therefore, might be the ultimate source of the motion which originated from within him, but the *psyche* moves not because it is itself in motion but because it is the pattern of full realization which the whole man, or the real man within the man, strives inevitably to achieve. As for the divine Intelligence, it, too, is pure, motionless Form, causing motion in precisely the same way: as the perfection desired by the universe as a whole.

We have little direct evidence that Plato actually ceased to believe in the description he gave of love in the *Symposium* and the *Phaedrus*. Indeed, the *Phaedrus* may well have been written fairly late in Plato's life. (It was, in any case, obviously written after the identification was made between *psyche* and self-moving motion, although, perhaps, not after the identification of intelligent *psyche* with circular motion.) But the direct development, from the theory of good and intelligence in Plato's middle dialogues to Aristotle's monistic, teleological explanation for the universe, does skip over the more physical visions of Plato's later works. If we must regret these later suggestions by Plato, however—and they were dead ends, and are indeed among the most bizarre notions in the history of philosophy—we may at least respect the profundity of the speculation which led him to these daring theories: his speculation on the nature of *psyche*, and above all his desire to come to grips with the reality of evil.

# CHAPTER 8

*The Theory of Love Modified by Aristotle. His Theory of Friendship. Love Made into a Cosmic Principle by Replacing the Self-moving* psyche *with a Theory of Universal Final Causation.*

TO BE A DICTATOR, Plato argues,[1] is the greatest of all nightmares, because dictators can have no real friends at all. The same is true, he felt, wherever one finds stupidity, vice, or selfish greed. Friendship, that which brings into being all order, unity and splendor—in society as in the cosmos as a whole[2]—is possible only between the good. The bad man, or the unjust man, as Plato habitually calls him,[3] is unjust because, within him, that which desires the well-being of the whole is not in command, and his *psyche* is therefore at war, one part with another. The man's character will show itself in desires for things which are not really desirable for his whole being. Under such circumstances, true friendship will be ruled out. A man attracted to something which is by definition opposed to his true well-being can only desire the kind of seeming power and self-gratification which confuses and destroys his intercourse with the world around him, not what binds and builds and creates ever higher co-operation.

The just man, unlike the unjust, loves himself. This was a Greek commonplace,[4] but it followed, Plato thought, from the peace and harmony within the just man's *psyche*, and from the fact that when a man is attracted to excellence in men and actions everywhere he is really only being drawn by an anxiety for the most valuable part of himself. There can never be a real conflict between a man's concern for himself and his concern for what is valuable in the world around him. This, Plato thought, was the secret of the powerful bond which unites all good men. If society could only be dominated by a group of true friends of this sort, Plato believed, there was no end to the order and happiness which could be brought into our lives.

This side of Platonic love suffered neither eclipse nor complication in the later developments of Plato's philosophy, nor even in the sweeping revisions made in his philosophy by some of his students in the next generation. Plato's letters show that the activities of the Academy were deeply suffused with this trust in the power of friendship. And, indeed, Plato's own circle of friends did bring enlightened order to many communities throughout the world. For a while Athens exported constitutions and political advice the way we export cars. There were failures, of course. The unhappy story of Plato's loyalty to Dion and the failure of his attempt to make the dictator of Syracuse, Dionysius II, worthy of the friends of the Academy, is well known. But the very epistle in which Plato tells the story of this catastrophe also gives the most vivid picture we have of the vigor and effectiveness of the conscious, intellectual friendships which Plato brought into being among the most intelligent of the younger men around him.[5] Dionysius, too dim and undisciplined to qualify for this select companionship, nevertheless perceived enough to be thrown into agonies of jealousy by his failure. His inability to win the good opinion and exclusive love of Plato himself roused despair and fury in him.

After Plato's death, many of his circle wrote treatises "On Friendship"—not only Aristotle, but also Philip of Opus, Speusippus, and Xenocrates. And friendship as a reality is one of the most notable and one of the finest things about the Platonic circle. Aristotle, although he spent his life revising Plato's philosophy from top to bottom, never shows the slightest disloyalty to the friendship which bound him to his master.[6] We even have a fragment of some elegiac verses by Aristotle which are said to be addressed to one Eudemus but offered in praise of Plato.[7] In these verses Aristotle speaks of someone (perhaps Eudemus, perhaps Aristotle himself, perhaps some other friend of Plato's)[8] coming to Attica and piously setting up an altar to holy Friendship (*σεμνὴ φιλία*), the friendship "of the man whom it is not pious for bad men even to praise: who alone or first among mortals revealed clearly, both in his own life and in the investigations of his discourses, that a man becomes good and happy at one and the same time (*ὡς ἀγαθός τε καὶ εὐδαίμων ἅμα γίγνεται ἀνήρ*)," "But now nobody can attain this ever again," he adds (*οὐ νῦν δ' ἔστι λαβεῖν οὐδενὶ ταῦτά ποτε*). The tangle of genitives (an altar *of* holy Friendship *of* Plato) is significant.[9] It means, presumably, an altar dedicated either to the ideal of friendship discovered and clarified by Plato, or to the friendships which Plato brought into being in the Academy—probably both. Also interesting is the formulation of Plato's message as the discovery of the identity between excellence and happiness.[10] And the last line is startling, because it suggests that a contrast could be vividly felt between the inspired goodness of Plato himself and the more humdrum world after the master's death.

Aristotle's own analysis of friendship, although it bears the unmistakable mark of his methodical mind, is an entirely orthodox Platonic analysis. In the *Eudemian Ethics* he puts the problem in terms of the puzzle which Plato discussed in the *Lysis*: is friendship the attraction of likes or of unlikes?[11] He solves the difficulty by dividing friendship into three kinds: that based on usefulness, which alone is the attraction of unlike, that based on pleasure, which is the desire for apparent good, and that based on excellence, which is desire for the real good. This is the most truly reciprocal and rewarding friendship. Only in this last kind, says Aristotle, does our pleasure in and good will toward another human being really amount to the same thing as our pursuit of happiness, the desire, as Plato would say, for *τὸ τῷ ὄντι φίλον*. These are not three species of one genus, friendship, however, because only the last is friendship in the primary sense, *πρώτη φιλία*, he says. This and this alone is the friendship between good men which it is the special business of the political art to produce.[12] Men experiencing the other two kinds of friendship have failed of this ideal in one way or another.

In the *Nicomachean Ethics* the same idea is elaborated at greater length, although the similarity to the language of the *Lysis* is a little more remote.[13] As in the earlier version also, the best kind of friendship, that on which all good political planning depends, is carefully explained on the personal level as a kind of self-love.[14] Here is how Aristotle describes that. All men want to live and to know that they live, he says. Life for a man *means* thinking and feeling; but above all self-awareness—contemplation, that is, of his own reality—is the real essence of a man's pursuit of happiness. Now to a good man this self-awareness is completely satisfying. (In other words, he "becomes good and happy at one and the same time.") Unlike God, however, no man, however good, is self-sufficient in this respect.[15] Man needs, therefore, to see his excellence reflected in another to experience the goodness in joint actions.[16] Thus it is that the pleasure which good men take in each other's company is identical with the pleasure which they take in life itself. To the bad man, on the other hand, what seems good is not really good, so he is neither attracted to excellence around him nor finds any within of the sort that can bring him real peace and self-respect.

I have said that this is an orthodox Platonic analysis of Friendship, but, of course, something vital is missing from Aristotle's description which we were accustomed to find in Plato's most brilliant dialogues. Plato liked to enlist in the aid of philosophy the great dangerous fires of the usually irrational emotions, especially sexuality. He always insisted, of course, that these sources of energy be transformed so that there was not a trace of bestiality left, but to kill them altogether would have once seemed as impossible to him as to ask a charioteer to kill his horses and walk the rest of his life. In Plato's last years, however, the paler word for friendship, *φιλία*, seems once more to have replaced *ἔρως*, his word for friendship in the *Symposium* and the *Phaedrus*. This shift back to the term of the *Lysis* was introduced, presumably, to play down the sexual element as much as possible. Indeed, in one noteworthy passage at the beginning of the *Laws*,[17] Plato draws a, for him unprecedented, distinction between heterosexual pleasure, which he calls natural, and homosexual pleasure, which he calls contrary to nature. Drinking parties among young men, students and their teachers, continued to be central in the ideals of education, as the first two books of the *Laws* testify.[18] But now there were elaborate rules to keep affections and good spirits under iron control. These parties must have been excellent in their way, for many of Plato's circle wrote their own treatises on the conduct of symposia;[19] but it is hard to believe that the party described in Plato's *Symposium* could have taken place at all under this new regime.

Aristotle, in Plato's later manner, used the word *φιλία* for true friendship and seemed to reserve *ἔρως* for excess in the direction of pleasure.[20] Apparently he also, like the rest of his contemporaries, wrote a treatise on the conduct of drinking parties.[21] In addition, as we have seen, he did most certainly believe in special and close friendships as well as in a community of friends. (Indeed, he complained that the form of communism described in the *Republic* would result in a "watered-down friendship" [*ὑδαρῆς φιλία*][22] and would unduly weaken the bonds of loyalty and love on which any successful society must depend.) But in Aristotle, as in the later Plato, there was never a question any more of harnessing the wild energies of Eros or Dionysus. Something was gone. The ideal of friendship that remained was fine and productive, but after it was no longer considered profitable to play with the irrational fires, a certain brilliance was inevitably lost.

As I suggested in the last lecture, the wider theory of *ἔρως* seemed to get lost in the bewildering complexities of Plato's later physical theories, and this, perhaps, is enough to explain why Plato lost some of his enthusiasm for *ἔρως* in human relations. But there were probably many things involved in this development, including the aging of Plato himself and the collapse of Spartan leadership. (For the ideal of male love seems to have been popularly associated with Sparta.) And the clarification of Plato's dualistic theory of motion would, in any case, have tended to throw doubt on the wisdom of trying to harness irrational energy. This dualism, as we have seen, grew much more distinct in Plato's later years, when he elaborated theories of a second source of energy in addition to Intelligence. Only a monist, after all, could have much confidence in the transformation of all of the ordinarily destructive drives in the darker parts of the *psyche*. A dualist would be more likely to condemn the passions outright.

Aristotle, on the other hand, was a monist; he did not believe in a second source of motion, a naturally irrational energy. Yet he, too, no doubt, had his own reasons for welcoming the deflection of emphasis away from the erotic. His own temper and that of his whole generation were against the idealization of male love. Compared to most of us today, indeed, he cherished the friendship of good men to an extraordinary degree.[23] But there was no question of tapping dark passions in order to climb to visionary heights. According to his philosophy a dark passion was by definition one of a pair of tendencies which one is obliged to steer between. And then, too, Aristotle was just a more ordinary man than Plato. As he says himself in his poem to Eudemus, Plato, both in his person and in his inspired words, was able to convince men that a dazzling goodness was possible and was the most worthwhile thing one could achieve, but after Plato was gone, all this seemed quite impossible ever again.

But what about the cosmic and impersonal side of the Platonic theory of love? This aspect of the theory, as we have seen, grew ever more obscure as Plato's dualist theory of cosmic motion and his concept of *psyche* as self-moving motion were clarified. But strangely enough, this side of Plato's idea suffered the reverse of an eclipse in Aristotle's hands. By rejecting both the dualism and the self-moving *psyche* and re-establishing the supremacy of final causation, Aristotle actually gave back to Love once more the rôle it had in the *Symposium*, the *Phaedo*, and the *Republic*.

To be sure, Aristotle does not usually call his teleological theory of causation a theory of Love, but that should not really surprise us. For one thing, the connection with human sexual desire, as I said, had been more or less discredited. For another, if every action in the world, from the falling of a stone to the fury of a madman, is attributed to the same cause, to call this ἔρως is simply not very illuminating. Also, Aristotle concentrated on Form as the good being striven for, not the striving as such. At one supremely important moment, however, when Aristotle describes the action of the First Mover in moving the universe as a whole, he does use the word ἔρως, and he shows then that he is quite conscious of the continuity between his explanation and that of his great predecessor. Let us look closely at this passage.[24]

To guarantee an eternal circular motion to the universe as a whole there must be a mover, Aristotle argues, which is itself immovable and without body or dimensions. But how could such a thing cause motion? That is the problem. Here is how it works, says Aristotle. The objects of desire and thought move us without themselves being in motion at all. The ultimate mover of both desire and natural will is the real good or the really beautiful (τὸ ὂν καλόν). (When a man is pursuing what he thinks he wants, as opposed to what is really desirable, his moves are caused by a false appearance of good only. Still, he must *believe* that it is the real good.) Notice, Aristotle says, that one assumes something to be desirable *before* the desire comes into being, not the other way around. The starting point of desire, then, is an intellectual understanding (ἀρχὴ γὰρ ἡ νόησις). But intellectual understanding is itself set in motion by the intelligible (νοῦς δὲ ὑπὸ τοῦ νοητοῦ κινεῖται). The object of desire, then, is the ultimate source of directed motion.

That which is intelligible, Aristotle goes on to say, belongs to one column in the list of opposites. What he is referring to is his custom of drawing up two columns of terms, two parallel lists in which positive things, like reality, unity, and so on, in one column are paired off against their negations, non-reality, plurality, and so on, in the other.[25] Now, only the things listed in the positive column, he argues, are objects of knowledge; their negations are known only by reference to these. But which of the things in this list is the *primary* object of thought? Of all the things in this positive column, Aristotle suggests, Reality (οὐσία) comes first, and of realities, that comes first which is simple and exists in actuality (ἡ ἁπλῆ καὶ κατ' ἐνέργειαν).[26] Now comes the surprise: the primary member in any class, Aristotle points out, must always be either the highest good itself (τὸ ἄριστον) or analogous to the highest good. In this case, however, the class of intelligibles, the primary member must *be* the highest good, because the Beautiful and that which is in itself desirable (τὸ καλὸν καὶ τὸ δι' αὑτὸ αἱρετόν) is one of the objects of intelligence and so a member of this very class. The primary object of thought therefore (Reality) and the primary object of desire (Beauty) must be identical—exactly as Plato had decided also! Simple, actual Reality, then, *is* the highest good, and, as the primary object of all directed motion, it has to be this which is the first cause of the motion of the universe.

Since this prime mover is among things which have no motion or change, Aristotle says, it cannot be that for the benefit of which (τινί) what is done is done; but there is another sense of "that for the sake of which," namely "that at which other things aim."[27] This is the sense in which the highest good is the final cause of universal motion while it itself remains unmoved. It causes motion, Aristotle says, by being the object of love (*κινεῖ δὴ ὡς ἐρώμενον*); all other things cause motion by the heavens thus carried round.[28]

Aristotle's insistence that there must be an eternal cause of motion, also his identification of the circular motion of the universe as the divine source of all other motion, are obviously both taken over directly from Plato's later theory.[29] Aristotle does not depart from Plato's description until Plato asserts that this circular motion is self-caused. This idea, Aristotle points out,[30] is full of difficulties, at least as it is worked out in the *Timaeus*. Aristotle's most important point, however, is that to guarantee absolutely eternal motion of the most uniform sort, you must have a cause which is itself incapable of change. It must, therefore, be not only without matter,[31] but also without motion,[32] separate from sensed things,[33] without magnitude,[34] without parts,[35] and incapable of being acted upon or altered.[36] The circular motion itself, then, must have a cause which is without place or motion, bringing the *δίνη* into being by *ἔρως* and nothing else.

Such a supreme object of love was recognized, Aristotle felt, by all men: it is divinity, *ὁ θεός*.[37] But to a fourth-century Greek, God was unthinkable except as eternal life, full of knowledge and completely happy, beyond all touch of change. And so it is with Aristotle's God also. He is not only Reality, Actuality, and Beauty but also Life (*ζωή*)[38]—life for ever and ever, Aristotle says, such as we mortals taste only in those fleeting moments when we are utterly happy. Now happiness, as we have seen, meant to Aristotle self-conscious knowledge, the knowledge that one exists and that existence is good. But we in our mortal state, he also pointed out, can sustain this awareness only in our attraction to excellence in another man. God, however, needs no companion, he says; his is the best and happiest knowledge, knowledge of the best,[39] knowledge of knowledge, *νόησις νοήσεως*,[40] and this turns out to be knowledge of himself.[41]

Life and intelligence, Plato believed, could reside only in *psyche*. Aristotle agreed. But *psyche*, Plato believed, was self-generating motion. Here Aristotle refused to go along.[42] *Psyche* is the cause of motion all right, but that which introduces motion does not itself need to be in motion, he argued. It can be the perfection being striven for. (Indeed, this is more obvious in the case of conscious, intelligent energy than elsewhere.) If we were to assume, he suggests, that a *psyche* is nothing more nor less than the main unifying Form of a living being, that which gives it its identity, then we could still account for all internally originating motions without requiring that there be any self-moving motion. Just as with all other phenomena, all we would have to do is to identify and describe the Form, the pattern of perfection which the matter is yearning to realize.

The action of the *psyche* within each living creature, Plato argued, and the action of the cause of universal motion within the universe itself must be identical. Again Aristotle agreed. But notice the superior elegance of Aristotle's system just here. The patterns of perfection in different kinds of things are different; the motions introduced, therefore, are different.[43] And so, if the First Mover affects the universe by introducing an eternal circular motion to it, that does *not* mean that our own *psyches* also reproduce this same motion in our heads!

Here we can get a fascinating glimpse of the development of Aristotle's ideas.[44] We can detect roughly three stages. First, in an early dialogue called *On Philosophy*,[45] Aristotle argued that the divine circular motions of the heavenly bodies, since they cannot be accounted for by natural tendencies of matter nor yet by violent interference, must be caused by intelligent will. He was more or less in agreement, in other words, with Plato's *Laws*, which assigned an intelligent *psyche* to move each heavenly body. By the time Aristotle came to write *De caelo*, however, he had abandoned the threefold division of motion into the natural, the interfering, and the willed, and had reduced the classifications to two only, the natural and the interfering.[46] The stars, he now suggested, are embedded in a fifth element, the *aether*, the natural tendency of which is to move in a circular fashion. No *psyche*, therefore, is required to account for the revolution of the heavens.[47] Or rather, no *psyche* is needed *in addition* to the natural motion of this sphere.[48] For, while the four elements which have merely rectilinear tendencies are not divine,[49] the fifth element is called divine, intelligent and immeasurably superior to the other four.[50] Aristotle had thus dropped Plato's suggestion of individual star souls,[51] but he had substituted for it merely a more elegant version of Plato's world-*psyche*.[52] But then, when he came to write *Metaphysics Λ*, he took a far more important step: he dropped the idea of a self-caused motion altogether, and substituted another version of *psyche*, a perfect Reality which causes motion as the object of desire.[53] This, of course, is a direct development of yet another, earlier idea of Plato's, the Form of the Good; but it is a development, not a mere borrowing, because it implies a revolutionary discovery about the nature of all *psyche*. Every *psyche*, human and animal as well as the divine, according to this new theory, is but a special kind of Form, and like all Form, it causes motion without itself having to be in motion at all.

The Platonists, Aristotle complained,[54] could not explain how Forms introduced motion inasmuch as they insisted that Forms were separate from the phenomena to which they were a key. If, however, you make the Forms imminent[55] then they *can* be the cause of local motion.[56] There are, as we have seen, only two factors in the universe as Aristotle understood it, Form and substratum, and of these only the first caused motion. All that we know of substratum is that it desires to realize the Forms.[57] But the Forms of individual things, Aristotle suggested, are right there, informing the substratum, nowhere else. The Form of the full-grown oak tree must already be there in the acorn, pulling it to its realization. Find the formula for a perfect specimen of a species and you have not only knowledge of what it is to be that sort of thing, but also the most important clue to the motions to be observed or expected in any example of the species.

It is true, of course, that the Form which is identical in all members of a species is never actually realized to perfection in any individual member, but this does not mean that the substratum has introduced a second motion of its own to cause this failure, as Plato thought.[58] The discrepancy between the Forms striven for and those realized can be accounted for by the fact that there is a contrariety between mutually exclusive Forms affecting the same substratum. This contrariety results from the fact that, although there is a hierarchy (*τάξις*)[59] in the order of different kinds of Form, it cannot be maintained in unmoving simplicity. The truth is that almost all Forms exist only embedded in substratum. The piece of matter struggling to realize such a Form, therefore, is subject also to an immensely complicated web of other influences. Indeed, Forms survive at all, not as Plato thought, because they are immune to flux in eternal stillness outside of time and place, but only insofar as they can achieve a sequential survival from parent to offspring (τῷ ἐφεξῆς).[60] A parent tree or human being stamps its Form on a piece of substratum and separates that off from itself. This new Form will then start motions aimed directly at realizing a full-grown member of the species. The Forms are permanent solely because, although individuals may disappear without leaving young, the species as a whole will never alter or die out. There is no other way in which these Forms are unchanging. No wonder, then, that we never actually see a Form fully realized except as our minds discern where things are tending.

But in order for even this less august kind of immortality to be guaranteed, we must have, first, an eternal mover which will insure perpetual motion—the revolution of the outer stars—and then at least one other circular motion, namely that of the oblique path described by the passage of the sun through the signs of the zodiac, that which introduces the rhythmical seasons and thus brings about the processes of birth and death.[61] At the periphery of the universe, as you get closer and closer to the outer sphere with its one simple motion, there are few imperfections. The magnificent precision of heavenly phenomena proves that, Aristotle thought. On the other hand, as you get closer to the center and farther from the First Mover, more and more confusion is introduced, he admitted.[62] This does not matter, however. As in a government or a household, Aristotle says,[63] he who is really in charge can be allowed no leisure or irrationality, but the lowliest of the servants can waste many hours in inactivity or foolish pastimes without damaging the order of the whole.

Picture the universe, then, as pulled this way and that by Forms of every kind.[64] Most of these are *psyches* of one sort or another.[65] (For the very earth contains an admixture of water with *pneuma*, and *pneuma* contains *psyche*-heat, θερμότης ψυχική), the essential ingredient of semen, analogous to the element of the stars.)[66] But there are also Forms of elementary stuff, fire, air, earth, and water, which affect the substratum, not in the way in which we identify a living organism, but, like the First Mover, in simple local motion.[67] We identify earth as that which desires to be at the center of the universe, fire as that which longs to be at the periphery, and so on. And then, between the simple bodies and the *psyches* which give life to whole organisms, there is a hierarchy of intermediate Forms: tissues, organs, and the limbs of plants and animals.[68] (After all, these sometimes display some powers of motion even after they have been severed from the main body.)[69] Thus, although Aristotle sometimes refers to a man's matter as though it were fire and earth,[70] for instance, or flesh and bones,[71] or sometimes as the head and other members,[72] these are all really only other Forms, informing the substratum at more or less elementary levels.[73] In fact, ultimate undifferentiated (that is, unformed) matter does not exist as such.[74] Every bit of the universe is informed by at least one Form, and the vast majority of stuff is pulled by more than one Form at the same time. That is why the result is sometimes delicate and productive co-operation, but just as often privation and destruction. In no case, however, is there a cause other than some Form or Forms.

The Forms in each case are called the actual realities, and all processes are toward them. It is the completely realized oak, nothing less, which is the cause of all the internal motions of the acorn and of the half-grown tree. There must, Aristotle argues, be a Reality prior to every motion, and, indeed, Reality preceding Reality all the way back to the pure Reality which is the ultimate cause of all processes in the universe.[75] That is *not* to say that prior to a particular father there must be Man, and prior to Man there must be Animal, and so on. Aristotle specifically denies that. What he means is that an individual parent must have reality prior to the coming into being of a new individual, and in addition, to make the generation possible, there must be the reality of the sun in its oblique course, and prior to that, the mover of the whole.[76] This is perhaps the most important of the several kinds of hierarchy which Aristotle sees in the universe.

Plants and animals, their tissues, organs, the simple elements, and the movers of the heavenly bodies: does this exhaust the kinds of Forms which initiate motion throughout the universe? Hardly. There are also tools, furniture, speeches, constitutions, poems and plays—the patterns of perfection, in other words, which, although they do not draw matter itself, draw men to shape matter.[77] (Indeed, in queer cases, like a physician healing himself, the process is almost indistinguishable from natural processes.) In expounding his theory of Form and Matter, Aristotle gives an artefact as an example as often or more often than natural objects.[78] Health, for instance, that which inspires a doctor in his typical activity, is often spoken of as a formal-final cause.[79] True, Forms which inspire human activities are the most obvious examples of things which cannot exist separately, in the way in which certain natural Forms can (namely the movers of the universe and the active intellect).[80] Nevertheless men do not invent the Forms House, Health, or Tragedy; these Forms are as ungenerated and indestructible as the species of plants and animals.[81] If a man turns to house building, that must mean that his mind has been informed by the Form "what is to be a house."[82] But how did the Form come to inform his *psyche*, if the man did not invent it?[83] Presumably because he saw another house and understood both the principle and the function. And the first person ever to build a house? Presumably he recognized the Form already implied in nature, for art but imitates and perfects nature, Aristotle thought.[84] This, by the way, explains why, in the *Poetics*, Aristotle is at pains to show that Tragedy is but a more perfect realization of the same Form which inspired earlier writers to compose epics, and that this, in turn, was but a superior realization of an activity, namely imitation, which is absolutely universal and had no beginning. Tragedies may only have been written for some three generations before Aristotle's time, but no Form can have a beginning in time, or it could not be a true universal and thus an object of true knowledge. It must always have been there, passed on from particular to particular somehow.

Plato thought that unless the Forms had a separate existence, quite independent of the particulars where they could be recognized, then they could not be permanent and exact—they would be no better than sensed things in their reality or knowability. On the other hand, he also assumed that the Forms were somehow among the causes of individual events.[85] The problems involved in reconciling these two requirements plagued him throughout his life. In fact he never did give a very satisfactory description of the way in which particulars "participated in" Forms. In the *Timaeus*, probably his latest attempt, he suggested that the sensed world is somehow a reflection of the other; but when he came to give an account of the Forms as causes of events, he had to introduce a Divine Craftsman who saw the Forms, understood their excellence, and was inspired by this to interfere with the sensible world.

Aristotle, on the other hand, by making the Forms immanent, did solve once and for all the problem of participation and causation. But he aggravated thereby the other problem, the requirements of permanence, precision, and perfection in the Forms as the objects of knowledge. Most of the remaining modifications which Aristotle introduced into the theory of Forms can be traced to this difficulty.[86] He accomplished his purpose (1) by separating the problem of universals and the understanding of Form, (2) by restricting the Forms *of* things (as opposed to the Forms *in* things) to the category of Reality (*οὐσία*), (3) by developing a new theory of knowledge to get around the metaphysical implications of Plato's theory of learning as Recollection, (4) by eliminating chance or uncaused events, indeed any cause other than Forms as goods striven for, and (5) by arguing, probably for the first time in all Greek thought, that the world as we know it has always been essentially just as it is. Let us take these one at a time.

First, the separation of the problem of universals and the understanding of Form. Aristotle frequently attacks Plato's understanding of Form and the arguments by which Plato supported his belief.[87] One of his most important complaints is that Plato's arguments prove only the existence of universals, things common to several particulars (*τὰ κοινά*).[88] Now, that universals exist somehow he does not wish to deny. The universal is to be prized (*τίμιον*), he says,[89] because it makes clear the causes of events. Even if we could stand on the moon and clearly see the earth blocking the light from the sun, he points out, we still would not be able to explain the eclipse if we could not connect what we perceived with other experiences —if, that is, we had no knowledge of universals. But it simply does not follow from this, he believes, that the Form of a thing, that which gives a thing its essential identity, has an existence somehow quite separate from the phenomena where it is recognized.

The most difficult of all problems and the one most necessary to investigate in First Philosophy, he says elsewhere, is this: "If there exists nothing besides (or separated from, *παρά*) individual things, how is it possible to acquire knowledge of an infinite number of things? For we know all that we know by virtue of something that they have in common, the presence of some universal."[90] If nothing existed besides individual things, nothing would be intelligible, nothing lasting. (And indeed there could not even be coming-into-being, since that implies a persistent substratum and something definite as the terminus of the process.) Socrates and Plato were right, he says in yet another place, insofar as they refused to identify reality with the infinite variety of sensible individuals.[91] Knowledge is of universals (*ἡ δ' ἐπιστήμη τῶν καθόλου*).[92] This is a cardinal principle with Aristotle. Even in the study of things like rhetoric, medicine, or politics, we acquire knowledge by seeing what things have in common, not by observing particular cases in isolated uniqueness.[93] Plato's mistake, however, was in assuming that the proof of the reality of universals was also the proof of the separate existence of Forms. This Aristotle flatly denies.[94]

The next step is to discover a criterion for distinguishing those universals which really are the Forms of things from those which are not. That is, if the Forms of things (1) as the causes of phenomena, must exist, not separate from matter, but only in the individual occurrences, and yet (2) as universals and the objects of knowledge, must be, not changing and unique like the individual occurrences, but permanent and ever the same, then those of *Plato's* Forms which (1) caused no events, or (2) appeared and disappeared erratically, simply have to be eliminated. These included some of Plato's most characteristic Forms—qualities, for instance, and relations, and sizes.[95] What Aristotle does then, is to develop a theory of Categories, an analysis of the different kinds of assertions which we can make. The chief result of this analysis is to uncover the uniqueness of Reality (*οὐσία*) as the only truly important assertion.[96] Only those universals which are the descriptions of *what things are*, he suggests, never those which describe qualities, quantities, relations, and the like, are the Forms of things. It is then only these Forms (or species) which must be shown to be simultaneously eternal and unchanging, and yet existing only in sequential material realizations. We can afford to remain uncertain about the mode of the existence of the other kinds of universals, perhaps, because they are neither the causes of phenomena nor the answers to the question of what things are. Not so with the Forms, however. As the Reality of things and that which causes all events, the manner of their existence is of greatest importance.

"That which is sought for now, in the past and always, and is ever raised as a difficulty," says Aristotle,[97] "namely 'what is the real?' is the same as 'what is Reality?' " Now what *is* the reality of something? Certainly it is never a quantity, quality, relation, position, or anything of that sort. Aristotle recognized only three claimants: the Forms by which we identify a thing, the substratum which makes it unique, and the compounds of the two—units of informed substratum.[98] The claim of the persistent substratum, however, is weak, because, being in itself undifferentiated, it can never be a very clear answer to the question, what really is the true nature of some thing.[99] But of the other two, each had a strong claim to the title Reality, Aristotle felt. Since the separate existence of the Forms is denied, it is obvious that the individual man or horse is the most real thing in the world.[100] Nevertheless, if it were not for the fact that Forms are *not unique*, that a given Form is logically indiscriminable from a number of other Forms which inform other pieces of substratum,[101] they would not be universals and we could therefore not be acquiring knowledge of things when we apprehended their Forms. If we investigate any object in our experience, no matter how certainly unique it is in many ways, the content of our intellectual grasp of it, Aristotle points out, will be essentially equivalent with its Form as a universal.[102] The Forms as mentally abstracted from their matter, then, may also be called the ultimate Realities.[103]

This turns out to be a very elegant suggestion. The problem raised by the discovery that knowledge is of universals is solved by Aristotle without Plato's desperate assumption that Forms have an existence separate from their occurrence in particulars. Forms *of* things, the species of plants and animals, the elements, and the ideal types of men's creations, do not appear and disappear in the alarming way in which qualities and quantities do. Before you have a man or a horse you must have a parent man or horse, before fire, you must have other fire,[104] and before a man is moved to build a house he must become aware of the Form house, either in a structure built by another man or in nature. But it is still possible for these Forms to be "universal," common, that is, to more than one experience, if the Forms which inform various members of a species are identical[105]—that is, if the Form which is the chief cause, the τέλος, of each member of a species is in fact identical with the cause of all of the other members. To be sure, the degree of realization is in each case unique, but this is only because each individual is surrounded by other substrata headed for different Forms of every sort, and also, as we have already noted, there is invariably a complex of Forms working together on the same substratum whenever it is organized into a complicated being. The Form Man is exactly the same as it affects each of us, therefore, but the influence of yet other Forms nevertheless makes each of us unique as well. Even our uniqueness is knowable to some extent, however, because our more elementary Forms—Flesh, Fire, Water, and so on—are "universal" in the same sense that the unifying *psyche* is.

The third step in the modification of the theory of Forms is the development of a new theory of knowledge to replace Plato's theory of recollection. We are born, Aristotle asserts,[106] not with knowledge of the Forms, but with a capacity to discriminate (δύναμις σύμφυτος κριτική), that is, sense perception, the ability to be impressed by the Forms around us without their matter.[107] In lower animals such impressions do not persist after the perceiver and the perceived are separated, but in higher animals they do.[108] A further distinction can be made between those in whom some system (λόγος) takes shape out of the residual impressions, and those that have a merely mechanical residue of repeated experiences. This higher ability, we learn elsewhere,[109] is limited to a man, and it amounts to the ability to infer, when he experiences an impression which coincides with a still persisting impression from the past, that he has in fact encountered that Form before. Experience, then, is "the stabilization of a universal in its entirety in the *psyche*—

that is, the one beside the many, that which remains one and the same throughout them all."[110] This, when concerned with what comes to be, yields skill (τέχνη), when concerned with that which is, yields precise knowledge (ἐπιστήμη). As when men turn and run in battle, Aristotle says, but one man stands his ground, then another and another, until they become as they were again, so in an initially confused *psyche*,[111] first one of these indiscriminable Forms is stablized (that is, the universality of one Form is inferred from repeated impressions of indiscriminable Forms in various particulars) and then another, and so on. Then a broader generality may be inferred by the same process, because of the identical features in two species of the same genus. From there we can climb to a yet higher genus, and so on, until we have filled out our analysis of everything. To be sure, the higher the genus the less reality it has in one sense,[112] because only the lowest species actually inform matter. (After all you will never find an "Animal," only men, tigers, and so on.) But that does not mean that higher genera are fictitious. On the contrary, although they are Reality only in a secondary sense (δευτέρη οὐσία), they are the key to knowledge, the analysis of how things are ordered, how things are like or unlike one another. As for Plato's assumption that we must have known all this before we were born, why do we need such an absurd suggestion? We need assume only three things: (1) the Forms informing members of one species are absolutely identical,[113] (2) the various species display a certain hierarchical order in relation to one another, and (3) the human *psyche* is simply so constituted as to be capable of responding to this order.[114]

The next step was to eliminate chance, the notion of uncaused events, or the suggestion that there was any cause at work in the world other than Forms as goods striven for. Aristotle points out that we are tempted to say that an event resulted "by luck" (τύχη) or that it "just happened of its own accord" (ταὐτόματον) when the result is one which either an intelligent agent or a natural process *might* have aimed at, even though as a matter of fact none did.[115] If the result is not in some sense an achievement, one which arrests our attention and arouses our desire to find causal connections, then there is no problem. But if the event does arouse our curiosity, and upon investigation we find that neither a man nor a natural process was aiming at just that end, then we say that it was chance or luck (in the case of the actions of adult human beings) or that it just happened (in the case of all other processes). These phrases, however, says Aristotle, must on no account be taken to refer to real causes; they are merely names for actions which, while they resemble purposive actions, are really only incidental results of agents bent on *other* purposes.

Aristotle maintains that all events, if analyzed correctly, can be shown to have been purposive. The trick is to find the regular processes, and then explain irregular results as unusual side effects of two or more of these regular events affecting the same substratum. Just because it did not rain *in order* to ruin a farmer's crop does not mean that there is no final cause for the rain at all.[116] Things which happen regularly, like rain in the rainy season or teeth in a jaw (grinders in the back, incisors in front),[117] cannot be said to happen by chance, and something which does not happen by chance must have taken place because of a tendency toward some end. Conscious deliberation is not present in natural processes, but neither is it in art.[118] The mark of a purposive act is that the end aimed at is evident throughout the process; step by step the final goal is realized in the most efficient possible way. But notice, this subordination of all actions to the final product is just as clearly observable in nature as in the conscious actions of an intelligent man. Spiders, ants, and birds, for instance, without a moment's inquiry or deliberation, nevertheless do what they do with remarkable efficiency toward clearly defined ends. Plants too, if we but notice, act for a purpose, sending out roots in the direction of the kind of nourishment they need, and so on. "And since 'nature' is used in two ways," says Aristotle,[119] "as matter and as Form, and since the latter is the end (*τέλος*) while all the rest are for the sake of the end, then the Form is the cause—that for the sake of which."

But what about mistakes in nature? Well, there are mistakes in art, too, but that does not disprove purpose in artistic processes. In fact, monstrous births and the like occur in nature precisely as they might in art.[120] The male supplies the Form, the female the matter.[121] The same sort of things can go wrong here, in the attempt to form matter, as say, in a craftsman's attempt to form iron into a saw: the actual stamping of the Form can be muddled, the matter can be unsuitable, or other entities can maim or destroy the product before it is finished. Why is it, Aristotle asks at one point,[122] that while the young of animals generally look very like their parents, human children often do not? Could it be, he asks, that animals concentrate when they copulate while men's minds sometimes wander? The creative act, if completely successful, notice, would produce, not a perfect specimen of what it is to be a man, but Man modified by all the minute privations which make the father unique. If the failure is in the act itself, then the result will be either a female child (an ἀναπηρία φυσική, a natural —because regular and necessary—lameness),[123] or a child that looks like its mother, or a child that looks like one of its grandparents, or a child which, however good-looking, resembles none of its relatives strongly, or, most serious of all, an actual monster.[124] If, on the other hand, the failure is in the mixture of fire, air, earth, and water presented by the mother, then the result will be a giant, a dwarf, or a child with malformed, redundant, or missing parts. In any case, we still need no separate cause for failure.

As for evil in human activities, this is a little more difficult to explain. When Aristotle speaks of the rational and irrational he never means, as Plato does, "caused by perception of the good" as opposed to "uncaused" or "caused by undirected energy"; the mark of irrationality is for Aristotle merely the absence of any possibility to act otherwise.[125] When a man is acting irrationally, then he is merely following a blind desire, precisely as a tree does when it sends out leaves, or as a stone does when it hurtles toward the center of the earth. After all, if there is no event in the entire universe which is not caused by a real Form pursued for its true excellence, then we cannot make an exception in the case of stupidity or passion. What then is a man doing when he finds it prudent deliberately to *fight* a temptation and go against a desire? Actually, says Aristotle,[126] a man is never presented with a single, isolated desire which it would be to his benefit to go against; he is always presented with a pair of mutually exclusive goals, both, however, quite real goals. Intelligence consists in so training oneself as to desire on every occasion that course between the two which takes the man directly to his true well-being. *Voilà* the famous theory of the Golden Mean. We *still* do not need any cause for evil. Every event in the universe is caused by the goodness of the Forms.

Will Aristotle's version of the philosophy of Form really work? Alas, in order to complete the system Aristotle had to introduce one more innovation,[127] one which seemed obvious enough to him, but which makes the whole vision collapse for us. In order for the Forms to be (1) the objects of exact knowledge, and (2) the causes of events and so existing for the most part only as they form matter, Aristotle had to assume that no species ever had a beginning in time—that the world always looked as it does now and that there was no real invention even in the pursuits of men. All Forms, natural and artistic as well, he had to assume, have always pulled their matter in exactly the way that they do now, and each pattern has achieved permanence by its ability to survive from parent to offspring forever. Unfortunately for his argument, it has become obvious in the last few centuries that this cannot in fact have been the case; neither the pursuits of men nor man himself and the other species have existed very long in their present appearances. And so, in one respect, Plato turns out to have been right after all: we cannot account for the preciseness and permanence of the objects of knowledge if we assume that they exist in the sensed world only, even if we assume that they are the perfections yearned for by the matter of the world.

For a long time, however, Aristotle's version of the idea of a world moved only by love of good had a wide and profound influence. It had its effect in several ways. First, in the ideal of the contemplative life.[128] For with all of Aristotle's criticism of Plato's Form of the Good,[129] and for all that he reduced the rôle of the supreme good to the mover of the outermost sphere,[130] he did identify man's highest and happiest activity with the tracing out of the highest splendor of the universe.[131] Aristotle's version of the Love of the *Symposium* is epitomized in the first sentence of the *Metaphysics*: "All men by nature desire to know." It is an ideal which we would call mystic if it were not based on a scrupulous analysis of daily events, and we would call scientific if it did not begin so obviously from a sense of the beauty of the whole world around us.

A second form in which Aristotle's vision influenced the world was in a feeling about nature, and above all the stars. Toward the end of Aristotle's life, some astronomers of his acquaintance figured out that we could account for all heavenly phenomena if we supposed that there were a number of different, perfectly regular circular motions, forty-seven or fifty-five, one inside another.[132] Aristotle accepted this observation.[133] For each of these many spheres there was, he thought, a different bodiless[134] unmoved mover like the First Mover. Each sphere, then, is moved, above all, by desire for its own unmoved mover, but it is affected as well by all of the spheres superior to it. We down here, therefore, are the products of a fantastically complicated choreography of star-studded spheres, drawing us, some in one direction, some in another, at different speeds, different angles of inclination, and different distances from the center. If only we knew how, we ought to be able to trace every movement in the world down here all the way out to these divine bodies moving through the heavens.[135] As for the stars themselves, do not think of them as the works of a giant clock; they are moved by love, love in the last instance for the highest beauty of all, that which draws the universe as a whole. This is the love of which Dante speaks in the last line of the *Paradiso*, the love that moves the sun and all the stars:

*l'amor che move il sole e l'altre stelle.*

# CHAPTER 9

## *An Evaluation of Various Aspects of the Platonic Theory of Love. The Claims of the Rival Theories Reconsidered.*

CHRISTIAN APOLOGISTS often speak as though it were in their different ideals of supreme goodness that the Christian and the Platonic understanding of love differed most essentially. This, as we have seen, is not quite right. On several occasions, most memorably in the *Republic*,[1] the *Phaedrus*,[2] and the *Timaeus*,[3] Plato singles out as the most notable sign of the supreme goodness of divinity that it acts without a trace of grudging (*φθόνος*). In the *Timaeus*, the divine Craftsman is said to have undertaken the task of making everything in the universe as good as it could be, for no other reason than that he himself was flawlessly good, "and in the good, no grudging can ever arise about anything (*ἀγαθῷ δὲ οὐδεὶς περὶ οὐδενὸς οὐδέποτε ἐγγίγνεται φθόνος*)." Aristotle repeats the idea, reproving the older poets for their crudeness in asserting the contrary.[4] Plato concludes that this universal good will is a complete explanation for all that divinity did in the beginning or does now. This, then, is what love would be at its best, according to Plato. It is hard to see how the most single-minded Pagan-hating Christian could quarrel with that as an ideal.

The Greeks, to be sure, were notoriously wary of matching their ambitions with those of divinity. But the Greeks also recognized divinity in the first place by the fact that it possessed all the things they admired most intensely. *Imitation* of divinity, *ὁμοίωσις θεῷ*, is also a deep and persistent feature of the Greek attitude. Indeed, after personal ambition, especially the kind which is likely to be expressed in unpredictable vindictiveness, was no longer thought to be a worthy possession for a god, the whole project of imitating divinity must have appeared to be less dangerous, and therefore, at last, the most attractive procedure. Plato himself was in any case the most conspicuous of the several Greeks who advocated making oneself over according to the standards of divine excellence.[5] When, therefore, he describes the nature of divine will as the desire to do good and nothing else, he is surely saying that love in a human being approaches this description also as the human being approaches ideal excellence.

And after all, is this not precisely the character of Socrates' love, which makes him almost the god of love himself in the *Symposium*? So purely is his love refined, to the point where he is motivated only by beauty and excellence itself, that he can feel not only no rancor toward his enemies but no favoritism even—no irrational clinging to any single person as a source of personal delight. Indeed, the similarity between Socrates and Christ in this respect has been felt vividly by countless readers over the centuries. For Christ, too, seems to have set an impossibly impersonal standard in his love. His demands on his followers were sometimes almost inhuman—as when he asked them to take no more thought for their parents if they were going to pursue God in him.[6] (Oddly enough, in both cases this demand for a love which would rise above personal inclinations, exemplified unforgettably in the life and death of the two masters, only kindled in their followers a deep, even fanatic devotion to the person of the master himself.)

In one version of the Socratic paradox, repeated by Plato from the *Lysis* to the *Philebus*, it is suggested that a god, inasmuch as he is perfect, and therefore presumably self-sufficient, could not want anything, and so must be incapable of love. We should not forget, however, that this was indeed offered as a paradox—an assertion, that is, which will be seen to be true only if we dislocate our associations with some of the terms in which the statement is couched. That it is not to be taken at its face value is proved, if proof is necessary, by the fact that not only the Craftsman in the *Timaeus*, but men themselves as they approach excellence, are invariably shown by Plato to be motivated, not less, but more than ordinary men are, by an intense devotion to beauty and perfection. The key to the paradox, as to all of Socrates' paradoxes, is in the new idea about the nature of rationality. As men became more splendid examples of what men should be, Plato suggests, they may indeed lose their need for irrational attachments—consolation, stimulation, help—but this is not because they feel the absence of desire; it is because they have come to desire that alone which is truly rewarding. Men think that to be rational is to be able coolly to discount all passions, but rationality really consists in a passion so powerful and happy that what most men conceive passions for is finally seen to be *really* irrational—that is, not rewarding at all.

Aristotle, although he hated paradoxes,[7] in effect created a new version of the old Socratic paradox when he argued that the man who had reached the highest level of impersonal justice was also the man who most loved himself.[8] It is this version of the paradox as much as any which has led Christians to the belief that the Greeks must have been incurably self-centered and deplorably ambitious for their own happiness, while only Christ seemed to have advocated rising above that. But Aristotle's paradox needs *interpretation*. What it means, it turns out, is that the man who is most alive to all that is precious in the world outside himself is by that very fact also the man who has seen most clearly which of his desires do and which do not arise unerringly from what must inevitably be his chief concern, his anxiety for what is most valuable in his real self. Such a man is certainly not "selfish" or "self-centered" in the usual meaning for these phrases. (In any case, Christ, too, is said to have quoted with approval the old injunction to love one's neighbor *as oneself*.)

The basic Christian paradox, on the other hand, if its absolute unlikeness to anything in the Pagan world is stressed too strongly, can become a paradox of the un-Socratic sort, namely a simple inconsistency. For there are those who would have the Christians say more than that we had better not consider the *usual* rewards when we choose and when we act, for if we do that we shall not be rewarded in heaven. They would glory in the mysterious inconsistency itself: we should choose the life not based on rewards because that is the most rewarding. But this is nonsense. ("When I am weak," says Paul, "then I am strong." Is he really weak, or does he only seem weak to those who have not comprehended his new source of strength? If the latter, then his is really another form of the love of true happiness; if the former, however, then he has spoken nonsense.)

Nobody could deny, of course, that somewhere there is a vital difference between the Platonists and the Christians in their understanding of love. It is just that this difference is not really noticeable in their ideals of human generosity. The place to look, rather, is in the practical advice implied in the two formulations. The most obvious peculiarity in the Christian version is the surprising demand that we pay no attention to the excellence or foulness, preciousness or worthlessness, of the object of our affections. Now, Socrates, too, denied the wisdom of the old command to love one's friends but hate one's enemies;[9] and, as we have seen, he argued that no man is ever justified in doing true harm to another, regardless of the apparent provocation. But there the resemblance to the Christian position ends. Socrates did not seem to feel that the requirement to experience only good will even toward one's most dedicated enemies involved a fundamental complication in our inevitable pursuit of the truly precious. To weaken one's special attraction to truly beautiful things would have seemed to Socrates to be not wisdom but suicide. When it comes right down to it, of course, it is not really true that an awareness of precious things is wanting in the *New Testament*, either. What there is, however, is a startling new emphasis on the value of that which anyone would have thought to be *without* value: a new tenderness for those who have not accomplished anything as yet, like small children, for those who never managed to achieve anything at all in life, like the foolish or the simple, and even for the social pariahs, like criminals, prostitutes, and lepers. In actual fact, therefore, Christ does not ask us really to pay no attention to excellence, but he does ask us to turn the values of society upside down—to take even brilliance, deep learning, style, and the achievement of happiness in society as signs not of success but of the very reverse. (If you actually *like* little children, is your tenderness *agapê*, or is it *eros*? Love only those whom you cannot love, Christ seems to say.)

Socrates, too, remember, was thought to turn the judgments of the world on their head. He was feared as a subversive no less than Christ was. Both, after all, were finally executed for their influences. Socrates, however, thought that society's real mistake lay, not in its failure to feel love for the mean and unimportant, but in its failure to demand more than a shabby appearance of brilliance and success. It comes down to a difference in what they hoped for from society in the future. Christ had little or no hopes for this source; he thought that men banked all too much on the values which were the product of social organization. Socrates, on the other hand, thought that men were ruining their very souls when they refused to trouble themselves about the stupidity and injustice of their organizations.

As I have said, the ideal was much the same for both theories of love, namely a completely selfless devotion to good which would show itself in universal benevolence. Plato, however, would realize this in the course of careful, rational improvement of human society, while Christ (although he was not consistent on the point) often betrayed a conviction that society as such was not worth bothering about, that we ought really to be able to live without planning even for the bare essentials, like the lilies of the field. It is not surprising, therefore, that the Socratic version, which tells us to become ever more exclusively devoted to true excellence and work diligently to isolate or eradicate stupidity, is of much greater use as a principle on which to build a working society than is the Christian version, which tells us to broadcast our good will indiscriminately and leave the wicked to heaven. In fact, so alarming is the Christian advice as a suggestion for consistent action in the world of men that one is tempted to wonder if the *New Testament* has not been made largely obsolete by the simple fact that the world did not come to an end so soon as the original Christians expected. Have we perhaps been adding a certain element of confusion to our lives these past two thousand years by trying —intermittently, half-heartedly, and inconsistently, to be sure— to guide our nations by a principle which was actually based on the assumption that the world would last only another generation anyhow? The Russians, for instance, stick blindly to their charming notion that if we but eliminate all private property, no other social problems will remain, and the Americans cherish similar simple-minded hopes from the eradication of class barriers and the separation of church and state.

But that is hardly the last word on Christian love. As a way to achieve the perfection of deep, ungrudging benevolence toward all men Christian love even has one advantage over the Platonic version. Plato's ladder to this goal is offered as an effective way up only for the gifted few, really, and then only with luck and years of hard work. Christ's way, on the other hand, can give worth-while power almost on the spot, and to the most limited of men. Even as a social force it can be a constructive procedure under certain conditions: when, as in the first century, there are as many or more good men among the underdogs and the "have nots" as there are among the influential. Certainly the Christian message has from time to time transformed what might have been a worthless crowd of wretches into a powerful force for justice and consideration for others.

It is a little unfair, I suppose, that we should be forced to judge Christian love by the element which a scholar might isolate as most truly peculiar to the original movement. For while our art, our morality, and our very way of looking at the world have been profoundly influenced by the Christians, this has rarely happened in any clearly definable way. If one were so inclined, after all, one could lay upon the Christians the blame for centuries of wars and stupid judgments, and such charges could not be proved untrue. But this procedure would be worth very little, for the Christian tradition has been complicated by too many influences and conditions to make it possible to assign blame crudely in this fashion. Nor would the case be different if we were to try to give Christianity the credit for our achievements. We had better content ourselves, therefore, with a less ambitious question: which of the vital elements of our civilization which can be traced *at least in part* to the Christian understanding of love, do we still hold in such esteem that we are not tempted to discard them even when we disown Christianity as a dogma? I would choose, I think, above all, the special awareness which Christian love has given us of children and very simple people. It must always strike a modern reader as a great blind spot in Plato, that he treats children as incomplete adults. If we substituted Plato's version entirely for the Christian, what (we might consider) would be left of our response to, say, that worshiper of children, Dostoevsky or to *King Lear*? What would Plato have made of the ties which bound Lear and Cordelia, or Lear and the Fool?

Several new English and American translations of the *New Testament* now represent *agapê* no longer as "charity" but as "love." This is but the latest symptom of an old confusion, the confusion between Christian love and Romantic love. In a way it is right that Paul's word and John's should be translated as "love," for the various ideals of love, or so I have been arguing, are not various kinds of love but various descriptions and recommendations concerning what is really basically one thing. But in all modern European languages, the most general word for love calls up the Romantic tradition far more accurately than it does any other, at least in most contexts. When, therefore, a modern churchgoer hears that, of the three most important attitudes he should take toward reality, namely faith, hope and "love," the most important of all is "love," he may no longer be puzzled, as he once was, by the apparent suggestion that the greatest of all things is to give alms to the poor; on the other hand, he will probably respond to the word "love" all too enthusiastically, for the word will touch *something* in him which he has felt very vividly indeed. But he will really be responding, alas, to memories which Paul would have referred to by *eros*, not *agapê*. Paul had much less use for ordinary sexual attraction than Plato did (to put it mildly), and he undoubtedly steered clear of Plato's word precisely for that reason. And here we are, calling up once more those warm and exciting feelings of enthusiasm for our neighbors—a wish to clutch them to our bosom somehow—as if *that* were what Paul was referring to! Of course, if Freud is right, even the selfless concern for the unloveable which Paul tried to awaken in us gets whatever power it has from unconscious sexual desire somehow subtly transformed, but that does not reduce to nonsense the very serious disagreement between the Christian and the Romantic advice. I confess that I always experience a shudder of horror when I hear a minister, arms outstretched as though to embrace all humanity in one great hug, cry that what the whole world is really longing for when it looks restlessly for love, love, love is the love of God in Jesus. It is as if he wished (to use the words of a certain West End revue) to get the violence off the streets and into the churches where it belonged. But this is really a triumph of the Romantic idea.

The Romantic understanding of love, the notion of love which is most readily called up by the use of the word "love" today, has certainly not been an uncomplicated success as an ideal which one could follow either to personal happiness or to social order and stability. Its dark alliance with failure and death has indeed sometimes made it a force in the destruction of our chances to create order in our own lives and in the world. It has always seemed, in the Romantic tradition, somehow profoundly *right* that in the end society should invariably crush the lovers—think of Romeo and Juliet, Antony and Cleopatra, Tristram and Iseult, Lancelot and Guenevere. A Freudian might say that this is only our satisfaction in the way in which our *super-ego* must punish us for our anti-social desires. But perhaps there is more to it than that. Even in the sexual act itself, the intense drive for life is followed immediately by a complete and welcome surrender of all will—a foretaste of the relaxation of death. Perhaps the ideal course of a love affair in the Romantic tradition must itself follow this same pattern. Romantic love, then, cannot be in or for society; society must be provoked to the point where it will crush the lovers.

Because of Christian and Platonic influences in the Romantic tradition, however, there has also been a desire to reconcile Romantic love with the highest values of God, humanity, and civilization. But not only is this a schizophrenic desire, it has not even shown itself to be capable of being worked out with any great realism. The chief effect of this ideal, apparently, has been to throw tens of thousands of people into needless despair. Only true love makes life really worthwhile, runs this ideal. But, it adds, only a few are capable of feeling true love. ("Have *I* ever experienced true love?" ask people by the millions.) Anybody can experience sexual hunger, but that is nothing at all compared to the profound, exclusive love which one person can have for another on rare occasions. ("Is *my* desire perhaps nothing but sex?" we ask.) The sign of sin, that is of mere sexual need, is that any one of several people might do for the fulfillment of our desires. ("Why does my eye wander?" we ask.) All happiness is supposed, by this form of the tradition, to come to us like the rain from the sky and make luminous all the rest of our days if we but find our true love. If happiness does not stay with us, therefore, in the way in which the best-sellers and the popular songs promise us it must, then we torture ourselves with the thought that we lack some quality within us which would give us the power to love more deeply. That our problem might be more general than our relation to this one person does not occur to us. And it must surely be obvious by now that the recent injection of Freudian ideas has not transformed the Romantic ideal into a highway to bliss either. Our feelings about sexuality in love may have been further relaxed, but that has just given us new worries for old. ("Have I what it takes to hang on to my mate?" we ask.)

Plato's criticism of the Romantic ideal, as in the case of the Christians, would be that it works, not *for* all that is good in the real world, but *against* it. Since that is also the heart of his criticism of the remaining position, the Freudian, let us postpone for a few minutes our final evaluation of that question. For the present, let us ask if there is anything which we can say in favor of the Romantics.

If, as I suggested, we might defend even Christian love, among other ways, by recalling all of the wonderful works of literature which would become senseless if we wanted to—or could—obliterate the Christian strain in our feelings, how much more easily could we defend the Romantic strain by this same procedure! Perhaps you are not one to be moved by an appeal of this sort, but consider at least what it must mean in theory to say that many of the achievements which seem to most of us to be wise and moving would seem empty and uninteresting if we subtracted the Romantic idea of love from the things which make sense to us. The Romantic ideal of love must really be not some silly surface notion but a very deep conviction indeed.

A friend in America to whom I sent a draft of my first lecture in this series wrote back a spirited defense of the Romantic heresy.[10] "You might say," he writes, "that this line of Catherine's in *Farewell to Arms* is somehow faint and sentimental: 'You won't do our things with somebody else?' " And yet, he asked, "why does her tenderness, which is a kind of greed, seem to me finer than the universal insights of Freud and Plato? That is belligerent, but so is Catherine. She is rebelling against a world where 'most women fit most men.' Plato and Freud accept and would refine what terrifies her. So Catherine is your adversary." I agree. This, if any, is the right way to defend Romantic love. In this alone of our traditions is the uniqueness of each individual love cherished and not belittled. Plato and Aristotle, as we have seen, did finally come to say that special, personal attachments need not be discarded as love is used in the pursuit of higher understanding and exhilaration, but they added this almost as an afterthought. More important, they reserved their really enthusiastic praise only for the non-sexual ties of male loyalty and devotion. As for the unpredictable sexual excitement which, if given a chance, can occasionally grow so intense that it will cause a pair of lovers to damn the world and go down to ruin rather than betray their love, Plato's sympathy never went farther than to hope that this passion could yet be harnessed in the interests of its enemy—in the interests, that is, of all that was best in the life of the community.

"Why did I fall so madly in love with just this one person in all the world?" asks the young lover. The other theories of love tend always to discount this puzzling phenomenon as not ultimately very interesting; only the Romantic theory makes it the central mystery. Most modern readers of the *Symposium* remember very vividly, even many years later, the strange myth told by Aristophanes, that we are each looking for the one person who is our other half. Very few respond with a similar enthusiasm to Socrates' correction of this myth, when he says that we are not looking really for any other person at all, but for the knowledge of eternal beauty.

Must the sexual love of men and women, when it is more than just a very satisfactory animal and social accommodation, inevitably be against society, and a source of danger to it? Plato and Aristotle do not actually say so, but, strangely enough, Freud does.[11] The sexual energy of women, he thought, is, as a rule, not "sublimated" nearly to the degree that it is in men. The energy which men expend in their loyalty to super-personal standards, therefore, seems to women to be an almost senseless loss. Society, in a way, becomes the woman's enemy. Love for her man and for her children, both intensely sexual bonds, will usually outweigh all other considerations with her. When the world is lost for love, notice, it is usually only the man who is torn between two bonds—as when Antony vacillates between Rome and Alexandria. When Cleopatra gets Antony to say "Let Rome in Tiber melt!" we know that the woman has won. Cleopatra will hardly even notice that her own empire is gone as well.

When we ask which side Freud is on, that of the Romantic lovers or civilization, we do not get a very clear answer. Left to ourselves we would all be only lovers, he says. But since sexual energy as such does not discriminate even between the two sexes, let alone between family and strangers, and since, not only protection against enemies and ease in gathering necessities, but also leisure, honesty, dependability, sensitivity, and culture are among the rewards of deflecting our solitary desires in order to organize men into groups larger than immediate families, we had just better reconcile ourselves, Freud thought, to the necessity of having our secret and only true desires mercilessly and continuously mutilated. Society is by definition unnatural if you define nature as our real desire. Society's tasks are largely doomed, therefore. The successful society, one gathers from Freud, is the one which does not actually explode too often or too suicidally.

In their attitudes toward reality and rationality, therefore, Freud and the Romantics are still one. Where Freud departs from the Romantic tradition is in his attitude toward the unpredictable exclusiveness of the rare, intense attachments of famous lovers. Freud takes the general demand for sexual pleasure as the basic phenomenon, and attempts to explain exclusive passions as merely a variation of that. The Romantic does not begin to call it love at all until it is exclusive, and until it involves far more than a desire for sexual release. For Freud, as for any philosopher or scientist, the general laws must be the key to power and understanding. For the Romantics, the individual and the unique are sacred and must not be violated by orderly thinking.

Plato takes every opportunity to call up in us our memories of whatever Romantic enthusiasm we have felt, but, like Freud, sooner or later he steers us toward a conception of love as a general—indeed a universal—phenomenon. What is distinctive about Plato's position, as opposed both to Freud and to Freud's

Romantic antecedents, is his attitude toward reality and rationality. He actually *defends* civilization—and not just grudgingly, either, as Freud does, but enthusiastically! Civilization to him means rational order, and rational order means the best arrangement for the achievement of true happiness. How, he asks, can anyone be against that?

A good way to see the nature of the difference between Plato and Freud is to compare the two philosophers on the lower drives within the human *psyche*. Take the spirited element first, what Freud calls the *super-ego*. Freud believes that this is the result of an internationalization of the threats of authority. It is that, therefore, which makes an individual a loyal member of his culture. By virtue of its presence within him, the "good" man avoids breaking the rules of his society, not because of any bestial fear of direct reprisal from without, but because he would invariably punish himself. He really *wants* to do the right thing; he is responsible and moral, says his society. But the commands of this drive in our *psyches*, Freud thought, are relative to our various cultures, and if the truth were known, the drive actually came into being in the first place solely as the result of a series of threats to our sexual appetites when we were children. Plato, trying to account for the same phenomena, suggested merely that there was that within us from birth which, if given a chance, would make us fight our more unruly drives whenever these threatened order and sanity —an anxiety, in other words, for all the things the value of which is more subtle and more remote than is the case with objects which yield instantaneous pleasure. Both philosophers attribute great benefits to this capacity within us, and both tend to judge a society by the way in which it molds this drive. But Freud thought that the very existence of this desire to do the right thing was a kind of wry joke on us, as it is really only a cryptic response to an intensely selfish and cowardly fear—a childish and groundless fear, above all—that society will literally castrate us. Plato, on the other hand, with neither Freud's interest in nor his information on the stages which this spirited element goes through in the child, accepted its existence simply as a fortunate fact. He defined it not by its past but by its function. As a result, while Freud tended to have a wary respect for the *super-ego* as a tendency to check our real desires, an irrational, anti-personal force which we had better step carefully around, Plato accepted it joyfully as that which should make it possible for us to educate and organize the whole of society in order to bring even very limited men to goodness and happiness.

When we look at their respective treatments of the *id*, we find a difference which amounts to much the same thing. Freud did more than any other man to explore the unconscious systematically. To this end he developed a brilliant new technique and accumulated hundreds of case histories. But what he was looking for in the first place was the source of that drive which could in some wretched people suddenly dominate altogether, cause them to lose contact with the external world, and destroy what to an outside observer would seem to be their best chances for happiness. Like Plato, Freud found a royal road to this unconscious through our dreams and, also like Plato, he discovered in this way that even seemingly happy and orderly men can often be proved to be harboring monstrous appetites just beneath the surface of their own awareness. But, as the result of a scientific prejudice in favor of the greater importance of the lowest common denominators which might link men with other phenomena in nature, Freud tended to treat this darker side of ourselves, not as the enemy, but as our real selves. He became so impressed with the autonomy of this drive, its obliviousness to the demands of society, and its power to revenge itself on the conscious man if it is not allowed to exercise its will at least in disguised fantasies, that the *ego*, the real self, the observer in all introspection, that which makes the conscious judgments and decisions, all but disappeared before Freud's eyes. It became, as we saw, a part of the *id* itself, modified by the laws of cause and effect but dedicated in reality to the energies below. Reasoning became mere rationalizing, and civilization merely the result of the physical impossibility of satisfying to the full all of our merciless demands for pleasure.

Plato began not with the problem of hysterical breakdowns but with the desire to clarify our understanding of that which makes the good man admirable and happy. Like Freud, he, too, realized that men betrayed a dangerous bestial element just beneath the surface, that civilization as it exists most often is a thin crust over a powerful and ugly subterranean world of irrational energy; but he assumed that our main task was to improve this situation as rapidly and as effectively as we could—not so much in the private lives of the hysterical as in our political and educational philosophies. Since he was much more interested in the gifted few who might be able to guide the rest than he was in the failures and the insane, he came to center his attention on extraordinary men, like Socrates, who showed that one could indeed rise above unreasoning desire for immediate pleasure, rather than on the men whom Freud worried most about. The finest men, Plato thought, seemed to overcome their childish appetites, not by bumping their heads against a cruel reality, but by seeing in remoter things other goals so much more exciting than the nearby ones that life in the real world became, not only not precarious, but wonderfully rewarding for their whole selves.

Over and over again our investigations have led to the same observation, that the unique and startling thing about Plato's thought was above all his suggestion that rationality, the activity of the real self when it is functioning as the guiding drive in a man, is not primarily a pursuit carried on in the interests of the irrational appetites; it is an overmastering desire to live in the world, a delight in the way the world really is. This, as we have seen, is why Plato equated love and philosophy, why the etymology of the word "philosophy" seemed to him to be so profoundly right. It is time at last to ask ourselves if this suggestion, basic to so much of Plato's philosophy, can possibly be correct. Our answer to this question can be, I think, neither a simple yes nor a simple no. It must be a mixture of enthusiasm with some very grave doubts. Let us look at the doubts first.

Rationality, Plato thought, was an energy directed toward a goal. As energy it is exactly like irrationality. The difference between rationality and irrationality must lie, he thought, first in the fact that rationality seeks the ultimate goal, happiness, while irrationality seeks only instantaneous satisfaction, and second in the fact that rationality is a process of making connections between experiences, while irrationality invariably recognizes only unique events. Plato seems to have concluded from these two observations that happiness, the distinctive goal of rationality, *was* the discovery of the patterns and connections behind the flux of unique events. He apparently thought he saw a confirmation of this idea in the common experience of heightened vision when we are especially happy —above all when we are in love—those days when a flower is not a flower merely, a cloud not merely a cloud, but all things somehow right and beautiful, and really unchanging, for all the flux at the bodily level. After all, Plato observes, when you look for a pattern by which to connect experiences and thus come to understand them, the process is in fact never one of detached statistical reckoning; you are *looking* for something, a key to success in the pursuit of happiness, and you conclude that you have made the right connections only if your analysis, when acted on, yields the best possible results. Are we not justified, therefore, asks Plato, in taking the lover's description of the world as the literal truth? Beauty is but a special, unlooked for hint of happiness and that it is which illuminates the lover's world. Inasmuch as happiness is our ultimate criterion for correctness in figuring out connections, must not beauty be an inevitable feature of all connections correctly seen?

That a man could live a good life who was utterly convinced of the metaphysical implications of Plato's line of thought seems hard to deny. Or even that we should prefer such a man to be the most influential in our society—in preference, that is, to someone who had respect really only for his momentary appetites. The trouble comes when Plato suggests that a complete and consistent description could be worked out on this metaphysics and communicated systematically in a state education. What *are* these beautiful connections? Plato hedges, finally, and says that, inasmuch as happiness cannot be described directly, and no connections can be made entirely clear without a true grasp of happiness, the final teaching of the nature of reality remains a mysterious process. Plato never succeeded in explaining the compelling power of the flux of individual phenomena in its claim to be true reality. Although phenomena owed everything to the Forms, he believed, the Forms owed nothing to phenomena. Try as he might, therefore, he could not devise a foolproof method for going through phenomena to genuine Forms.

But are we really any more convinced by Aristotle's modifications, as a result of which the true realities of things were looked for, no longer in unpredictable visions, but right there, pulling the sensed world itself this way and that? What do the Forms turn out to be in this version? The species of things, above all the apparent goals being striven for by organisms of every sort. This ingenious idea had a dazzling success for a while, but we have become thoroughly disillusioned with it by now. (At least all but a few biologists and Thomists, who are still trying to make it work.) The trouble is, not only do the species change in no demonstrably beautiful fashion from age, but our very decisions as to what perfection in any given species would be seems, if not entirely arbitrary, at least very slippery. (Heather, which may grow two feet tall here in Scotland, is sometimes found ten feet high in the Congo. Which is closer to the full realization of the Form? And why?) We are thrown back on Plato's paradox about the necessity to know what happiness is before we can call a realization good.

Let us consider the idea, common to both Plato and Aristotle, which reappears centuries later as the most famous of Aquinas' proofs of the existence of God, the idea that we must assume some more than merely analogous connection between the good which we seek in every decision and the good which is the cause of universal order. The argument goes as follows. In observing ourselves or a fellow human being we find that we *understand* only insofar as we judge the action in question to be rational in the Socratic sense—that is, only insofar as we see what goal was being pursued, why it should be thought that this action would win that goal, and above all why that goal should be thought to be worth pursuing. If we cannot answer this last question, we catalogue the person uneasily in one or another of the categories of known irrational types. When we go on to try to understand irrational things like animals, and even when we descend to plants, and eventually to molecules and atoms, we really attempt the same procedure, although, since we do not expect to sympathize with the goals apparently pursued by these things, we are not so shocked by their tendencies to drive toward realizations which we do not covet ourselves. Still, the understanding which we do achieve of these things consists of our comprehension of the goals which they are in fact aimed at, however pointless or monotonous some of them appear to be. And then on some days, if the weather is good, our liver sound, and our friends friendly, we seem to realize that the goals striven for even by the things which have no utilitarian value for us are nevertheless recognizably fine. A savage beast seems splendid, and a flower dazzlingly perfect. We wonder delightedly at the mechanism of a rat's kidney or a helium atom. Then we suddenly realize how very much of the universe really is intelligible and how all its strivings fit together with extraordinary intricacy and beauty. We may then feel that the key to our excitement lies in the fact that we have understood each thing only insofar as we have seen how the goodness which each is striving for is also the only good which we too are striving for. Or, if we keep in sight the fact that the patterns of perfection striven for by different kinds of things are different, we may still be deeply impressed by the discovery that excellence of one sort or another is the cause of all that happens, and that the various different patterns of perfection display a beautiful hierarchical order in their relations one to another.

The trouble is, alas, that the mood has passed. The vision of the sophists has triumphed after all. We can no longer count on seeing brilliance and order in the jungle; indeed we see the law of the jungle in our very cities. And when we have occasion to dwell on the intricate regularity of the motions of moons or electrons, we are as likely as not to feel that the universe is rather like a vast, mindless servo-mechanism, or a giant IBM machine, one which is, however, incapable of giving anybody any answers. We still enjoy and admire nature much of the time, for the Platonic version still operates to carry us through our thoughtless moments. But when we force ourselves to dig up our deeper convictions, we are more likely to side with Freud and one strain of the Romantic temper: reality as such is, if not monstrous, at least no edifying teacher, no demonstrator of a benevolent intelligence or innate goodness.[12]

We know a thing, Plato points out, only insofar as we know what assumption it would be to our benefit to make about it; it must follow, therefore, he concludes, that our own true good is what gives not only significance but reality as well to all that we come into contact with. To this we now shrug our shoulders and reply: not proved. There is still a logical possibility, we say, that the world is truly mechanical, and that when we see actions toward ends (which, by the way, we really find only in living organisms) we are merely noting analogies to some of the less interesting drives which we know all about in ourselves, the drive to survive, for instance, or to avoid pain and experience pleasure. For the rest: we observe, catalogue, and offer bizarre hypotheses. "Little we see in nature that is ours." Plato's paradox about knowledge and the good only makes us realize the more vividly how much more vast is that part of the universe which we have no hope of understanding in the way in which we would like to understand things, than is the corner which we can understand. In this respect we are closer to the vision of the *Timaeus*, a semi-cosmos haunted by the specter of a blind, unknowable Necessity, than we are to the vision of the Form of the Good or the Prime Mover.

Next, consider what has become of our enthusiasm for clarity and planning in human affairs. Ever since Plato first suggested that it was our duty to see that those who understand most should be in the positions of greatest influence, we seem to have suffered under a long series of ideological tyrants, from Alexander to Lenin and from Hadrian to Cromwell. We began some time ago to wonder if the sad compromise implied in that other Greek idea, democracy, bolstered up by compulsory education in mathematics and a thousand checks on those who think that they know more than the government, is not preferable after all. To be sure we realize from time to time that, with all our occasional advances in technology and the like, we have still left utterly untouched our terrible tendencies toward war, greed, injustice, and waste. But we have been stung too many times by now. Whenever we have given someone the power to plan ahead and do better, it has always seemed to end up worse: regimentation, exploitation, genocide, and revolution. To Plato's assertion that most men must be helped, even against their will, in order to make their appetites match their real desire for happiness, we reply that we would rather retain the right to make ourselves unhappy than surrender our present confusion in favor of any tighter scheme which we have seen yet.[13] Plato suggested that a well-planned state should display a power structure precisely like that in the soul of a wise and happy man, but so cynical have we become as to what is probably really going on in the unconscious—that is, the plebs—of even the happiest man, that we find a magnified version no very pleasing prospect.

Plato's condemnation of the poet's right to sing whatever he pleased has become a symbol of what we feel is most dangerous in the vision of a nation run by the truest lover of the good. Aristotle, because he denied the existence of a genuinely irrational energy anywhere in the universe, was forced to reinstate poetry as a natural phenomenon with its formal and final cause like any other, but his Platonism shows through uncomfortably in the patronizing tone he takes toward the poets. Now, where precisely do we ourselves stand on this ancient quarrel between poetry and philosophy? If you ask a man, "Who is the wisest of us all?" what will he answer? Not the philosopher; that is certain. Philosophers are likely to prefer to be called mathematicians or lexicographers now, and to disown their ancient role as teachers of wisdom. Who then? Priests and rabbis are passé; scientists are known fools, politicians are panderers to vulgar conceptions and demands, psychiatrists of use only when things really break down. But surely the winners are not the poets and novelists either, are they? We would not be so mad as to ask Yeats or Dostoevsky how to order our lives. The right answer, it seems, is the men who know how to read the poets and novelists correctly. (In other words, the literary critics!) In a way, then, we are not really so far from Plato after all. Plato's chief complaint against the Greek habit of looking for wisdom in the poets, remember, was that one had to be wise already in order to recognize wisdom when one saw it. The madness of a poet is divine, for the doors of his perception may be cleansed when ours are blocked; yet turn a fool loose on all that passes for poetry, Plato points out, or ask the poets themselves to isolate the true excellence lurking in the mass of their output, and you will get some very strange observations. Our literary critics, as I say, actually talk very much the same today. But when Plato concludes boldly that poets must therefore put themselves into the hands of the men who have true understanding, our heads reel. Surely life is so complex, we say, and poetic power so rare, that we had better suffer the nonsense and be grateful for whatever really wonderful things may come along. (And after all, we add more than a little sadly, the poets do not have all that much influence in our lives anymore.)

Well now, if we reject the theory of Forms, the World Soul, the assumption of a divine Intelligence or any real beauty and order in the cosmos at all, also the possibility of introducing intelligence systematically into human affairs or ever clarifying once and for all what is involved in the pursuit of happiness, is there anything left of the Platonic theory of the universal pursuit of good? Plato, we can be fairly certain, would have been disgusted with such a question. We would have seemed to him to be throwing out almost all of what he had accomplished. If we but go back to the texts, however, and read again any of Plato's greater works, we are instantly restored in our confidence that there is still a very exciting idea there, a little too brilliantly worked out, but growing from an incredibly deep understanding of life and humanity.

For example, consider Plato's emphasis on the lover's habit of rising above his petty plans and narrow concerns, conceiving instead ambitions to do great and beautiful deeds. What right have we to laugh at lovers, after all? May we not be wasting a fine and valuable capacity by our degrading tendency to trace out the biological and egocentric origins of such visions? Might we not consider whether or not there is some fallacy lurking in our obsession with the natural history of each urge?

And what about Plato's observation that life and the world look fine on fine days and mean only when we feel miserable in some way? Should we not perhaps examine what is involved in our odd assumption that we are being "realistic" only when we are suffering from jaundice? The difficulties we see in Plato's conclusion are real, to be sure. Not only is the theory of Forms unworkable as it stands, but there is also something not quite right about the link which Plato tries to demonstrate between happiness and the correct description of object, events, and experiences. We tend to think of all of the relatively happy people whose judgments are *not* accepted as true—that is, their conclusions would work only for themselves. Such people avoid coming to grief simply by being isolated from more general problems—in extreme cases by being committed to asylums! Plato asks us to look rather for a man who has made assumptions which have not only led him to lasting pleasure in the course of his own long and active life, but assumptions which would also be capable of leading all of us to happiness as well. Such a man, we should have to admit, had achieved happiness and correct judgment of the world at one and the same time. We simply do not believe that such a man can exist, however. Socrates once suggested that no good man could survive with his life if he did not deny himself direct political action; we say, yes, and no happy man could survive with his zest for life if he did not deny himself a clear view of the mortal state, for it is poor, "mean, nasty, brutish, and short." And yet our attitude is just that—an attitude. Not only is it not proved; it should not even be dignified by being called a theory. The problem is full of interest and a long way from being settled. And yet, so far are we from concentrating our energy on this fascinating question, we pour contempt on anybody who does not content himself with spelling out the implications of vulgar opinions.[14]

And there is the extraordinary suggestion that in all that we do we are just trying to convince ourselves that we really exist and that existence is good. If Plato and Aristotle are right, we ought to be able to explain better than we have why so many people who would like nothing better than to be good fellows and well-liked by all, nevertheless end up snarling, torturing, domineering, and destroying. When we are not sure whether or not we really exist, we are driven to making an impression on the world around us, to prove to ourselves that we are really there. But, alas, it is easier to make an impression by turning a knife in someone than by trying to bring happiness into his life. We talk glibly about aggressive instincts and the functions of neurotic patterns of behavior, but perhaps this physician's approach is causing us to miss the more interesting questions which lie beneath these phenomena.

As for the suggestion that what we long for when we pursue our dearest goal is immortality, this may not be so wild as it seems. We may be conscious only of a desire for pleasure, and we certainly do not feel joy in direct proportion to the number of children we find ourselves bringing up or the number of articles which we have manufactured, but consider the horror which we should feel if we were convinced that we *were* our momentary pleasures, that there was no lasting continuity in the core of our persons. And could we really contemplate with equanimity the destruction of the world by hydrogen bombs a minute after we and our last friends had died? Does such a prospect not seem like a personal failure even when we tell ourselves that we would not be around to know anything about it? The surprising discovery of an element of sexual pleasure in our love for our children and in our other actions and achievements can, after all, be explained in any number of ways. Surely the larger, more conscious phenomena and the sexual drives ought each to throw light on the other. Perhaps we really are trying to do with our whole lives what each of our cells does night and day, to circumvent inevitable dissolution by new creation.[15]

What shall we say about Plato's notion of beauty, the idea that beauty is a sudden, unexplained glimpse of what we are really always after in our pursuit of happiness? If Plato is right, it would mean that aesthetic theory as it is often explored today, divorced, that is, from all attempts at constructing a metaphysical system, must be doomed. If Plato is right, we shall never have anything very illuminating to say about beauty until we try to connect it with our understanding of what makes a thing good and what we want when we want to be happy. Are we so satisfied, after all, with our talk about tone or metaphor, our talk about the ordinary uses of words like "dainty" and "dumpy," or our talk of disguised audio-visual sexuality?

And Plato's general tendency to hang on always to the rare, the special, and the valuable in humanity might be just the thing we need to put in opposition to the Freudian approach and so raise the discussion to a more intelligent level. Is it perhaps only our Romantic prejudice—a prejudice in favor of that within our submerged imagination which links us with the vicious tendencies of detestable people, with the uncompromising appetites of our own childhood, and with the thoughtless savagery of nature—which has led us to this startling new picture of ourselves: the depressing conclusion that we are all really after organ pleasure and nothing more, and that our concern for others is but an anxiety to hang on to a "love object"? Why should we not start rather with the observation that we sometimes do in fact manage—as animals never begin to do—to transform our infantile instincts into far more satisfying pursuits, and that the naturalness and excellence of the usual transformations of our energies are more basic facts than are the details of the history of our energies as they were manifested in childhood? The Freudian hypothesis is at least not proved to be true beyond all shadow of doubt.

Since the Platonic theory of love is really a theory about life, it is an idea with almost endless ramifications. Everybody will have his favorites. I could have mentioned the ideal of teaching, the call to base government on a high standard of friendship, the insistence that the way to greater sureness in life lies in the restriction of our greatest tenderness to the finest things only, the warning that the way we have been taught to look at things and to talk about them may be far more crude and misleading than we have suspected, or the ideal of philosophy as nothing less than life itself when it is lived most bravely and most wonderfully.

But the last word, perhaps, should be reserved for that most characteristic of all of Plato's suggestions, the idea which is the link between the paradoxes of Socrates and the metaphysics of Aristotle, that calculation is not the interesting thing about rationality at all, that perception of goals which are genuine goods is what we really value intelligence for. For one thing, this suggestion might offer an interesting solution to the strange mystery of the disappearing *ego*. What would happen if we took more seriously than we usually do the assumption that what embraced and employed the *id* and the *super-ego* in the healthy man was his correct grasp of the world as a fine and happy place?[16] More important, Plato's suggestion might offer a way to rehabilitate the notion of intelligence in an honorific sense in our never ending battle against stupidity, violence, and vulgarity. Intelligence in the Socratic sense would include, notice, even the simple, slow, uneducated people who nevertheless somehow come to understand the important things, and it would exclude the fast, accurate calculators who nevertheless fail in all the major tests in life. Might it not have a salutary effect in some ways if we could just persuade people to withhold the attribution of intelligence from anyone who failed to see what he ought to be doing for his own happiness? You and I, here and now, trying to do the best for ourselves, cannot sit back and hope that we are among those rare people who do the right thing without ever having thought things out; we had better calculate. On the other hand, correct calculation carried out in pursuit of the desires we are now experiencing will be valuable only if we are experiencing desires for the most desirable things. On this interpretation of intelligence and rationality, philosophy, love, and the art of living itself really do become one and the same thing.

Plato's assertion that the pursuit of happiness is the pursuit of one goal, a single good, should not put us off, I think. To be sure, it does seem more likely that good is the same in different experiences only insofar as various experiences are in fact rewarding, that life presents us with many possible goals, indeed that we would be better off to assume that we must divide our energies and look for no single description of success. Once we have said this, however, we have not said very much. Listing and mulling over the plurality of activities which might or might not be worth trying, or throwing up our hands in weariness at the discovery that it is precisely the biggest questions which are the hardest to answer, will certainly not get us very far. We might still listen to Plato's call to wake up —to see that our desires may in fact be ill-conceived, that the exercise of intelligence can change desires, and that there may be experiences which, if we could but taste them, would make our present goals lose all desirability.

# NOTES

## Notes to Chapter 1

1. *De l'Amour* (Paris, 1952). Translated by P. Mairet as *The Many Faces of Love* (London, 1955).
2. *The Four Loves* (New York, 1960). Cf. also Erich Fromm, *The Art of Loving* (New York, 1956).
3. *Platon* (Berlin, 1919), I, 384.
4. *Agapê and Eros,* P. S. Watson, trans. (Philadelphia, 1953).
5. Luke vi, 27, 32, 35.
6. *Op. cit.*, p. 126.
7. "Love not the world. . . . If any man love the world, the love of the Father is not in him" (I John ii, 15). See Nygren, pp. 151–9. There is also the forbidden selectivity in Christ's special love for John (John xxi, 7).
8. *Op cit.*, p. 176.
9. *L'Amour et l'Occident* (Paris, 1939). Translated by Montgomery Belgion as *Love and the Western World* (American paperback edition, New York, 1956). This is a very controversial book, however, and needs to be balanced by other studies on the subject: e.g., A. J. Denomy, "An Inquiry into the Origins of Courtly Love," *Mediaeval Studies* VI (Toronto: Pontifical Institute, 1944). The fullest account is by R. R. Bezzola, *Les origines et la formation de la litterature courtoise en occident* (Paris, 1960), vol. 3 still in preparation. There are indeed those who would throw doubt on the very existence of Courtly Love as a serious ideal, e.g., D. W. Robinson, *Modern Philology* 50 (1953), pp. 146–61.
10. M. C. D'Arcy, *The Mind and the Heart of Love* (London, 1945), (2nd ed., revised; New York, 1956). See also R. A. Marcus, "The Dialectic of Eros in Plato's *Symposium*," *Downside Review* 73 (1955), 219–30, and Marcus and A. H. Armstrong, "Love and the Will" in *Christian Faith and Greek Philosophy* (London, 1960), pp. 78–96.
11. *Op. cit.*, p. 99.
12. *Op. cit.*, p. 84.
13. de Rougemont (*op. cit.*, p. 108) claims this title for the letters of Abélard and Héloïse. I have not slighted Apollonius Rhodius without forethought.
14. I do not believe for a moment C. S. Lewis' account of the rôle which Ovid played in the development of Courtly Love, *The Allegory of Love* (Oxford, 1936).
15. de Rougemont, *op. cit.*, p. 107 n. 55. In older times AMOR was a secret name for ROMA without any sinister connotations; cf. Fedor Schneider, *Rom und Romgedanke in Mittelalter* (Munich, 1926), pp. 57, 246. See also J. H. Oliver, "The Ruling Power," *Transactions of the American Philosophical Society*, N.S. 43, part 4, 883–6.
16. *On Love,* trans. H. B. V. (New York, 1927).
17. *Über die Liebe* (Berlin, 1933), trans. by Tolby Talbot with the title *On Love* (New York, 1957).
18. *A Psychologist Looks at Love* (New York, 1944), now once more available in a volume called *Of Love and Lust* (New York, 1959). Fromm, *op. cit.*, n. 2.
19. I cannot really recommend any; they are mostly rather awful. There is

one, however, which gives scrupulous references and an immense bibliography: V. W. Grant, *The Psychology of Sexual Emotion, The Basis of Selective Attraction* (New York, 1957).

20. A. Ellis, "A Study of Human Love Relationships," *Journal of Genetic Psychology* (1949), pp. 61–71, and G. V. Hamilton, *A Research in Marriage* (New York, 1929), p. 210. I owe both references to Grant, *op. cit.*

21. "The most striking distinction between the erotic life of antiquity and our own no doubt lies in the fact that the ancients laid the stress upon the instinct itself, whereas we emphasize its object. The ancients glorified the instinct and were prepared on its account to honor even an inferior object; while we despise the instinctual activity in itself, and find excuse for it only in the merits of the object." Sigmund Freud, *Three Essays on Sexuality*, trans. James Strachey (London, 1949), n. 28.

22. *Collected Papers*, eds. J. Riviere and J. Strachey (New York, 1959), IV, 81.

23. *Three Essays on the Theory of Sexuality* (4th ed.; Vienna, 1920), p. 35 n. 1. *Cf.* also *Civilization and Its Discontents*, trans. Joan Riviere, (New York, 1958), p. 25.

24. S. Nachmansohn, "Freuds Libidotheorie verglichen mit der Eroslehre Platos," *Internazionale Zeitschrift für ärztliche Psychoanalyse* III (1915), 65–83. There have been other comparisons of this sort also, none very good, e.g., O. Pfister, "Plato, a Forerunner of Psychoanalysis," *International Journal of Psychoanalysis* III (1922), 169–74, H. Kelsen, "Platonic Love," *The American Imago* III (1942), 3–110, and Garfield Tourney, "Empedocles and Freud, Heraclitus and Jung," *Bulletin of the History of Medicine* XXX (1956), 109–23, esp. 114–16; and many people, e.g., Cornford and Dodds, are fond of making the comparison just in passing.

25. *Three Essays*, preface to the 4th ed.

26. Freud has an interesting note on his consistency in this regard throughout the many changes in his analysis of the στάσις: *Beyond the Pleasure Principle*, trans. J. Strachey (New York, 1959), n. at end of Chap. VI, pp. 105–6. He has frequent soul searchings on this point. Cf. *The Ego and the Id*, trans. J. Strachey (New York, 1960), p. 63 ff., and *Collected Papers*, V, 132 (against Jung's monism).

27. Plato *Republic*. See the beginning of Book IX.

28. *The Future of an Illusion*, trans. W. D. Robson-Scott (London, 1928), p. 95.

29. *Collected Papers*, V, 300.

30. *Op. cit.*, V, 297. "Our mind, that precious instrument by whose means we maintain ourselves alive, is no peacefully self-contained unity. It is rather to be compared with a modern State in which a mob, eager for enjoyment and destruction, has to be held down forcibly by a prudent superior class. . . . Consequently, made wise by our sufferings, we have developed organizations in our mind which, in the form of inhibitions, set themselves up against the direct manifestations of the instincts . . ., etc." Cf. also the last chapter of *Civilization and Its Discontents*.

31. Others have attempted to spell out social criticisms latent in Freud's theories, most recently Herbert Marcuse, *Eros and Civilization* (Boston, 1955), N. O. Brown, *Life Against Death* (New York, 1959), and B. Brophy, *Black Ship to Hell* (London, 1962).

32. Cf. Brown, *op. cit.*, p. 49.

## Notes to Chapter 2

1. One of the best books on the *Symposium* even bears this title: Gerhard Krüger, *Einsicht und Leidenschaft, das Wesen des platonischen Denkens* (2nd ed.; Frankfurt, 1948). Of the books heavy with Existentialist and anti-Existentialist language, this one is easily the most rewarding for readers who usually find that world uncongenial.

2. *Phaedrus* 264c.

3. *La théorie platonicienne de l'Amour*[2] (Paris, 1933), p. 9. A similar attitude is taken throughout the very much fuller accounts of these speeches in Robin's edition of Plato's *Symposium* (Paris, 1951), xxxvi–lxxii. So also in Bury's edition (Cambridge, 1909), xxiv–xxxvi and lii–lx.

4. *Paideia* (Berlin, 1944), II, 244 ff. In the translation by Gilbert Highet (Oxford, 1944), II, 174 ff. Krüger, *op. cit.*, also treats the preliminary speeches with great respect.

5. *Symposium* 177a.

6. *Op. cit.*, 177d.

7. Euripides *Hippolytus* 525–34. Euripides gives cautious praise of Eros, however, in fr. 897 and fr. 136 (Nauck). See Athenaeus XIII 561a ff.

8. Sophocles *Antigone* 781–99. Plato may even have had this chorus specifically in mind when he wrote Phaedrus' speech. E.g., *σὺ καὶ δικαίων ἀδίκους φρένας παρασπᾷς ἐπὶ λώβᾳ. / σὺ καὶ τόδε νεῖκος ἀνδρῶν ξύναιμον ἔχεις ταράξας.*

9. E.g., Alcman fr. 36 (Diehl); Sappho frs. 172 and 188 (Page and Lobel); Anacreon frs. 2, 27 (with which cf. Sophocles *Trachiniae* 441–2), and 34 (Diehl); Simonides fr. 24 (Diehl); Archilochus fr. 112 (Diehl). *τύραννος* as a title for Eros actually appears before Plato (*Republic* IX. 573b–d) only in Euripides—*Hippolytus* 538 and fr. 136 (Nauck)—but it may, for all we know, have been quite common.

10. E.g., Alcman fr. 101 (Diehl); Sappho fr. 54 (Lobel and Page); Anacreon fr. 5 (Diehl). Cf. Aristophanes *Birds* 574, 696, 700, 1737. Although some of these may have been fairly earnest hymns (cf. Euripides fr. 136, especially) the general impression left by these and other fragments is of a more lighthearted tradition.

11. E.g., Ibycus fr. 7 (Diehl).

12. Cf. Sappho frs. 159 and 198 (Page and Lobel), Theocritus 13, 2, Apollonius of Rhodes 3, 26, Pausanias IX. 27, 2, also Hesiod *Theogony* 201.

13. E.g., Pindar viii Nem. 5 and fr. 122, 4 (Snell); Bacchylides ep. 9 (8) 73 (Snell); Euripides *Medea* 627.

14. *Amatorius* 20.

15. *Vid. s.v.* Eros in W. H. Roscher (ed.), *Ausführliches Lexikon der griechischen und römischen Mythologie* (Leipzig, 1884), also *s.v.* Eros in Pauly Wissowa. There is evidence also that statues of Eros were common in gymnasia: Athenaeus XIII. 561d, Pausanias VI. 23, 3, and 5.

16. Cf. Krüger, *op. cit.*, p. 21. Consider, above all, the ordinary uses of the verb *ἐρᾶν*. Also, Pausanias (I. 43, 6) says that in a temple to Aphrodite in Megara there were statues of Eros, Himeros (desire), and Pathos (yearning), *εἰ δὴ διάφορά ἐστι κατὰ ταὐτὸ τοῖς ὀνόμασι καὶ τὰ ἔργα σφίσι.* Cf. Hesiod *Theogony* 201. Professor Dover, on the other hand, suggests that while Aphrodite stood for simple, undirected sexual arousal (cf. the inscription on the "Ischia Cup"), *ἐρᾶν* referred to the mysterious desire *for a particular person.* The closest that Plato comes to a discussion of Aphrodite in this sense is the *Philebus.* Cf. 12c and the frequent references to "the goddess" thereafter, also 65c. Philebus (though not his young apologist Protarchus, perhaps) is apparently drawn to hedonism above all because of the

intensity of the pleasure at a sexual climax. (Note how readily Protarchus accepts the suggestion, at 27e, that pleasure is *ἄπειρον*—entirely without demarcation, order, hierarchy, limit, arrangement, all that characterizes thought and understanding. Cf. also 47 and 65e–66a. Perhaps Philebus himself is made to turn over the argument to his "boy" Protarchus precisely for this reason—because his brand of hedonism was too crude to allow any progress in a conversation.)

17. *Works and Days* 11 ff. The procedure is actually quite common in Greek literature. Cf. *Hippolytus* 385.

18. *Symposium* 178a–180b.

19. Hesiod *Theogony* 120 ff.; Parmenides B 13 (Diels-Kranz[8]).

20. These lines haunt modern commentators, too, because they seem so easily detachable. It is only the effect of the lines as they stand, however, which is important to us here.

21. *Symposium* 180c–185c. The known facts about all these speakers have been collected by R. G. Bury, *The Symposium of Plato, Edited With Introduction, Critical Notes and Commentary* (Cambridge, 1909), xxiv–xxxvi.

22. Cf. Xenophon *Symposium* VIII. 32. On the other hand it is possible, of course, that Xenophon wrote his *Symposium* after Plato published his, and that he is actually only alluding to our passage in Plato's version.

23. A temple in honor of Aphrodite Pandemos is described by Pausanias I. 22, 3; one in honor of Aphrodite Urania, I. 14, 6. (Cf. Herodotus I. 105.) In the cults, "Pandemus" had no derogatory force, of course. It means "worshipped by the whole *demus*", or something of the sort.

24. Cf. *Gorgias* 464–5.

25. Cf. Nietzsche, *Homers Wettkampf* and J. Huizenga, *Homo Ludens* (New York, 1950).

26. The *καὶ ἐν Λακεδαίμονι* at 182a7 has caused much trouble. Some, like Winckelmann and Bury, bracket it; others, like Robin and Burnet, transpose it to b 1, so that it is included among the backward states which show no hostility at all. Even those, like Jaeger (*op. cit.*, II. 181–2), who accept the text as it stands, are hard put to explain it.

27. In fact, on one level, Pausanias' speech is a parody of elaborate rhetoric for its own sake. Cf. Léon Robin, *Platon: le Banquet* (Paris, 1951), XLI.

28. 183a–b.

29. E.g., Page and Lobel, frs. 31 and 94.

30. For the lying on the doorsteps, *κοιμήσεις ἐπὶ θύραις*, 183a6, cf. Horace *Odes* III. 10 or Ovid, *Art of Love* II. 238.

31. E.g., Lord Avebury, *The Origin of Civilization and the Primitive Condition of Man* (London, 1911), p. 70; F. Müller-Lyer, *The Evolution of Modern Marriage: A Sociology of Sexual Relations* (New York, 1930), p. 50; W. G. Sumner and A. G. Keller, *The Science of Society* (New Haven, 1929), III. 503, 509; R. Briffault, *The Mother: A Study of the Origins of Sentiments and Institutions* (New York, 1927), II. 150; I. Bloch, *The Sexual Life of Our Time* (London, 1914), pp. 25–6.

32. This is an impression of Anacreon's tone and tastes rather than an interpretation of any of the fragments. One might compare, however, 27 and 79 (Diehl).

33. 185e–188e.

34. 186d7–e1.

35. B 51 (Diels-Kranz).

36. See the pseudo-Hippocratic *On Diet*, Chap. 1. That Plato is ridiculing some scientific theories seems clear. But see Ludwig Edelstein, "The Role of Eryximachus in Plato's *Symposium*," *Transactions of the American Philological Association* 76 (1945), 85–103.

37. So Diels-Kranz[8] in their notes to B 63 and 64. Also Bury, *op. cit.*, xxxiii f.

38. B 20, 4 (Diels-Kranz), although in the plural: *'Ερίδεσσιν*.

39. At 176 and 214b he champions

sobriety, and at 223b, after Alcibiades and then the revelers have banished sobriety altogether, he is the first to slip away from the party—with Phaedrus, his *παιδικά*, in tow.

40. 189c–193d.

41. There is, to be sure, a similar myth in the ninth century *Brihadâranyaka-upanishad* I, 4, 3 (Heinrich Gomperz, quoted in Freud, *Beyond the Pleasure Principle* [New York, 1959], p. 101 n.), and Karl Ziegler traces the myth to Babylonian origins, "Menschen- und Weltenwerden," *Neue Jahrbücher für klassische Altertumswissenschaft* XXXI (1913), 529.

42. *Symposium* 190e 1. Rettig, Bury, and many others condemn the phrase, but on insufficient grounds, I believe. The idea recurs in Plutarch *Amatorius* 24, where it appears to be a proverbial phrase for something that is very easy to do, like our "falling off a log." For the custom in modern times see K. P. Hasse, *Marselius Ficinus über die Liebe oder Platons Gastmahl* (Leipzig, 1914), p. 234 n.

43. 191c1. *τέττιγες* were symbols of Athenian autochthony (Thucydides I. 6).

44. 193b 7. Cf. Robin, *Le Banquet* LXI f.

45. "At no point in one's analytic work does one suffer more from the oppressive feeling that all one's efforts have been in vain and from a suspicion that one is 'talking to the winds' than when one is trying to persuade a female patient to abandon her wish for a penis on the grounds of its being unrealizable, or to convince a male patient that a passive attitude towards another man does not always signify castration and that in many relations in life it is indispensable." Freud, *Collected Papers*, V, 356.

46. 192e 10, *τοῦ ὅλου οὖν τῇ ἐπιθυμίᾳ καὶ διώξει ἔρως ὄνομα.*

47. *Beyond the Pleasure Principle*, pp. 100–2.

48. P. 100. The italics are Freud's.

49. 189c 2, *ἄλλῃ γέ πῃ ἐν νῷ ἔχω λέγειν ἢ ᾗ σύ τε καὶ Παυσανίας εἰπέτην*. Cf. 193d 8.

50. 194e–97e. That Plato should have made Agathon's speech the climax of the series has disturbed many commentators, because they are repelled by Agathon. A. E. Taylor, for instance, suggests that Plato means us to perceive "the barrenness of thought which all this euphuism cannot conceal." (*Plato, The Man and His Work* [London, 1926], p. 222). This is a very common view. Cf. Bury, *op. cit.*, liii f. Krüger suggests ingeniously that Plato had to put Agathon and Socrates side by side in order to bring out *der Streit des Philosophen mit dem Dichter über das Wesen des Eros* (*op. cit.*, p. 81). For an interesting use of Agathon's speech in the Roman period see J. H. Oliver, *loc. cit.*, Chap. 1, n. 5.

51. See the *Thesmophoriazusae* of Aristophanes, e.g., 191–2, also 200–1 and 130 ff.

## Notes to Chapter 3

1. 791.

2. Thus in *Phaedo* 97 f., Socrates interprets Anaxagoras' *νοῦς* as that which would invariably guide everything *ὅπῃ ἂν βέλτιστα ἔχῃ*.

3. *Birth of Tragedy.*

4. "*Wo in der Litteratur diese zwei Begriffe* (i.e., *das Dionysische und das Apollinische*) *überhaupt eine Rolle spielen, hat man es fast immer mit Dilettantismus zu tun.*" H. Pfister, Bursian: *Jahresbericht*, suppl. 229 (1930), 136, quoted with approval by W. K. C. Guthrie, *The Greeks and Their Gods* (London, 1950), p. 145 n. Traces of legends concerning an opposition between Apollo and Dionysus are mostly limited to rivalries over musical invention and oracular seats. See, however,

Aeschylus' *Bassarids* (frs. 23 ff. [Nauck] or 10 ff. [Lloyd-Jones]).

5. Cf. *Phaedrus* 245b, and *Laws* II. 665 to the end of the book. (At 672 Plato shows that he is aware that genuine, destructive irrationality was associated with Dionysus, but in effect absolves the god of responsibility. Cf. *Epistle* VII. 335c where Plato absolves the true Aphrodite of the bestiality associated with her name. Similarly at *Philebus* 12c.) Notice, by the way, that in the *Phaedrus*, Zeus, not Apollo, is the philosopher's special deity.

6. *Republic* III. 399e 1–3: *κρίνοντες τὸν Ἀπόλλω καὶ τὰ τοῦ Ἀπόλλωνος ὄργανα πρὸ Μαρσύου τε καὶ τῶν ἐκείνου ὀργάνων*. At *Laws* VII. 812, however, Plato speaks of a chorus in honor of Dionysus (made up of sixty-year-old men!) learning to play Apollo's instrument, the lyre.

7. See especially Erwin Rhode, *Psyche*, trans. W. B. Hillis (London, 1925), pp. 282–303, Euripides *Bacchae* ed. E. R. Dodds (Oxford, 1944), introduction, and Guthrie, *op. cit.*, pp. 145–82.

8. *De Iside et Osiride* 35.

9. Stories of resistance to Dionysus, such as the one which constitutes the plot of Euripides' play, used to be explained solely as remembrances of the late and troublesome introduction of this cult in Greece. Now even Homer's lack of interest in Dionysus is no longer taken to be very significant, especially since the discovery of Dionysus' name in Minoan Linear B tablets. See Michael Ventriss and John Chadwick, *Documents in Mycenean Greek* (Cambridge, 1956), p. 127, and Mabel Lang, "The Palace of Nestor Excavations of 1960, Part II," *American Journal of Archaeology* (1961), p. 152. (W. F. Otto, on the other hand, in *Dionysus* [Frankfurt, 1933] goes too far in the other direction when he denies that Dionysus is an alien at all.) The main reason for the continued interest in stories of such resistance is now correctly understood to be the psychological truth implied. See the references in Guthrie, *op. cit.*, p. 172 f.

10. E.g., Anacreon fr. 2 (Diehl). Statues exist showing Eros and Dionysus together: Roscher, *op. cit.*, I a 1141–3. Notice that two of the favorite decorations for wine vessels were satyrs in obscene postures and confrontations between an older man and a pretty boy. Groups showing Eros with Dionysiac figures were apparently very common in later antiquity: e.g., 110591 at the Museo Nazionale in Naples (Pompei) and 9645 (Herculaneum).

11. Cf. Heraclitus, fr. 15 (Diels–Kranz).

12. 177 d–e. If Athenaeus is right (V 217a), the occasion of Agathon's victory was the Lenaean, not the Great Dionysia. But this lesser celebration, for all the mystery which surrounds it, was certainly just as closely associated with the god Dionysus as the more famous festival was. See Sir Arthur Pickard-Cambridge, *The Dramatic Festivals of Athens* (London, 1953), pp. 22–40.

13. Cf. Krüger, *op. cit.*, pp. 86–92.

14. 223d. For a superb study of this final scene and what it means, see H. H. Bacon, "Socrates Crowned," *Virginia Quarterly Review* 35 (1959) 415–30.

15. 176a.

16. 176e.

17. 176c.

18. 220a. See 214a.

19. 223d.

20. 212d.

21. 175e.

22. 213e.

23. 215a ff.

24. Socrates speaks of "*silenoi*" and may, of course, refer not to busts of Silenus, the companion of Dionysus (cf. Pindar fr. 57 and Herodotus VII 26, etc.), but, as often, to *silenoi*, a type of satyr of which Marsyas was one, also. The carved *silenoi* of which Alcibiades speaks are mentioned nowhere else, nor have any examples

ever been found by archaeologists. Either they were made of some perishable material like wood, or (more likely) their popularity was brief and local—they were something which Plato remembered seeing in the shops when he was a child, perhaps.

25. 174d.

26. 220f.

27. 218f.

28. Certainly Xenophon assumed Socrates to be very susceptible indeed to sensual beauty: see his *Symposium*, especially *ad fin.* See also Aeschines' *Alcibiades* fr. 4 (Krauss), and cf. G. C. Field, *Plato and His Contemporaries* (London, 1948), pp. 149–50. Plato himself, at *Charmides* 155, has Socrates confess, although in a comically exaggerated tone, that he was inflamed at the accidental glimpse which he got inside the young man's garment. At *Phaedo* 89 Phaedo tells how Socrates used to stroke his hair and press it on his own neck (cf. Xenophon's *Apology* 28). According to a story which may go back to a dialogue by Phaedo himself, Zopyrus the physiognomist read a number of vices in the face of Socrates. When the rest of the company present hooted in derision, Socrates came to his rescue, saying that he was indeed inclined toward these vices, although he had conquered them by reason. See Cicero's *Tusculan Disputations* IV. 37, 80 and the note *ad loc.* in the edition by T. W. Dougan and R. M. Henry (Cambridge, 1934). In any case this fits very well with what Socrates has Diotima tell him on the occasion of one of their meetings in his youth (*Symposium* 211d): that *now* he was all too excited by the company of good looking boys, but *later* he would rise far above that, etc.

29. 177d: *οὔτε γὰρ ἄν που ἐγὼ ἀποφήσαιμι ὃς οὐδέν φημι ἄλλο ἐπίστασθαι ἢ τὰ ἐρωτικά.* So also at *Theages* 128b.

30. 194.

31. 198f.

32. As Alcibiades reminds the company, 216d3.

33. 199–201.

34. 201d–212a. Plato had to choose someone of the right generation, with a reputation for wisdom (presumably: we have no other references to this Diotima), but someone about whom not too much was known. By choosing a woman he avoided the suggestion that the wise one was the youthful Socrates' real "Platonic" lover. By choosing a priestess he could leave the origin of *her* knowledge obscure.

35. 221d.

36. 496d.

37. 405e. (This dialogue is almost certainly not by Plato himself, however.)

38. *Lysis* 220b. On Socrates' habitual insistence that *τὰ καλά* and *τὰ ἀγαθά* should not be taken to be different things see *Lysis* 216d, *Protagoras* 360b, *Hippias Major* 297b, c, *Philebus* 64e, as well as *Symposium* 197c–e (Agathon) and 204e, 206a–b (Diotima).

39. 202a. This is a favorite Socratic distinction. Cf. *Republic* V. 477, *Meno* 99, and the whole of the latter part of the *Theaetetus*.

40. The passages are collected and very sensibly discussed by Léon Robin, *Amour*, pp. 129–68, to which should be added the cautious remarks of Paul Friedländer, *Plato*, trans. Hans Meyerhoff (London, 1958), I, 32–44.

41. *Apology* 24b, *Euthyphro* 3b.

42. 508a.

43. 99c.

44. 462b. The purpose of *Eros*, according to Freud, is "to form living substance into ever greater unities, so that life may be prolonged and brought to higher development." *Collected Papers*, V, 135. Cf. Marcuse, *op. cit.*, p. 211.

45. 32c.

46. 188.

47. 204c.

48. *De Iside* 48.

49. *Enneads* III. 5.

50. See Robin, *Amour*, pp. 194–6, and others whom he cites there.

51. 204d.

52. 205a: *οὐκέτι προσδεῖ ἐρέσθαι ἵνα τί δὲ βούλεται εὐδαίμων εἶναι ὁ βουλόμενος, ἀλλὰ τέλος δοκεῖ ἔχειν ἡ ἀπόκρισις.*

53. 206b.

54. 206d 6. "Ces images se lient à des observations zoologiques concrètes," says Robin *ad loc.*

55. *Essays on Sexuality*, pp. 34–6.

56. E.g., Bronislaw Malinowski, *Sex and Repression in Savage Society* (New York, 1955), p. 183 ff.

57. 207a.

58. *Metaphysics* 1069a21. (Remember Macbeth's anguish at the thought that Banquo's sons, not his, would succeed to the throne of Scotland, III, sc. 1. 60 ff.)

59. 208a 4.

60. 208e.

61. "If one were to yield to a first impression, one would be tempted to say that sublimation is a fate which has been forced upon instincts by culture alone." *Freud, Civilization and Its Discontents* (New York, 1960), p. 43. On the earlier history of the word *sublimieren* see W. A. Kaufmann, *Nietzsche: Philosopher, Psychologist, Antichrist* (Princeton, 1950), pp. 190–1.

62. 209d 1.

63. 209b1, literally not "gifted" but "divine," *θεῖος*. Burnet and others accept Parmentier's conjecture, *ἤθεος*, "of age but not yet married." Bury and Rettig defend the MSS reading.

64. See Freud's papers, "Some Psychological Consequences of the Anatomical Distinctions between the Sexes" and "Female Sexuality," *Collected Papers*, V, 186–97 and 252–72.

65. See, for example, *Group Psychology and the Analysis of the Ego*, trans. James Strachey (New York, 1960), pp. 43–4, and *Collected Papers*, V, 134.

66. *Three Essays*, p. 22.

67. 210a ff.

68. 212b.

69. 220a.

70. *κἂν σμικρὸν ἄνθος ἔχῃ*, 210b9. Cf. 216d8 and 217a2 (Alcibiades).

71. 221c.

72. 175 c–d.

73. 217e–218a.

## Notes to Chapter 4

1. *Lysis* 204b, *Theages* 128b, *Gorgias* 481–2, *Charmides* 154b, *Phaedrus* 227c, 257a. Cf. Xenophon, *Memorabilia* II. 6, 28, *Symposium* VIII. 2.

2. 274–7.

3. 263c–e.

4. 122.

5. *Symposium* 216.

6. 20c. Cf. *Symposium* 218e.

7. 20d.

8. 23a–b.

9. 21c–23e.

10. 38a.

11. 33c.

12. 36d.

13. 29d–e, 36d, 41e.

14. 30d ff.

15. 30c–d, 40d, *Phaedo* 58e, 64a, *Republic* 613a.

16. *Symposium* 204a.

17. There has been a long controversy between Max Pohlenz and Hans von Arnim as to whether or not the subject of the *Lysis* is identical with that of the *Symposium:* Pohlenz, *Aus Platos Werdezeit* (Berlin, 1913); von Arnim, *Platos Jugenddialoge* (Leipzig, 1914); then in the *Göttingische gelehrte Anzeigen* 1916 and 1921, *Rheinisches Museum* 1916, and *Nachrichten . . . zu Göttingen* 1917. Mr. David Robinson of the University of Edinburgh, in sympathy with the suggestions of von Arnim (and Wilamowitz, *op. cit.*, II, 68), has made a careful study of *φίλος*, *φιλία* and *φιλεῖν*, also an analysis of the *Lysis* on the basis of the assumption that the various uses of *τὸ φίλον* are of the utmost importance to the argument of that dialogue. He has convinced me that there are indeed some confusions in the *Lysis* which do not re-

appear when the term is dropped in favor of ἔρως. In particular, so long as Plato asked *τί ἐστιν τὸ φίλον*, he had trouble connecting the phenomenon of mutual friendship with the notion of value seen in something cherished. The important thing, however, is that this is precisely the connection which Plato cares about most when he investigates ἔρως in the *Symposium*. In the *Phaedrus*, indeed, the problems of the *Lysis* come out with great clarity although the verbal tangles of the earlier work are avoided completely. Wilamowitz himself (I, 196), as Pohlenz points out (*Gött. gel. Anz.* 183 [1921] 9), complains that Plato transports the force of ἔρως into his conception of φιλία in the *Lysis*. That, and the fact that in both dialogues Plato deliberately links the experience of human ties with the striving for a good, surely make it impossible for us not to consider the *Lysis* and the *Symposium* together. (Cf. also *Lysis* 218a with *Symposium* 204a, and see Wilamowitz, II, 69, and Pohlenz, *loc. cit.*).

18. 212 ff.

19. 214a. The right answer was that somehow love at its best had to be of the good for the good: see *Laws* VIII. 837 and Aristotle *Nicomachean Ethics* IX. 9.

20. 215c.

21. 215a7, 218a3.

22. 217–18.

23. 219.

24. 221.

25. 223a.

26. 219.

27. 465a, 467a.

28. At 472 ff., and 511a much is made of the way Socrates seems to invert all common sense. At 474a–b, however, Socrates asserts that he is only saying what everybody *really* believes and must believe.

29. 466.

30. 468c.

31. 499e–500a. The language here sounds almost Aristotelian.

32. 463.

33. 517b, 521d–e.

34. 492c.

35. 499.

36. 493.

37. Especially in the myth, 523 ff.

38. *Republic* VI. 485d, IX. 588–9; see also F. M. Cornford, "The Doctrine of Eros in Plato's *Symposium*" in the *Unwritten Philosophy* (Cambridge, 1950), pp. 68–80 and W. K. C. Guthrie, "Plato's View on the Nature of the Soul," *Recherches sur la Tradition Platonicienne* III (Vandoeuvres-Geneva, 1958), pp. 3–22.

39. 96a ff.

40. 96a9–10: *εἰδέναι τὰς αἰτίας ἑκάστου, διὰ τί γίγνεται ἕκαστον καὶ διὰ τί ἀπόλλυται καὶ διὰ τί ἔστι.*

41. 97a7–b1.

42. That is, as Socrates says in the preceding sentence, the two phenomena are not explained by the same cause but by opposite causes.

43. 97b6–7. This whole sentence is in the present tense and must therefore refer to Socrates' present state of mind. But it may either be taken as an entirely ironical reference to a solution which Socrates really believes to be final and right, as R. D. Archer-Hind, *The Phaedo of Plato* (London, 1894), and John Burnet, *Plato's Phaedo* (Oxford, 1911), do, or it may be taken more literally to mean that Socrates, although he does have a unified procedure for explaining things, still feels his method to be a little forced and not ultimately satisfactory. The latter interpretation is closer to what Plato has Socrates say in the next few pages. I am not sure what R. Hackforth, *Plato's Phaedo* (Cambridge, 1955), intended by his translation, "in its place I am gaily substituting a new sort of hotch-potch of my own." "Gaily" is rather daring for *εἰκῇ*, I think.

44. *κατὰ νοῦν ἐμαυτῷ*, 97d7.

45. 97c6–d3. Cf. Friedrich Solmsen, *Plato's Theology* (Ithaca, 1942), p. 100.

46. fr. B12 (Diels–Kranz).

47. 97c–98b.

48. 98c–99b.

49. Cf. 98b2–3.

50. 97d5–98a6, 99b6–8.

51. 98a6–b6.

52. 99c2–6. On the *δέον συνδεῖν* see, or instance, Hackforth *ad loc.*

53. *Physics* II. 8, especially 199b28.

54. 99c6–9.

55. 99c9–d2. The use of the phrase in Menander, fr. 241, suggests that *δεύτερος πλοῦς* means a more laborious way of getting to the same port. Other occurrences (e.g., *Politicus* 300c, *Philebus* 19c, Aristotle's *Politics* 1284b19, *Nicomachean Ethics* 1109a34) sometimes suggest that the original goal is partly forsaken. As a number of commentators have pointed out, our phrase, *τὸν δεύτερον πλοῦν ἐπὶ τὴν τῆς αἰτίας ζήτησιν* seems to rule out the latter implication.

56. 99d4–100a7.

57. 100b1 ff.

58. R. S. Bluck, *Plato's Phaedo* (London, 1955), p. 165, suggests that up until 100a7 Plato attempts to make Socrates talk as he really did, but that from that line on he has him expounding the doctrine of the *χωριστὸν εἶδος*, which is a development of Plato's own. Although it cannot be proved, it is a very attractive idea. Bluck has in any case come closer to a completely satisfactory explanation of this passage than any of the numerous scholars who have tried.

59. 97b7. On Bluck's interpretation, this would refer to the *λόγοι* but not the *ὑποθέσεις*.

60. 100a 5–7.

61. 100b6.

62. 101b7 ff.

63. *ἕως ἐπί τι ἱκανὸν ἔλθοις*, 101e1.

64. 73 ff.

65. 74e–75a.

66. 75a–b.

67. 75b4, a phrase bracketed by many editors, but for insufficient reasons.

68. 105c9 ff.

69. *Metaphysics* A987a29–b14, M1078b9–32.

70. Cf. Bluck, *op. cit.*, p. 199: "The Forms are already sometimes spoken of as though they were severally—to use Aristotelian language—final as well as formal causes." In Chap. VII I have more to say about Aristotle's relation to the doctrine of the *Phaedo*.

71. The St. Andrews Heresy—that is, the assertion by John Burnet and A. E. Taylor in their various works that the Socrates of the *Phaedo* and *Republic* is a completely faithful portrait of the historical Socrates even when Plato has him talking about a realm of separate Forms—has been dealt with most succinctly by W. A. Heidel in his contribution to the discussion in the *Proceedings of the Sixth International Congress of Philosophy* (1927), pp. 559–88. For a list of other places where this theory is attacked, see Bluck, *op. cit.*, p. 5 n. 1. The argument is not simply closed, however. The line between Socrates and Plato is drawn differently with every different interpretation of the one or the other.

## Notes to Chapter 5

1. Letter to Goethe, November 1815.

2. Cf. Bertrand Russell's essay, "Logic and Mysticism."

3. Cf. e.g., *Laws* V. 731c7–d6.

4. E.g., John Mill, *On Liberty*; Isaiah Berlin, *Two Concepts of Liberty*.

5. *Republic* II. 370a7 and frequently thereafter.

6. VI. 493.

7. V. 473c–e.

8. Cf. V. 472d–e.

9. VII. 538c.

10. VII. 538d–e.

11. V. 479–80. See the excellent analysis of this passage by J. Gosling, "Republic Book V: *τὰ πολλὰ καλά*, etc." *Phronesis* V (1960), pp. 116–28.

I do not believe that Gosling is successful in proving that Plato was not ambiguous in these words, but he is certainly successful in finding the main sense of the passage.

12. V. 474b, ff; VI. 485b1, 490b2, 501d2.
13. V. 480a3–4.
14. V. 474c, ff.
15. V. 474d4–475a2.
16. V. 475b8.
17. V. 475c–d.
18. V. 476e7, ff.
19. VI. 501d2.
20. VI. 485d6–8. Cf. F. M. Cornford, *op. cit.*, p. 73.
21. VI. 488.
22. VI. 489.
23. VI. 490–2.
24. VI. 492d5–7.
25. VI. 494–5.
26. VI. 496c–e.
27. VI. 499.
28. VI. 501d2. Cf. *Philebus* 58d.
29. VI. 500b–c.
30. VI. 500e–501b.
31. VI. 505a2–4.
32. 343b–c.
33. E.g., *Gorgias* 499e–500a.
34. *Nicomachean Ethics* III. 1–5.
35. VI. 505b–d.
36. VI. 505d5–9.
37. VI. 505d11–506a2.
38. VI. 506b2, ff.
39. VI. 506e3, ff.
40. VI. 507b, ff. Cf. V. 475e, ff.
41. VI. 508b10.
42. VI. 508d4–5.
43. VI. 508d6–9.
44. VI. 508e–509b.
45. See R. L. Nettleship, *Lectures on the Republic of Plato* (London, 1955), pp. 212–37, for an excellent appreciation of Plato's concern for the Good.
46. VI. 509d4–11e5. The literature on this passage is enormous. The soundest and most intelligent approach is still, I think, Nettleship's, *op. cit.*, pp. 238–58. A large bibliography and a fairly clear account of the traditional differences can be gathered by comparing H. W. B. Joseph, *Knowledge and the Good in Plato's Republic* (Oxford, 1948), pp. 34–40, W. D. Ross, *Plato's Theory of Ideas* (Oxford, 1951), pp. 39–77, John Gould, *The Development of Plato's Ethics* (Cambridge, 1955), pp. 165–81, and J. E. Raven, "Sun, Divided Line, and Cave," *Classical Quarterly* N.S. III (1953), 22–32.
47. There is unfortunately some difficulty in deciding whether we should read *ἄνισα* or *ἴσα* at 509d6. (But see Jowett–Campbell *ad loc.*) It does not make too much difference, however. If we read *ἄνισα* we still have the problem of deciding whether the bottom segment should be the longest or the smallest. If we make the division according to the number of people represented, the bottom part will be the largest; if according to reality or clarity, the bottom part will be the smallest.
48. VI. 511b7.
49. VI. 510b5.
50. VII. 517.
51. VI. 511c6.
52. VI. 510c2–3.
53. VII. 520c3–6, VI 500d7, 505a3, etc.
54. VII. 517d8–e2.
55. IX. 577a.
56. III. 402–3. Cf. IV. 443c4–5, VII. 522a3, ff., IX. 586b–c and 587c9, X. 595–9, 602.
57. III. 401e–2a.
58. E.g., *Metaphysics* A 987b–88a.
59. Aristoxenus, *Elementa Harmonica* II. 30–1.
60. Cf. *Eudemian Ethics* 1218a 15, ff.
61. VII. 523–32.
62. VII. 514–20.
63. VII. 520c.
64. VII. 518b–19a.

## NOTES TO CHAPTER 6

1. *Republic* IX *ad fin.*
2. *Parmenides* 130b–d.
3. *Timaeus, passim.*
4. *Republic* X.
5. 249a.
6. 80–84.
7. *Gorgias* 469, ff., *Laws* IX. 859e–60a. Cf. *Crito* 49a4–e1 and *Republic* I. 335b2–e10.
8. *Gorgias* 521d.
9. *Epistle* VII. 324d–5c.
10. E.g., *Laws* V. 731c7–d6.
11. *Phaedo* 78c–9a, *Symposium* 207d–8b, *Republic* VI. 485a–b, *Theaetetus, passim*, *Sophist* 249b, *Timaeus* 52a, 27d–9d. The *Phaedrus* and *Laws* X. will be discussed later.
12. See the eschatological myths of the *Gorgias*, the *Phaedo* and the *Republic*. Cf. *Republic* I. 353d–e, IV. 444d–e, *Sophist* 227d ff., *Timaeus* 42b–d, *Laws* X. 904.
13. 248e–9a.
14. Cf. *Cratylus* 397d ff., *Phaedo* 98b, ff., *Republic* I. 353d. The more explicit theories in the *Phaedrus*, *Timaeus*, and *Laws* will be examined shortly.
15. *Phaedo* 66c, 67a, 79ff., 83, 94e, *Republic* X. 611, *Cratylus* 403e, *Politicus* 272e, *Timaeus* 42a–b, 86, 88a–b.
16. *Republic* IV. and IX.
17. Cf. *Republic* VI. 485 and X. 611.
18. *Timaeus* 42a7, 69d ff., 89e, and cf. 77c.
19. Cf. *Republic* IV. 436, and *Laws* IX. 863b (where it is casually left open as to whether the *θυμός* is a *πάθος* or a *μέρος* of the *ψυχή*).
20. *Republic* IX. 571, ff.
21. "Narcissism," *Collected Papers* IV, sec. I, and *Beyond the Pleasure Principle*, p. 91.
22. *The Ego and the Id*, p. 45 n. 1.
23. *New Introductory Lectures on Psychoanalysis*, trans. W. J. H. Sprott (London, 1933), pp. 100–1. Cf. "Analysis Terminable and Interminable", *Collected Papers* V, especially pp. 326 and 337.
24. E.g., Paul Friedländer, *Platon* (Berlin and Leipzig, 1928–30), I, 202 and II, 485 ff, Also Zeller, *Die Philosophie der Griechen* (Leipzig, 1889), II, a 4, pp. 609 ff.
25. 230a.
26. 230d.
27. 230e–234c. On the traditional arguments for and against attributing this speech to Lysias himself, see the references in R. Hackforth, *Plato's Phaedrus* (Cambridge, 1952), pp. 16–18. My own confidence that the speech is Plato's invention is based mainly on its too perfect appropriateness to the discussion.
28. 232a.
29. 233d.
30. 237b–c.
31. 237c–d.
32. *παῖς, μᾶλλον δὲ μειρακίσκος, μάλα καλός*, 237b2.
33. *οὐδενὸς ἧττον ἐρῶν*, 237b4.
34. 237d3.
35. 237d4–5.
36. 237d8.
37. 237d8–9. For this nontechnical use of *δόξα*, see Hackforth's excellent remarks, *op. cit.*, p. 42.
38. 238a6–7.
39. 238b–c.
40. *θεῖον πάθος πεπονθέναι*, 238c6.
41. 238d1.
42. Cf. Robin's *Budé* edition (Paris, 1933), LXXI.
43. 238e3–4.
44. 239c4–5.
45. 238e4, cf. 231d2 and 236b1.
46. *μανία*, 241a4.
47. 240b–d.
48. 241a3.
49. 241c8.
50. 241e.
51. 242b–c.
52. *μανικόν γέ τι καὶ ἡ ψυχή*, 242c7.
53. 243c.

54. θεὸς ἤ τι θεῖον, 242e2. The qualification is no doubt added to take care of readers who remember the *Symposium.*

55. 242c6, d2.

56. 242d4.

57. 243a3.

58. 241a. Hackforth, *op. cit.*, pp. 47–8, misses the point.

59. W. H. Thompson, *The Phaedrus of Plato* (London, 1868), p. 150, finds remarkable parallels between our speech and that which Xenophon gives Socrates in his *Symposium*, viii.

60. This is all clearly implied in Socrates' definition of the wrong kind of love, 237d–238c.

61. 243e–245c. Socrates here uses σωφρονεῖν for uninspired plodding (244a5, d5, 245a8, b4), but this will not stop him from using the same word for a positive and inspired thing when he is being less shockingly paradoxical. Cf. 247d 6. See also the σωφροσύνη θνητή at 256e5. It has often been noted that Plato's praise of inspired poetry is here carefully limited to the kind of poetry approved of in the *Republic* (607a), and in a few moments (248d) he will take his usual caustic tone in talking about poetry as imitation. The other kinds of μανία mentioned here are equally low in Plato's final catalogue.

62. 245c, ff.

63. 245c8.

64. 246a6–7.

65. 246b7. That both the horses and the charioteer are winged is proved by 251b7. This description, like that of the Sun in the *Republic*, is said to be not οἷον μέν ἐστι (a4) but ᾧ δὲ ἔοικεν (a5). The image was a natural one for a Greek. Cf. Anacreon fr. 4 (Diehl). Also, Plato was no doubt drawn to this image of the *psyche* by the fact that Eros, too, was traditionally depicted as a winged boy, from the sixth or fifth centuries on. See Adolf Greifenhagen, *Griechische Eroten* (Berlin, 1957).

66. 246b6–7.

67. 247a7. Cf. 253b7. The resemblance of this love without φθόνος to the Christian ideal will be examined later.

68. 247c3.

69. 247d 6–7.

70. 248a 6–7.

71. 248b2, κακίᾳ ἡνιόχων.

72. 248d.

73. 249b6–c1, accepting Badham's ἰόντ' for ἰόν.

74. 249a 1–2. Hackforth, note *ad loc.*, thinks that only one person is being described, but the most obvious way of taking ἀδόλως above is to assume a contrast. W. J. Verdenius agrees with Hackforth and quotes some parallels for this use of ἤ, "Notes on Plato's *Phaedrus*," *Mnemosyne* (1955), p. 279. It is the force of ἀδόλως, however, which makes his interpretation improbable.

75. 249 d–e.

76. 250 b–d.

77. 250d1.

78. 250c4–5.

79. Cf. Robin, *Amour*, pp. 220 ff.

80. 250e. Cf. *Laws* VIII. 837c, 841 d–e.

81. 256e5.

82. ἐφαπτόμενοι αὐτοῦ τῇ μνήμῃ ἐνθουσιῶντες ἐξ ἐκείνου, 253a2–3.

83. 253a6.

84. 253c–256e.

85. 254 b 1.

86. 255b1–2. This, of course, is the right answer to the puzzle of the *Lysis*.

87. 254. Hackforth, *op. cit.*, pp. 107–8, points out quite rightly that the healthy respect shown here for the incorrigible violence of the lowest part of the *psyche* has no real parallel in the *Republic*.

88. 255b–e.

89. 256c, ff.

90. Cf. note 74 above, on 249a1–2. In any case, Aristotle agreed with the form of the doctrine given in the *Phaedrus: Nicomachean Ethics* VII–IX.

91. I owe this last suggestion to Mr. Ian Kidd of St. Andrews. Cf. also J. Stannard, "Socratic Eros and Platonic Dialectic," *Phronesis* IV (1959), 120–

34. It has always seemed to me that readers of the *Republic* miss an important point when they complain about Glaucon and Adeimantus being mere "yes men." The encounter between Socrates and Thrasymachus may be more dramatic and believable than that between Socrates and the two brothers, but see how much more is accomplished with the two devoted disciples than with the bitter opponent! The founder of the Academy would probably have had much more inclination toward such careful explorations carried out among friends than toward the stormier cross-examinations which must often have occurred in Socrates' market place existence.

## Notes to Chapter 7

1. *Physics* I. 9.

2. 192a16–17. This is the orthodox interpretation of this line, guaranteed, it seems to me, by the clause, *οὔτε αὐτὸ αὑτοῦ οἷον τε ἐφίεσθαι τὸ εἶδος διὰ τὸ μὴ εἶναι ἐνδεές* in the next sentence. Cf. W. D. Ross' edition (Oxford, 1936), *ad loc.*

3. 50c–51a.

4. 192a15.

5. 192a18.

6. 192a19–20.

7. 192a21.

8. 192a22–5.

9. The most important passages for the theory of *στέρησις* are *Physics* I (especially Chaps. 7–9) and *De Generatione et Corruptione* I. Chap. 3. See also *Metaphysics Z* Chap. 7, *Γ* 1004a13–16, *Δ* Chap. 22, *Θ* Chap. 1, and *Categories* 12a26–13a37. Harold Cherniss, *Aristotle's Criticism of Plato and the Academy* (Baltimore, 1944), I, 90, has a similar interpretation.

10. *Metaphysics Θ* Chap. 9 (which does *not* contain a fallacy, as Bonitz and others have thought), and *De Generatione Animalium* II. 732a4–6. Cf. Cherniss, *op. cit.*, pp. 96–7.

11. *Physics* I. 190b35. That there is no opposite to reality (*οὐσία*): *Categories* 3b24–7, *Physics* V. 225b10–11.

12. Cherniss, *op. cit.*, I, 84–97 finds many difficulties in Aristotle's description of Plato's system here, but he defends Plato, illegitimately as it seems to me, by quoting the *Phaedo* in reply to a criticism of the *Timaeus* (p. 91). Also, the formlessness of the *χώρα* (*Timaeus* 50–1) does not prevent it from being uncooperative in the realization of formal perfection. For other similarities between the *Phaedo* and *Physics* I. 9 see Friedrich Solmsen, *Aristotle's System of the Physical World: A Comparison with His Predecessors* (Ithaca, 1960), pp. 83 ff., and the notes to Cherniss there. I am delighted to be able to refer the reader to this new study of the many passages which bear on the relation between Aristotle's system and his teacher's. Solmsen's investigation should be taken as a corrective to mine, as it explores the problem with far greater fullness than I can allow myself here, and with more learning than I would be capable of.

13. *Metaphysics Z* 1041a25–32, H 1044a32–b3, *Physics* II. 198a22–35, *De Generatione et Corruptione* II. 335b4–7, *De Partibus Animalium* I. 641a25–32, *De Generatione Animalium* I. 715a1–10.

14. *Physics* II. Chap. 1. That in art the Forms are in the psyches of individual men: *Metaphysics Z* 1032b1, *De Generatione Animalium* I. 730b16. That they are the first causes of men's activities: *Politics* III. 1282b15–16. That men cannot invent these Forms: *Metaphysics Z* Chap. 8. That art imitates nature: *Protrepticus* fr. 13 (Ross), *Meteorologica* IV. 381b6–7, *Politics* VII. 1337a2, *Physics* II. Chap. 8.

15. *Physics* I. 9. Cf. the evidence cited in Chapter VI in favor of the assumption that Plato wanted to exclude Forms of foul or trivial things.

On the exclusion of purely negative ideas from the Forms, see the fragments of *περὶ ἰδεῶν*. I do not see how *Republic* V. 476d can be interpreted to mean that Plato accepted Forms of evil things. It is true, on the other hand, that Aristotle's references to an "unwritten doctrine" in Plato confuse this picture somewhat.

16. *Metaphysics Λ* 1072b3.

17. *Timaeus* 29–30. Cf. *Republic* VI. 500e–501b where the guardians, also called *δημιουργοί*, are described in precisely similar terms.

18. 48a3.

19. 53b.

20. 57d–58c.

21. 52–3.

22. A fair idea of the problems involved, the theories possible, and a bibliography can be gathered by comparing Jaeger, *Paideia* II, 414–16, and Cherniss, *op. cit.*, I, 603–10. Jaeger emphasizes the necessity for believing that the various aspects of divinity, intelligence, and goodness must be connected on some level; Cherniss emphasizes the difficulties in any attempt to spell this out.

23. 64–8.

24. 79.

25. 105–7. Cf. Cherniss, *op. cit.*, pp. 508–9.

26. Especially close to Plato's theory is Alcmaeon A 12 (Diels–Kranz). Cf. Aristotle, *De Anima* I Chap. 2, where the general idea is attributed to a large number of earlier physicists. Cherniss, *op. cit.*, I, 433–5, collects passages in Plato's own earlier dialogues that at least show that the idea was always one of the more obvious possibilities in Plato's mind.

27. There is, as has often been recognized, a kinship between the proof of the *Phaedrus* and the final proof in the *Phaedo*, inasmuch as both hinge on the idea that psyche cannot violate its essential nature. But at least the proof in the *Phaedrus*, by adding a description of what this essential nature is, is not circular in the same way that the earlier proof was. Cf. Hackforth, *op. cit.*, p. 68, Cherniss, *op. cit.*, I, 436–7. To be sure, neither the *Timaeus* nor the *Laws* uses the identification of psyche with self-motion to prove its immortality, as the *Phaedrus* does, but cf. Cherniss, *op. cit.*, pp. 429–31 n. 365.

28. Aristoxenus, *Elementa Harmonica* II. 30–1, and Simplicius, *In Phys.* 453, 25–455, 14. The nature of this lecture and Plato's so-called "unwritten doctrines" (*Physics* IV. 209b14–15, which Simplicius, *ad loc.*, identifies as the lecture on the Good) is hotly contested now. I have nothing new to add to the controversy. Cf. also *Metaphysics A* 987b14–988a15, N 1091a29–b15, and the *Eudemian Ethics* 1218a. The literature on the subject is large and growing. For the extreme position in the direction of scepticism, see Cherniss, *The Riddle of the Early Academy* (Baltimore, 1945). For a more matter-of-fact interpretation see Ross, *Plato's Theory of Ideas* (Oxford, 1951).

29. See the passages quoted above in the notes to Chap. III, numbers 42–6.

30. 23–7 and 64–6.

31. 53b. Cf. 87c–d.

32. We might also think of *Phaedo* 74–5 and many passages in *Republic* V–VII.

33. 46d–e, 89a. The first of these passages distinguishes emphatically between Intelligence as a cause and induced motion as a secondary cause. Cherniss, *Aristotle's Criticism of Plato and the Academy* I, 428–9, discusses other passages (missing these two) where the identification of *ψυχή* as self-generating motion may be implied. Cherniss rightly emphasizes Plato's reluctance to spell out this definition as clearly as he did in the *Phaedrus* and *Laws* X.

34. 34a, 43.

35. This is, of course, based on an error. The truth is that the friction caused by whatever contains the whirlpool causes the fluid to move more slowly on the outside than it does at the center. If the *δίνη* had no

walls, there would be no centripetal tendency.

36. 50–1.

37. 52–3 and 57–8 respectively.

38. 34b.

39. Cf. Cherniss, *Aristotle's Criticism of Plato* I, 429 n. 364.

40. 57d–58c.

41. See note 33, above. Plato's failure to be more straightforward on the point proves, if any proof were necessary, that he is well aware of the inconsistency.

42. 46e1.

43. See Cherniss, *Aristotle's Criticism of Plato* I, 421 ff.

44. Cherniss (444) cannot be right in saying that the inconsistency is entirely explained by the Academy's suggestion. The form of the *narrative* is not what forced Plato to assume that without Intelligence the world would reveal restless rectilinear motion. Nor was it the form of the *narrative* which forced Plato to assume that psyche was needed to guarantee all motion, rectilinear as well as circular.

45. 89e.

46. 69c–d. On the rectilinear character of these mortal sources of energy, see Aristotle, *De Anima* I, 407a6.

47. An extraordinary number of theories have been offered as to the nature of Plato's theory of evil. References to earlier writings may be found in the commentary by Karl Steinhardt in Müller's translation, *Platon's sämmtliche Werke* (Leipzig, 1850–66) VII (1859), 315. See also Zeller, *Die Philosophie der Griechen* (Leipzig, 1922), IIa$^5$, p. 769 n. 5. The major lines of interpretation were already clear in Plutarch's *De animae procreatione in Timaeo*. References to more recent works may be found in Cherniss, "The Sources of Evil According to Plato," *Proceedings of the American Philosophical Society* XCVIII (1954), 23–30.

48. *Theaetetus* 176.

49. *Republic* 379c, *Politicus* 273c–d, *Timaeus* 29e–30a.

50. See Cornford's excellent remarks, *Plato's Cosmology* (London, 1937), pp. 43–9.

51. 893b–4c.

52. There is some overlapping, and Plato will use one of these distinctions to make a subdivision beneath another; but the list as a whole obviously cannot have been arrived at by an orderly *diaeresis*. See the brave attempt by Jula Kerschensteiner, *Platon und der Orient* (Stuttgart, 1945), pp. 70, 72. See also M. Guéroult, "Le X$^e$ livre de Lois et la dernière forme de la physique platonicienne" in *Revue des études grecques* XXXVII (1924), 27–78, especially p. 35.

53. These two motions are elaborately described. We shall examine these descriptions later.

54. In terms of the *Timaeus*, change of *ἕξις* presumably means the breakup of the particles into their triangles, as opposed to mere local shift by the various regular solids. But see the next note.

55. The description of genesis here is very complex; it is not, as we might have expected, simply the appearance of a new *ἕξις* every time an old one is disturbed.

56. A distinction between *ἀλλοίωσις* and *φορά* appears at *Theaetetus* 181b–e and *Parmenides* 138b–d. But *ἀλλοίωσις* must either be "motion in one place," or it is really locomotion of parts, and so not a true opposite of *φορά*. As we shall see, Plato had good reason to reserve "motion in one place" for something quite different from *ἀλλοίωσις*.

57. 894d–6c.

58. *Timaeus* 79–80.

59. 891c.

60. 896d.

61. 896e.

62. The only similar reference to evil soul outside the *Laws* (except for disparaging remarks about the lower parts of the human *psyche*, of course) is *Epinomis* 988e, which is a brief, uninformative summary of the argument in the *Laws*. Attempts to identify the evil soul with the Other in the

world *psyche* of the *Timaeus* have been unconvincing. See Gregory Vlastos, "The Disorderly Motion in the *Timaeus*," *Classical Quarterly* XXXIII (1939), 78. My own interpretation of evil *psyche* was first offered and discussed in 1955, at a meeting of the Society for Ancient Greek Philosophy, in Chicago. I especially profited from the criticisms of Philip Merlan and G. M. A. Grube.

63. Cf. E. B. England, *The Laws of Plato* (Manchester, 1921), II, 467: " 'soul,' 'psychic force,' not *a* soul." And see *Laws* 897b: *γένη*. Cf. also Perceival Frutiger, *Les Mythes de Platon* (Paris, 1930), pp. 130–4, on *ψυχὴ πᾶσα* at *Phaedrus* 245c.

64. 897a. Perhaps the production of these latter qualities should be connected with the description of the genesis and destruction which involve changes in *ἕξις*. Otherwise generation and destruction are the only motions in the original list of ten not mentioned subsequently.

65. 893c–e.

66. 897b, ff.

67. 897e–8e.

68. Various editors have added *καθ'* or *ἀνά*.

69. So far as I know, no one has seen this quite clearly, although one of the standard explanations does begin with the assumption that *ψυχὴ κακή* is somehow irrational motion, not an evil intelligence. Cf. Wilamowitz, *op. cit.*, and Kerschensteiner, *op. cit.* Also Franz Susemihl, *Die genetische Entwicklung der platonischen Philosophie* (Leipzig, 1860), II, 2, 601. Also, perhaps, August Boeckh, quoted in Steinhardt, *loc. cit.*

70. 893 d–e.

71. That this is a subdivision of rectilinear motion is proved by the fact that any other interpretation yields eleven motions, whereas the Athenian specifically asserts that there are only ten. See Solmsen, *Aristotle's System*, p. 177, where the fate of this and other distinctions in *Laws* X. are traced out in Aristotle's *Physics*.

72. 903–4.

73. With the terms *οἰκίζεσθαι*, etc., at *Laws* 904b, cf. *Timaeus* 69d and 89e.

74. *Timaeus* 70b, 89e. Cf. *Laws* 904b–c: "The causes of genesis (*αἰτίαι γενέσεως*) of any particular kind he left to the wills (*ταῖς βουλήσεσιν*) of each of us." I.e., each of us is responsible for becoming intelligent or the opposite in our *ἦθος* as a whole.

75. 906c.

76. 906a.

77. See especially *De caelo* I–II.

78. Already in the *Republic* (IV. 436) and *Parmenides* (138b–d) some paradoxical aspects of rotation were mentioned. J. B. Skemp, *The Theory of Motion in Plato's Later Dialogues* (Cambridge, 1942), pp. 36–51, 82 ff., traces the pre-Platonic history of ideas linking soul, motion, and circularity, but the evidence is not so clear as one could wish. In the *Politicus* the *σωματοειδές* is said to have a natural tendency to move in a direction opposite to that which divinity gives it, but this opposite tendency is circular, too. This would seem to me to indicate that Plato did not make up his mind in favor of the scheme in the *Laws* until very late.

79. 34a–b, 37c–8c.

80. Cf. Solmsen, *Plato's Theology*, p. 86.

81. See A. D. Steele, "Über die Rolle von Zirkel und Lineal in der griechischen Mathematik," *Quellen und Studien zur Geschichte der Mathematik*, Abteilung 13 (Studien). Band 3, Heft 3 (1936), 287–369. Cf. also *De caelo* 268b.

82. *Timaeus* 44. See also 80a–b, where a detailed and technical explanation of harmonic consonance is given, which works *only* on the assumption that the mind is in circular motions. Cf. *De anima* 407a where Aristotle complains that Plato ought not to have had such a spacial notion of *psyche*.

## Notes to Chapter 8

1. *Republic* I. 351–2, and IX.

2. *Gorgias* 507e–8a.

3. Cf. *Gorgias* 470–1, 477, *Republic* I. 335, 351–2, X. 609.

4. *τίς γὰρ ἐσθλὸς οὐχ αὑτῷ φίλος;* says Oedipus, *Oedipus Coloneus* 309. And see the other passages quoted by Jebb, *ad loc.* At *Laws* V. 731d–e Plato has some very critical words for "self-love" in its ordinary sense, however.

5. *Epistle* VII should be read closely in this regard. True and false notions of friendship are mentioned in almost every paragraph. See also *Epistle* VI.

6. See especially *Nicomachean Ethics* IX. 1164a35–b6 for moving words on what one owes one's master in philosophy. See also the words with which Aristotle opens a criticism of Plato's Idea of the Good, Book I, Chap. 6.

7. Olympiodorus, *In Platonis Gorgiam* 41, 3. Cf. the *Vita Marciana* 26.

8. That it is Eudemus himself was proposed by Wilamowitz, *Aristoteles und Athen* II. 413 ff. But Jaeger, "Aristotle's Verses in Praise of Plato," *Classical Quarterly* XXI (1927), 13–7, objects that this would have to be *εἰς Εὔδημον* not *πρὸς Εὔδημον*, and proposes that an unknown student of the Academy is meant. Cf. his *Aristotle*, trans. Richard Robinson (Oxford, 1934), p. 107. Ingemar Düring, *Aristotle in the Ancient Biographical Tradition* (Göteborg, 1957), p. 317, suggests that Aristotle is referring to himself in the third person, as in some Hellenistic poems. The reference, he thinks, is to Aristotle's return to Athens in 334. The Eudemus to whom the elegiacs are addressed might be either the Cyprian, who was killed in Dion's expedition against Syracuse in 354, or the Rhodian, a much younger man, a student of Aristotle himself.

9. In interpreting the double genitive, Jaeger (*Classical Quarterly* XXI, 14) adduces as a parallel the altar to Friendship set up by the Roman Senate with statues of Tiberius and Sejanus on either side (Tacitus, *Annals* IV. 74). Wilamowitz (*loc. cit.*) would make the dedication of the altar to Plato *because of* holy Friendship, but this strains the word order. Wilamowitz is better (as Mr. David Robinson points out to me) in *Platon*² (1920), I, 708 n. 1. See also Otto Schroeder, "Aristoteles als Dichter," *Neue Jarbücher für Wissenschaft* N.S. I (1925), 31–5, esp. p. 32.

10. Cf. *Republic* I. 354a and *Laws* II. 660e.

11. VII. Chaps. 1–2. On the identification of the *Eudemian Ethics* as an earlier but authentic version of the *Nicomachean Ethics* see Jaeger, *Aristotle*, pp. 228–58. For an argument against this identification see G. E. L. Owen, "Logic and Metaphysics in Some Earlier Works of Aristotle," *Aristotle and Plato in the Mid-Fourth Century* (Göteborg, 1960), p. 165 n. 3.

12. E.g., 1234b24–5. For the insistence that only good men can be friends, see *Laws* VIII. 837a ff., as well as *Phaedrus* 255b. The phrase *πρώτη φιλία* at 1236b28 is, of course, *not* the same as *πρῶτον φίλον* at *Lysis* 219c. The idea of a *πρῶτον φίλον* is, as we shall see, rather more prominent in Aristotle's metaphysics than it is in his ethics. The notion is latent, however, in his conception of *εὐδαιμονία* as a single *τέλος* for man.

13. VIII and IX. Mr. Robinson has convinced me that the philosophical interest of these books is considerably greater than is usually suspected. I regret that I must dismiss *φιλία* so briefly in this study of Love.

14. *Eudemian Ethics* VII. Chap. 12, *Nicomachean Ethics* IX. Chaps. 4–9.

15. Cf. *Metaphysics Λ* Chap. 9.

16. With *Nicomachean Ethics* IX. 1170a4 cf. *Phaedrus* 255b–e.

17. I. 636. But see *Phaedrus* 250e, which *may* hint at the same judgment.

18. See especially I 641a–b and cf. Jaeger, *Paideia* III, 222–3.

19. See Plutarch, *Quaestiones conviviales*, introductory remarks, and Athenaeus V. 186b. Cf. J. Martin, *Symposion: Die Geschichte einer literarischen Form* (Paderborn, 1931), and Jaeger, *Paideia*, II, 177. The symposium was a convention in education of a sort long before Plato, of course: cf. *Odyssey* I. 338, Xenophanes fr. 1 (Diehl) and Theognis 239.

20. *Nicomachean Ethics* VIII. 1158a12 and IX. 1171a11. (Presumably utilitarian friendship is the defect if virtuous friendship is a *μεσότης*.) At *Eudemian Ethics* 1235b20–2 *ἔρως* is identified as desire (*ἐπιθυμία*) for pleasure as opposed to will for good. Similarly also at 1245a24. Cf. *Nicomachean Ethics* VII, Chap. 3. Eros, according to Aristotle, is an excess peculiar to hot-headed youth! Cf. also *Rhetoric* I. 1370b14 ff., and *Laws* VIII. 837a: *τῶν λεγομένων ἐρώτων*. The ideal of *φιλία*, once so closely tied to *ἔρως*, has from Aristotle onward a separate history of its own—especially among those who were influenced by the Stoics. Cf. e.g., Cicero's *De amicitia*, Ailred of Rievaulx' *De spiritali amicitia*. For awhile, to be sure, the Stoics themselves spoke of *ἔρως* in a vaguely Socratic sense, e.g., III. 650 ff., and 716 ff. (von Arnim), but their tendency was to make it into *amicitia*, a sober, political bond, and to reconcile it with conjugal love (see however I. 248 [von Arnim]). The cosmic version of Platonic *ἔρως* was much more important to the Stoics.

21. Athenaeus V. 186b.

22. *Politics* II. 1262b15. As we have noticed before, by the time Plato came to write the *Phaedrus* he, too, had decided that a good man need not leave behind the personal love which led him to the philosophical vision.

23. Cf., for example, Aristotle's eulogy of Eudoxus, *Nicomachean Ethics* X. 1172b15–8.

24. *Metaphysics Λ* Chap. 7. For other passages in Aristotle (and Theophrastus) where this identification of the motive power in nature with the Good is alluded to, see Ross, *Aristotle's Metaphysics* (Oxford, 1924), II, 374–5. *Metaphysics* A Chap. 4 is also of special interest because Aristotle there recognizes the continuity between his analysis and that implied in the earliest thinkers—he quotes, indeed, the very passages from Hesiod and Parmenides which were quoted in the first speeches of the *Symposium*. With *Λ* Chap. 7 we must also compare *De motu animalium* Chap. 6, although that discussion is much more modest and limited.

25. See above all *Metaphysics* A 986a23 and Ross' note *ad loc.*

26. At this point Aristotle distinguishes between simplicity and unity (*τὸ ἕν*). Could this be an attempt to clarify a difference between his Good and Plato's *ἕν*? For a different suggestion see Alexander *ad loc.*

27. Accepting Christ's *<καὶ> τινός*.

28. The MSS have *κινουμένῳ δὲ τἆλλα κινεῖ*, which Jaeger prints in his recent Oxford text, explaining "sc. *τῷ οὐρανῷ*." Ross, on the other hand, says that this is "hardly possible Greek," and conjectures *κινούμενα*, explaining: " 'while all other things move by being moved,' i.e. simply transmit the motion impressed on them."

29. 1072a21 ff. In addition to *Metaphysics Λ* see especially *Physics* V–VIII.

30. 1071b37.

31. 1071b21.

32. 1072b3.

33. 1073a4.

34. 1073a5.

35. 1073a6.

36. 1073a11.

37. 1072b25.

38. 1072b26.

39. 1072b18 ff.

40. 1074b33.

41. See the whole of Chap. 9 in *Metaphysics Λ*.

42. *De anima* I. Chap. 3, II. Chap. 4 and *De motu animalium* Chap. 6 (also *Physics* VIII. Chap. 2–6).

43. *Metaphysics Λ*. 1075a16–17.

44. Jaeger, *Aristoteles* (Berlin, 1923), originally proposed that Aristotle had developed away from the theory of the Unmoved Mover, resembling as it does Plato's form of the Good, toward a more mechanical theory. Von Arnim, however, in *Die Enstehung der Gotteslehre des Aristoteles* (Vienna, 1931), showed that, on the contrary, the Unmoved Mover was a later development and did not appear in Aristotle's earlier writing. Ross, *Aristotle's Physics* (Oxford, 1936), pp. 94–102, and Guthrie, "The Development of Aristotle's Theology," *Classical Quarterly* XXVII (1933), pp. 162–71, XXVIII (1934), pp. 90–8, and in his Loeb edition of *De caelo* (London, 1939), XXIII–XXXVI, modified von Arnim's theory in the direction of a greater continuity in Aristotle's ideas throughout the development. My own account goes even further in the same direction.

45. See the fragments, edited by Ross, pp. 90–1. They are preserved especially in Cicero's *De natura deorum* (II. 15, 42; 16, 44).

46. The three-fold classification appears at *De natura deorum* II. 16, 44. See, however, *Metaphysics Λ* 1071b35–6, where there seems to be a dichotomy between motion by nature on the one hand and motion "by violence or intelligence or something else" on the other. Alexander and Themistius do not agree on the interpretation of ἤ . . . ἤ.

47. II. Chap. 1.

48. So Ross, *Physics* 96–8.

49. *De anima* I. 411a7, ff.

50. *De caelo* I. Chaps. 2–3, II. Chaps. 1–2 and 12.

51. See *Laws* X. 899 and the *Epnomis*.

52. *De caelo*, too, may be closer to *Laws* X. than is usually supposed. In the latter work it is decided that "motion in one place" rules the heavens. But how can this be a description of the motion of a given star? Is it a description of the *path* taken by that star—or of the circle in which the star is embedded?

53. As von Arnim showed, *De caelo* must have been composed before the acceptance of this idea. (See especially I. 279a30–b4, II. 284a15–16, and 286a10.) On the other hand, even here (e.g., II. Chap. 6 and IV. Chap. 3) there seem to be references to final causation for heavenly motions. Perhaps Aristotle attempted to patch up an earlier work and bring it up to date. It is one of Jaeger's greatest contributions, after all, to have shown that Aristotle often did this.

54. E.g., *Metaphysics A* 991a8–31, *Z* 1033b19–1034a8, *Λ* 1075b27, *M* 1086b6–7.

55. *τὸ εἶδος τὸ ἐνόν*: *Metaphysics Z* 1037a29–30. Cf. 1033b5–7, and *De anima* III. 432a3, ff.

56. See *Metaphysics Z* Chap. 17.

57. In *Metaphysics Λ* Chap. 10 Aristotle repeats the criticism he made at *Physics* I. Chap. 9, which we have already examined. See also *Metaphysics N* Chap. 4 and *De generatione animalium* II. 732a4–6. The "love" of the substratum for Reality may also be equated with one sense of *δύναμις*.

58. Cf. *Metaphysics Λ* 1071b34: *οὐδὲν γὰρ ὡς ἔτυχε κινεῖται, κτλ.*; and the analysis of *τύχη* and *ταὐτόματον* in *Physics* II. Cf. also Aristotle's analysis of *ἀνάγκη*, e.g., *Physics* II. Chap. 9, *De partibus animalium* 642a2, ff., etc. One takes account of it in a given event, but not in Nature as such. That Aristotle agreed with Plato on the inevitable imperfection of Forms as they are realized in phenomena is clear. Cf. *Metaphysics Γ* 1010a3–4, *Z* 1034b7–19, *Θ* 1050b25–6, etc.

59. *Metaphysics Λ* Chap. 10.

60. *Metaphysics Λ* 1069a20. See 1071a21–9: "Speaking generally, Man causes Man. But 'Man' does not

exist: Peleus causes Achilles and your father you. The cause of things in the same species (or Form) is the same, but in each individual is different: your substratum and Form and cause of motion (τὸ κινῆσαν) is different from mine, although they are the same in universal formula." Cf. *De partibus animalium* I. 640a24–33 and *De generatione animalium* IV. 767b30–768a3.

61. Cf. *De generatione et corruptione* II. Chap. 10, *Physics* II. 194b13, *Physics* VIII, *Metaphysics Λ* Chap. 5, *De caelo* II. 286b2–9, *Meteorologica* I. 346b22–32, *De generatione animalium* I. 716a17, II. 731b31–5, *De anima* III. 415a25 ff.

62. *De generatione et corruptione* II. 336b25–337a2.

63. *Metaphysics Λ* 1075a11–25.

64. For the *scala naturae* or "Great. Chain of Being" see *Historia animalium* VIII. 588b4–16 and *De partibus animalium* IV. 681a12–16.

65. *De motu animalium* 700b11–13, *De generatione animalium* III. 762a22. (See, however, *De anima* I. 411a7–23.)

66. *De generatione animalium* II. 736b33–737a1, III. 762a19 ff.

67. *Physics* II. 192b8–15, *Metaphysics Δ* 1017b10–14, *De caelo* I. Chap. 2 and III–IV. The feeling is beautifully captured by Dante, *Paradiso* I, 104 ff.

68. *De partibus animalium* II. Chap. 1, *De generatione animalium* I. Chap. 1, *De motu animalium* 703a28–b2.

69. *De longitudine et brevitate vitae* Chap. 6, *De iuventute et senectute* Chap. 2. See also *Metaphysics Z* 1040b5–16.

70. *Metaphysics Λ* 1071a14.

71. *Metaphysics Z* 1034a6.

72. *Metaphysics Λ* 1070a19, although the text is difficult here. See the remedies proposed by Ross and by Jaeger. See also *De generatione animalium* II. 735a4–9 and *Metaphysics Z* 1035b14–27.

73. Other examples of elementary Forms referred to as matter: *Physics* II. 194b9–15 (sinews, bronze), *Metaphysics H* Chap. 4 (wood, wool).

74. For the hierarchy of "matter" from the ultimate to the proximate (ἐσχάτη) see *Metaphysics H* Chap. 6, *Θ* 1050a15–16, *De anima* II. 412b6–9.

75. *Metaphysics Θ* Chap. 8, *Λ* Chaps. 4–5.

76. See note 61 above.

77. *Physics* II. Chap. 1.

78. *Metaphysics Z* Chap. 7–9 and 17, *H* Chap. 3–4, *Θ* Chap. 3, 7–8, *Λ* Chaps. 3–4, *De partibus animalium* I. 640a27–33, *De generatione animalium* I. 730b8–23.

79. E.g., *Rhetoric* I. 1356b29–1357a4, *Topica* 111a1, 116a29, *Metaphysics Z* 1032b13, 1034a8, *Λ* 1070b28, 1075b10.

80. *Metaphysics B* 999b17–20, *H* 1043b18–21, *K* 1060b23–8. For the "active intellect," whatever we are to make of that, see *De anima* II. 413a3–10, 413b24–7, and III. Chap. 5.

81. *Metaphysics Z* Chap. 8, also H 1043b15–22, *Θ* 1046b28–1047a4.

82. *Metaphysics Z* 1032b1, *De generatione animalium* I. 730b16. Cf. *Politics* III. 1282b15–16.

83. *Metaphysics Z* Chap. 8, etc.

84. *Protrepticus* fr. 13 (Ross), *Meteorologica* IV. 381b6–7, *Physics* II. Chap. 8, *Politics* VII. 1337a2. Cf. S. H. Butcher, *Aristotle's Theory of Poetry and Fine Art* (London, 1898), pp. 116–20.

85. In addition to the *Phaedo* passages which we examined in Chapter 4 there is the definition of εἶδος given by Xenocrates, which Proclus says was "a definition satisfactory to the founder," *in Parmenidem* 691 (Stallbaum). Form, according to Xenocrates, although it was separate (χωριστή), was also a divine cause (θεία αἰτία). It is "a pattern cause (αἰτία παραδειγματική) of the things which are continuously being compounded by nature."

86. Aristotle, of course, frequently dissociated himself from "those who assert the existence of Ideas," but his εἶδος, however modified, is obviously

a direct development of Plato's theory, and there is no reason to doubt that Aristotle was aware of this. Cf. Nocolai Hartmann, "Zur Lehre vom Eidos bei Platon und Aristoteles," *Abhandlungen der preussichen Akademie der Wissenschaften*, Philosophisch - historische Klasse (1941), No. 8. Hartmann's examination is seriously crippled, however, by his assumption that Plato did not really believe the εἴδη to have an existence apart from particulars.

87. The most important passages are *Posterior Analytics* II. Chap. 19, *Physics* I. Chap. 9, *Metaphysics A* Chaps. 6, 9, *Z* Chaps. 13–14, *M* Chaps. 4–5, περὶ ἰδεῶν (Alexander *in Met.* 79–89, 97–8). The best discussion of these passages is Cherniss, *Aristotle's Criticism of Plato* I, 223–317. Further bibliography will be found in G. E. L. Owen's "A Proof in the *ΠΕΡΙ ΙΔΕΩΝ*," *Journal of Hellenic Studies* LXXVII (1957), 103 n. 1.

88. Alexander, *In Met.* 97 and 80 (περὶ ἰδεῶν pp. 122–3, Ross). Cf. *Posterior Analytics* I. 77a5–9.

89. *Posterior Analytics* I. 88a5.

90. *Metaphysics B* 999a24–9.

91. *Metaphysics M* 1086a37–b7.

92. 1086b33.

93. *Rhetoric* I. 1356b29–1357a4, *Nicomachean Ethics* X. 1180b15–16, VI. 1141b14–23.

94. *Posterior Analytics* I. 77a5–9, *Metaphysics H* 1042a21–2, *Z* Chap. 13, also 1040b23, I. 1053b16.

95. On Plato's procedure for determining the existence of a Form see especially *Republic* X. 596a5–7, *Epistle* VII. 342d3–8, and Aristotle, *Metaphysics M* 1078b32–4. References to various discussions on this point can be found in Ross, *Theory of Ideas* 167–75.

96. *Categories* Chaps. 1–5. Compare Plato's τὸ τί.

97. *Metaphysics Z* 1028b2–4.

98. E.g., *Metaphysics Λ* 1070a9–13, *Δ* Chap. 8.

99. *Metaphysics Z* Chap. 3. That matter is only potentially a "this": *Metaphysics H* 1042a27–8. On τὸ χωριστόν as a requirement for "Reality" see *Metaphysics Z* 1029a27, *Δ* 1017b23–4; on τὸ καθ' αὑτό, 1022a24–36.

100. *Categories* Chap. 5, *Metaphysics Z* 1040b23–9, *Λ* 1086a32–b13, *De generatione animalium* II. 731b31–732a2, IV. 767b30–768a3.

101. *De caelo* I. 278a19–22, *Metaphysics Z* 1034a5–8, *Λ* 1074a31–5.

102. Cf. *Metaphysics Δ* 1016b33, *Z* 1037b1–2, 13–15, 1038b18, 21, *Θ* 1047a2, I. 1052a32–4, *M* 1086b32–7, *Posterior Analytics* I. 77a5–9.

103. *Physics* II. 193b7–8, *Metaphysics* I. 1052a32–4.

104. *Physics* VIII. 257b9, and *De anima* II. 417a7–9.

105. See, above all, *Metaphysics M* 1087a10–25, on the interpretation of which see Cherniss, *Aristotle's Criticism of Plato* I, 340–7. Cf. *Physics* VII. 247b4–7, *Metaphysics Z* 1035b27–1036a9, 1037a5–10, *H* 1043b2–3, *De anima* III. 430a26–31. Also *Posterior Analytics* II. 100a15–100b1.

106. *Posterior Analytics* II. Chap. 19.

107. *De anima* II. Chap. 12, also III. 425b23–5, and frequently thereafter in that book. The language of *Posterior Analytics* II. Chap. 19 almost suggests that we *sense* the Form-species directly. This is clarified, however, in *De anima* III., especially Chaps. 4 and 5. What we sense is the roundness and brownness of the acorn or the imperfect tree—the sensible forms without the matter; but to account for the fact that our minds are eventually informed by the Form "what it is to be a perfect oak" we need to assume the existence of some other agency, the "Form of Forms" (III. Chap. 8) which may or may not be the same as the "active intellect" (III. Chap 5). The literature on this very important question is enormous.

108. Cf. *Metaphysics A* Chap. 1.

109. Aristotle, *De memoria et*

*reminiscentia*, especially 453a10, ff. But see Note 107 above.

110. *Posterior Analytics* II. 100a6–8.

111. Again, cf. *Metaphysics* A Chap. 1.

112. *Categories* Chap. 5.

113. *Metaphysics* *Δ* Chap. 6, I Chaps. 1–2, *De anima* II. 412b6, ff., *Metaphysics* *B* 999a2–4, *Z* 1035a5–8, 1035b27–31, *Λ* 1071a21–9, 1074a31–4.

114. *Posterior Analytics* II. 100a13. (Much depends, however, on what we are to make of the "active intellect" in *De anima* III. Chap. 5.)

115. *Physics* II. Chaps. 4–6.

116. *Physics* II 198b16, ff.

117. Cf. Xenophon, *Memorabilia* I. 4, 6.

118. *Physics* II 199b26–8.

119. *Ibid.* 199a30–2.

120. Put together *De generatione animalium* IV. Chap. 3–4, 6, *Metaphysics Z* Chap. 9, *Physics* II. Chap. 8, *Nicomachean Ethics* III. Chap. 5; also *De generatione animalium* II. 737a25–30, Chap. 7–8, *De anima* III. 432b22–4, *Problemata* X. 10, IV. 13, X. 12, 41, 61.

121. *De generatione animalium* I. 729a10.

122. *Problemata* X. 10. (This may well be the work of one of Aristotle's pupils, but that does not matter.)

123. *De generatione animalium* IV. 775a16.

124. *De generatione animalium* IV. Chap. 3.

125. Cf. *Metaphysics* *Θ* Chap. 2 and 5. The greater the rationality, the greater the possibility of error. Cf. Aldous Huxley, *Texts and Pretexts* Vol. 17 in *Collected Works*, London 1949, p. 137 f.: "Zuckerman has shown that even the apes and monkeys must *learn* the sexual behaviour which is normal in their respective communities. Isolate a new born rat, then, when it is mature, introduce it to another rat of the opposite sex. It will know exactly what to do—will behave as all other rats behave. Not so an ape. Instinct does not tell it how to behave. Congenital ignorance is the condition of intelligence. The ape is intelligent, therefore knows fewer things by instinct than does the rat. It is not born with a knowledge of normal sex-behaviour, it must acquire this knowledge from its fellows." This is not really as paradoxical as it sounds, however. Consider the following. A rock will never err in desiring to go to the center of the earth nor ever miss a chance to do so. (Throw a rock upward ten thousand times and you will still not begin to pervert it from its true desire. Cf. *Nicomachean Ethics* II. Chap. 1.) But this rock cannot move itself even a fraction of an inch toward the edge of a cliff in order to realize its aim the better. Plants, on the other hand, are capable of many accommodations to their surroundings. If the bark of a tree were to be attacked by a goat, however, the tree would be powerless to prevent it. But the goat could do something about a hostile wolf: fight or run away. Yet the goat cannot forgo its present pleasure in eating grass in order to plan against future wolf raids. A man could. Thus man may, on Aristotle's analysis, be, by reason of his rationality, the most irrational creature in the sublunary world, the one most likely to go against his own best interests, but that is because he has the most, not the least, power to realize his aim.

126 *Nicomachean Ethics* II.

127. To be sure, Plato at least toyed with the idea (*Timaeus* 28b), and, as we have seen, some of his students asserted that he had assumed the world to be ungenerated; others denied it.

128. The Platonic origins of this ideal are lovingly described by A. J. Festugière, *Contemplation et vie contemplative selon Platon* (Paris, 1950).

129. Cf. *Metaphysics* *N* 1091a30 ff., *Nicomachean Ethics* I. Chap. 6, and *Eudemian Ethics* I. Chap. 8. The criticism amounts to this: Good, as it exists in the category of Reality (which Aristotle identifies as "God or Intelligence," *ὁ θεὸς καὶ ὁ νοῦς*, *Nicomachean Ethics* I. 1096a25), activity so

pure that it is without motion (*Nicomachean Ethics* VII. 1154b26–30, *Metaphysics* 1047a30 ff. Cf. *De caelo* II. 292a22), is not the cause of the goodness of all other Forms. Its only effect is to guarantee their continued existence τῷ ἐφεξῆς. Of course, existence is better than nonexistence (*De generatione et corruptione* II. 336b28). But the Forms act as final causes, each species in its own way. They cause motions which, in the universe as a whole, produce more order than disorder; but there are a variety of individual processes (πάντα δὲ συντέτακταί πως, ἀλλ' οὐχ ομοίως, *Metaphysics Λ* 1075a16–17). They produce "swimming things, flying things, plants," and so on. We do not get very far as scientific investigators, he says (*Nicomachean Ethics*, Chap. 6), by reducing every problem to a contemplation of the Good; we must investigate the good appropriate to each subject.

130. Although at *Metaphysics Λ* 1075a11 ff. he does say that the Good exists both as the Unmoved Mover and as order within the universe. And then, of course, there is the problem of the "active intellect" again.

131. See especially *Nicomachean Ethics* X. Chaps. 6–9, also VI. 1144a1 ff., also *Metaphysics A* Chap. 1.

132. *Metaphysics Λ* Chap. 8.

133. Apelt, in a review of Jaeger's *Studien zur Entstehungsgeschichte der Metaphysik des Aristoteles* (Berlin, 1912), in the *Berliner philologische Wochenschrift* (1912), p. 1590, first proved the late date of Chapter 8. Jaeger (*Aristoteles* III, 3), still convinced that Chapters 7 and 9 were early (because of the similarity between the First Mover and the Form of the Good), then set about to prove that Chapter 8 was of a later origin than 7 and 9, and that it was mistakenly inserted where it is by another editor. His main arguments are (1) that there is a disruption in the train of thought, (2) that there is a change of style (on which, however, see Guthrie, *Classical Quarterly* XXVIII, 94 and Nolte, *Het godesbegrip bij Aristoteles* [Nimergue, 1940], pp. 147–8), and (3) that the theory of multiple bodiless movers is incompatible with the theory of a single Prime Mover. In fact, this last is the only serious threat to the assumption that Aristotle himself inserted Chapter 8 where it is. But see Philip Merlan, "Aristotle's Unmoved Movers," *Traditio* IV (1946), 1–30. At 1073b1–3 Aristotle implies that the multiple unmoved movers are ranked in a hierarchy, which means that they are specifically different. Unlike things specifically identical, therefore, they need no matter to be numerically different (cf. *Metaphysics Δ* 1016b35–6). Aristotle often speaks of unmoved movers in the plural (see, even in *Physics* VIII. 258b12–13, and cf. Joseph Owens, *The Doctrine of Being in Aristotle's Metaphysics* [Toronto, 1951], p. 411 ff., especially, although with some caution, the passages he cites at p. 415 n. 38). On the sense in which immanent Forms are unmoving see *Physics* V. 224b10–15. At *Physics* VIII. 260a5–10, on the other hand, there is a very complicated description of the sense in which only the mover of the first sphere is entirely unmoved. See *De caelo* II. Chap. 12 for an extraordinary attempt to explain why the movements of the spheres do *not* get more and more compounded as you move inward from the outermost sphere. See also *De motu animalium* Chaps. 1–5, where it is explained that there are unmoved movers on every level.

134. Implied at 1073a37–b1. Cf. a3–13.

135. 1074a29–31.

## Notes on Chapter 9

1. Notably at the end of Book II and at the beginning of Book III.

2. 247a.

3. 29d–30d.

4. *Metaphysics A* 982b32 ff. Cf. Aristotle's praise for the love that a god may have for worshippers, a good ruler for his subjects, or a father for his son: *Nichomachean Ethics* VIII. Chaps. 7 and 10–12.

5. Plato in effect summarizes his whole philosophy in these terms at *Theaetetus* 176–7.

6. E.g., "If any man come to me and hate not his father and mother and wife and children and brethren and sisters, yea and his own life also, he cannot be my disciple." Luke xiv, 26. Cf. Matthew x, 34–9.

7. See, e.g. *Nicomachean Ethics* VII. Chap. 2.

8. E.g., *Nicomachean Ethics* IX. Chaps. 4–9. Cf. *Symposium* 204d–205a.

9. *Republic* I.

10. Mr. Robert Bagg, the poet. One might compare J. L. Stocks, "Desire and Affection," *Hibbert Journal* XXVII (1929), 511–25, also the distinction between "I-thou" and "I-it" relations in Martin Buber's famous essay, *I and Thou*, and many a similar distinction in Existentialist writings.

11. E.g., *Civilization and its Discontents*, p. 50.

12. I have never understood how audiences are able to accept with such equanimity and even delight the vision of nature presented by Walt Disney in his films on natural life: one unbelievably hideous insect, rodent, or reptile is for ever being shown in the process of swallowing another in slow, short, ugly gulps. Cf. Aristotle's eulogy of the repugnant in nature, *De partibus animalium* I. 645a.

13. Nowadays it is usually only when Plato is being attacked as the father of illiberal political philosophy that he is treated as a live person and a philosopher to be reckoned with. Among the most readable and intelligent of these attacks are K. R. Popper, *The Open Society and Its Enemies* Vol. I: "The Spell of Plato," (London, 1945), and E. A. Havelock, *The Liberal Temper in Greek Politics* (London, 1957).

14. It is interesting to compare the exhilaration to which Plato was led by a philosophic analysis of the way things are, with the exhilaration which can be brought about by mescalin, religious exercises, or other ways of lowering the sugar level of the blood in the brain. See Aldous Huxley, *The Doors of Perception* (London, 1954) and *Heaven and Hell* (London, 1956), and the references to medical papers in these essays. The chief trouble with narcotics, apparently, is that, not only do they often bring nightmarish visions instead of ecstasy, but they also make one lose all interest in the pursuits of life among men. With the vanishing of the sense of time comes, not only a vanishing of anxiety for flux, but a loathing for the problems of justice and cooperation. There is a parallel in the experience of Aquinas, also in the reluctance of Plato's philosopher kings to re-enter the Cave. Plato insists, however, that once the philosophers get used to the darkness of our miserable ways down here, they will understand more of our world than we do. Peyotl eaters bring permanent perceptions back to their ordinary lives, but their new observations do not appear to be of very much use in making long-range practical plans for the whole community. Plato's philosopher-kings and Indians under the influence of peyotl both lose some of their enthusiasm for the ordinary concerns of society, but the philosophers—or so Plato affirms—arrive at this state by a conscious and rational distillation of their ever more

intense passion for life correctly understood, while the Indians turn their backs on all things which call either for effort or for ratiocination.

15. "As regards the sexual instincts . . . what they are clearly aiming at by every possible means is the coalescence of two germ-cells which are differentiated in a particular way. If this union is not effected, the germ-cell dies along with all the other elements of the multicellular organism. It is only on this condition that the sexual function can prolong the cell's life and lend it the appearance of immortality." Freud, *Beyond the Pleasure Principle*, pp. 78–9.

16. This is certainly not the tendency in the new fashion for "ego-psychology."

# INDEX